LOOKING FOR GOD IN THE SUBURBS

JAMES HUDNUT-BEUMLER

LOOKING FOR
· G O D ·
IN THE SUBURBS

The Religion of the American Dream
and Its Critics,
1945–1965

Rutgers University Press

New Brunswick, New Jersey

Library of Congress Cataloging-in-Publication Data

Hudnut-Beumler, James David.
Looking for God in the suburbs : the religion of the American
dream and its critics, 1945–1965 / James Hudnut-Beumler.
p.   cm.

Includes bibliographical references and index.
ISBN 0-8135-2083-5 (hard) — ISBN 0-8135-2084-3 (pbk.)
1. United States—Religion—1945–1960. 2. United States—
Religion—1960–   3. United States—Church history—20th century.
4. Religion and culture—United States. 5. Suburban churches—
United States. I. Title.
BR526.H83   1994
277.3'0825—dc20   93-41778
CIP

British Cataloging-in-Publication information available

For Heidi

Contents

■

Preface

∎

This is a book about the social, moral, and religious problems of a people who got nearly everything they had ever dreamed of. It is a book about American culture in the early postwar years and the popularity of religion within that culture. It is also about the competing visions of what religion should be and what role, if any, it should play in society. Here you will read extravagant claims made for the moral virtue of America and charged critiques of that same society for its spiritual poverty.

This book had its origin in a question raised over twenty years ago by Sydney Ahlstrom in an essay entitled, "The Radical Turn in Theology and Ethics: Why It Occurred in the 1960s."[1] The question in its most basic form amounted to this: How, given the relatively placid Eisenhower years, can the deeply divided 1960s be accounted for religiously? Ahlstrom's own answer to that question—that theology in the fifties was poised for a radical turn when faced with the dramatic social challenges of the 1960s—was, for me, simultaneously too impressionistic and too narrowly focused on theology. The historical background to the story of American religion in the 1960s, I was convinced, was to be better found in the interplay of religious, social, and intellectual forces in the years leading up to the outburst of issues and enthusiasm we call the sixties. This work, therefore, has been guided by the attempt to explain the religion of Americans in the 1950s both for its own sake and for the sake of understanding what has happened to American religion and society in the years following.

Some of the people who read this book in early drafts wondered where I stood in relation to the ideas, people, and trends chronicled and analyzed in the book. Did I like the fifties? Did I agree with the critics? Did I prefer the world they prescribed, or the world they decried? I have been circumspect about offering too much of a moral judgment about fifties' religion and its critics in this narrative. The work of the historian loses much of its value when it simply becomes a brief for one side of a debate. Nevertheless, I do have a viewpoint on postwar religion and its critics that I now make explicit.

I chose to write about religion and culture in the fifties and early sixties because I think that the issues that surfaced in that period are vital ones. This era gave us the first broadly affluent generation in American life. Extending rights beyond roles was terribly important in realizing part of the American Dream. People were no longer confined to exercising the freedoms considered appropriate to their roles in life—housewife, businessman, Negro. Affluence and consumer individualism made that possible. Yet the extent to which American culture became in the fifties a culture premised on consumption is disturbing on its own and in light of how we now see that basis for culture slipping away. I do worry more for a culture based on what people own, buy, or do at work than I would for a family-oriented society, or a culture that based its identity on craftspersonship, healing, duty, or aesthetic achievement. The critics analyzed in this book shared that worry and anticipated it by thirty years. Therefore, the points they made against easy religion, other-direction, racism, and classism deserve a hearing today as much, and perhaps more, as in their own time. To be clear, I am sympathetic to what the critics tried to do to correct their culture.

And yet, I must confess that I, like most historians, find myself writing in the trope of irony. I am unable to portray the churches and synagogues of the era as simply implicated in a tragedy of cultural conformity. There is much that went right in the fifties. Nor am I able to depict the critics as unalloyed heroes. Like John Dewey, who maintained that the cure to the limitations of democracy was more democracy, these critics often recommended greater individual independence as the cure for every malady of the day, including those that in retrospect grew from a burgeoning individualism. If hypocrisy was found in the church, the individual should leave the church and maintain his or her integrity. If the roles in marriages, families, and businesses were found stifling, perhaps they should be renegotiated or severed. Today's empty churches, broken families, and troubled relations in business and families make us pause in our appraisal of the critics. If social criticism has a central, predictable flaw, it is its tendency to go to the extremes in recommending tomorrow's problems as solutions to those of today. Even so, these critics were more right than wrong, and I must underscore my sympathy for what they did.

Readers searching for heroes and villains will, for the most part, be disappointed. What they will find instead are the more interesting species of men and women, the fools and buffoons, the long-suffering and the dreamers who try as best they can to come to terms with questions of human purpose and divine intention.

In writing this book, I incurred debts of gratitude to many friends and colleagues. John F. Wilson assigned a writing task to me on another aspect of religion in the postwar era that enabled me to spend a year reading broadly in the religious literature of the period. Albert J. Raboteau, Peter Williams, and John Gager stimulated and encouraged my interest in popular religion. John Mulder, Benton Johnson, Craig Dykstra, and Conrad Cherry paid the highest compliment for which a scholar can hope by taking seriously the ideas and analysis in this book. Linda Watson Kaufman and Janice Strohl worked diligently to produce accurate transcriptions from tapes dictated on the road. I was blessed by their good humor. Marlie Wasserman at Rutgers University Press championed the project and was a model of professionalism at a university press. My wife, Heidi, has gone beyond what love requires again and again to read and respond to drafts with intelligence and good sense. Any faults that remain in the work are mine alone, and are probably the result of rejecting her good advice. Finally, my daughter, Julia, has nurtured in me an understanding of what people of the fifties held most dear in seeking to orient their lives around family and children. The earnest desire of both the American Dream's critics and defenders to make the world a better place for their children strikes me today as a form of nobility too lacking in our own time.

LOOKING FOR GOD IN THE SUBURBS

1

Life in a Suburban Culture

■

The 1950s stand as a high point for the place of religion in the United States. Never before in national history had as many Americans belonged to, attended, or associated themselves with religious institutions. Not only in adherence, but also in status, religion experienced a popularity that was without parallel. Terms like "religious revival" and "theological renaissance" were used by contemporary observers to describe the phenomenon. To understand the unique situation of religion in the postwar years, it is necessary to probe the unfolding of faith's fashionability in the context of developments in the wider culture.

The years immediately following World War II, commonly called "the fifties," form a watershed period in American life and culture. So much of what is now characteristic of contemporary life began in the fifties. Suburbs, transportation by car, television, rock music, paperback books, exceptionalism in foreign affairs, and the struggle to end racism all became dominant social realities in the years 1945–60. All are with us still. Yet the fifties are also distant to us today. From fashions in dress to patterns of speech and from assumptions about sexuality to gender relations, the fifties project a kind of staid certainty that is unfamiliar and even quaint to people of the 1990s.

Rediscovering the religion of the 1950s and the way it reshaped not only religion itself but also broader American culture requires an attempt at recovering the mentalité of the era, because sooner or later, the major questions and events of the day all involved religion. Four apparently secular social facts provided the context for the resurgence of religion in the 1950s and for subsequent criticisms of that revival of religious interest. Suburbanization is the most obvious. Joining it was scientism—a conviction that all aspects of life and nature could be explained and controlled scientifically. Also critical to the making of the postwar ethos was the homogenization of culture and experience wrought by the development of a national mass media. Finally, the return to religion was set within a major debate about the American character in which the desire to claim that Americans were moral exemplars to the world had to contend with false worries about Communist subversion and the real cancer of racism eating the society from within.

Suburbanization

The suburbanization of America involved much more than simply an increased number of people living on the fringes of large cities. Suburbanization was first of all the result of the decay of the nation's private housing stock from 1929 to 1945. During the Great Depression, new housing starts fell dramatically due to a lack of demand and capital. In the war years, building materials were diverted to the war effort to build ships, planes, tanks, base housing, and hospitals. All the while, the nation's housing was aging and in many places it was truly substandard—lacking adequate heating, plumbing, electricity—or structurally unsound. Moreover, because it reflected the demographic and building patterns of twenty to fifty years earlier, the existing housing stock was often in the wrong place for the needs of the postwar population. There simply was not enough suitable housing in and near the large cities where America's jobs were located.

Added to the dearth in the supply of housing that fed suburbanization was the swelling of the demand for housing created by the combined effects of the Depression and war. Normally when a group of young men and women reach a certain age they will move out of their parents' homes, begin a career, marry, secure housing of their own, and begin a family in fairly predictable patterns and intervals. The Depression had interrupted these patterns. Demographers watched as both the average age at marriage and percentage of married adults living with parents climbed, while the average number of children per family plummeted. The war exacerbated this trend as marriage and family life were further deferred by millions, as the phrase went, "for the duration" of the war. This trend had the effect of compressing several birth cohorts into one huge generation of men and women all eager to get on with their lives at the same time when the war came to a close.

The final important factor promoting the phenomenon of suburbanization was the low cost and availability of large tracts of farmland around most major cities. These lands did not have to be cleared and were inexpensive compared to urban acreage. Better yet, from the developer's view, this property was often found in unincorporated areas having little or no taxation, nor land use regulations. Once the GI bill was in place to finance the millions of veterans who wanted to buy a house (and once developers like William and Alfred Levitt and Philip Klutznick showed how colossal profits could be made in providing affordable, predesigned housing), suburbanization was underway.

Who were the people who lived in suburbia? They were largely young married couples, not old enough to have put down roots. They were mostly college educated, though less so as time went on. Their incomes came primarily from white-collar jobs in large corporations. Their lives had been shaped by a childhood in the Depression, but also by an adolescence of national success. Those who came to age as young adults in the 1950s were in no small measure the products of the fears and expectations of Depression-era parents. The uncertainty of employment, the elimination of nonessentials from daily life, even the terrifying possibility that one's only child might survive childhood illness only to be stolen from the crib like the Lindberghs' baby, all conspired to encourage parents to urge safety upon their offspring. As Benita Eisler wrote of this generation: "All parents want the best for their children. Ours seemed more determined that we avoid the worst: Don't get hurt, get pregnant, marry the 'wrong' girl, get in with the 'wrong' crowd, start your own business, try to make it in the arts or in sports. Stick with the union, the civil service, the corporation, the Navy. Uncertainty was the worst scenario. They knew. They had been there."[1] Yet if they were the kind of people who instinctively sought out safety in employment, relationships, and housing, this did not mean that the suburbanites were a pessimistic lot. Indeed, William H. Whyte, author of *The Organization Man*, wrote of them: "For the younger couples, there has been an almost unbroken momentum; they came to adolescence at a time of rising hope, and throughout their early adult years they have known nothing but constantly increasing prosperity, personal as well as general. Suburbia has further confirmed them in their optimism. Here they are surrounded by others like themselves—too young to have failed."[2]

Traditional was a good word in the fifties. What are we to make of a time when female college students told pollsters that they wanted babies, not careers? Or when men chose to spend their evenings at home joining the do-it-yourself craze? One possibility is that the culture was embracing the values of the pioneer era with a vengeance. The do-it-yourself homeowner, fixing anything from a lamp to a lawnmower with only a single trip to the hardware store for parts, was living out the role of the frontier settler. Self-sufficiency was to be praised. The role of homemaker, too, was valued as it had been on the prairie. To take a ranch house without curtains, landscaping, or carpeting and make it a family home was as important to suburban pioneer women as it had been to their great-grandmothers setting up a home in a house of sod.

In embracing the traditions and mythology of one period in American history, the young adults of the fifties were, of course, rejecting others. The smart sophistication of the 1920s would not do; it was too bound up in the myths of the cause of the Depression. Neither would the Victorian period and the Gilded Age, with its paid servants, silver tea service, and formal dinners, inspire the family culture of the 1950s. For this was a middle-class revolution. The American dream applied at least theoretically to everyone, and in the American economy's partial shift from a wealth to a wage economy, the real value of labor had risen to levels that both made the dream's fruits possible and precluded the employment of domestic servants on a wide scale. Moreover, the large majority of the suburbanites had neither the experience of nor the desire to experience such an aristocratic lifestyle.

The suburban frontier's men and women were also engaged in the positive appropriation of a ritual from other periods of American history; a ritual of marking out and defining their living spaces. Pilgrims, revolutionary soldiers with war bonus land grants in the Western Reserve, families homesteading at the end of the Oregon Trail, and even the residents of the nineteenth century's utopias had all found themselves in a wilderness lacking not in natural features but in the social structures and boundaries that they had left behind. The settlers in each new "wilderness" marked out spaces for laundry, waste disposal, cooperative food production, marketing, and for government, worship, and social interaction. If the suburban settlers had most of their physical needs for roads and public services planned for them, then their social needs were all the more emphasized. Family, motherhood, fathers involved with day-to-day running of the home, the Parent-Teacher Association, the block club, the playground and parks committees, and, of course, the church or synagogue were all parts of the exciting process of community building. Indeed, the high level of churchgoing may be related to the phenomena of being part of an institution's first generation and therefore feeling a higher degree of responsibility for its success. This people, in short, had rediscovered and embraced the voluntarism so evident to Tocqueville and other observers of Jacksonian America and of later frontier area towns.

That this pioneer metaphor is no mere motif imposed upon the fifties by the historian is confirmed by contemporary sources. William Whyte was one who noticed suburbanites leaning heavily on analogies to the frontier or to early American colonial settlements in describing their communities. At other times they might use different figures of speech— "a sorority house with kids," "a womb with a view," "a Russia, only with money"—or make comparisons to Army base or college dormitory life. Still, the bass note sounded was communalism. On a featureless plain the suburbanites were banding together to create a rich communal life complete with all the institutions city dwellers took for granted—schools, pools, parks, churches, clubs.

On the religious front, many of the same economic realities that had affected the domestic housing inventory faced church building trends. Robert Wuthnow has calculated that, in 1929, roughly "10 cents of every dollar given to religion was spent on construction," but that between 1932 and 1936 the figure dropped to only 2.5 cents. This continued through the war years when construction material was diverted to defense use. "Of the $7.1 billion taken in by religious organizations between 1941 and 1945, only $131 million, or 1.8 percent, went for construction," and this was despite a significant increase in religious contributions during the war of 64 percent.[3] Religious building, like home construction, had failed to keep up with the needs of society. Quite naturally, when the move to build came at the end of the war, the greater part of new religious construction took place in the outlying and suburban areas.

Although the most famous suburbs were those of the Boston-Washington corridor, southern California, and the industrial Midwest, suburbanization was a truly national phenomenon. Church building in new outlying residential areas was a part of it. For example, at the beginning of the 1950s, Omaha had thirty-five major religious building projects underway, including seven new Protestant churches, but not counting eleven more that had recently been completed.[4] Nearly all of Omaha's residential growth in this period occurred within the municipal limits of Omaha, which would have excluded it from being counted as suburbanization by the federal government's statisticians. Yet, although the owners of new homes and members of new churches in Omaha would have belonged to the same political jurisdiction as people in the central city neighborhoods, their experience was very much like that of the residents of the technical suburbs of the nation's older cities. Just like Levittowners, they banded together to lobby for the extension of services—schools, sewers, utilities—to their neighborhoods and engaged in community building on the fringe of an established urban area.

Fifties' suburbanization was primarily a Protestant and Jewish phenomenon because of the religious background of the people who moved to the suburbs. Those who bought a station wagon and a house with a picture window were, initially, overwhelmingly middle to upper-middle class, concentrated in the Northeast, Far West, and industrial Midwest, white, of British or German ancestry, and college educated. These were precisely the same demographic characteristics associated with liberal or mainline Protestantism.[5] Early sociological studies of the suburbs also demonstrated a propensity of intellectuals and professionals—academics, doctors, dentists, lawyers—to move to the suburbs. These were occupations that a large proportion of Jews occupied, so while Jews were a small part of the overall number of people moving to the suburbs, a sizable proportion of the American Jewish population made the transition from urban to suburban living, and made it early on in the process of suburbanization. Suburbanization, therefore, was a dominant social reality in the institutional life of mainline Protestantism and American Judaism from the early 1950s forward. This fact proved to be not always a pleasant one for some representatives of these religious groups.

In their 1950 series, "Great Churches of America," the editors of the *Christian Century* posed the promises and dilemmas of suburbia as they saw them: "The residents of Suburbia are, by and large, Protestant in tradition and by natural addiction. They want to have Protestant churches in their communities and will support them generously. They send their children to Protestant church schools, and more often than not they maintain a church membership for themselves. But in too many instances Suburbia breeds a sense of self-satisfaction, of complacency, on occasion even of self-congratulation, which tends to look on the church as little more than a social convenience. Suburbia is the home of those who have arrived."[6] Only one of the twelve churches chosen as a "great church" was a suburban church, and in their description of the First Church of Christ (Congregational) of West Hartford, Connecticut, the editors repeatedly expressed their concerns and doubts about the suburban situation, asking, "But are such suburban churches and ministries strong in terms of spiritual influence? Are the suburbs themselves strong in their influence on American life? Or are they parasite communities whose inhabitants are trying to buy their escape from the hurly-burly of the American social and political struggle at the price of a somewhat costlier standard of living? And are their churches more than chaplaincies to such a parasitic existence?"[7] Reading between the lines, it was clear that however great the Congregational Church in West Hartford might be, the editors of the *Century* believed that suburbanization and real Christianity were opposing forces in the lives of Americans.

Suburbia was also a concern to Jewish social observers. Morris Freedman, an associate editor of *Commentary*, wrote a feature article for his magazine about a new Jewish community in formation in Hillcrest, Queens, which was located in the inner ring of the new suburbia on Long Island. The only sizable pocket of wealth between Forest Hills and Great Neck, Long Island, the Hillcrest community was the site of burgeoning postwar residential construction, with some houses costing as much as $100,000. The ethos of home ownership was what most immediately impressed Freedman. He quoted the Hillcrest Jewish Center's rabbi, Dr. Israel Mowshowitz: "It's very important in understanding our character to realize that this is a congregation of home-owners. But even more important is the fact that these are their *first* homes—and probably their last. They don't have the sense of being apartment dwellers who might move away any time. Our members feel that for the first time in their lives they have let roots down here."[8] In putting down roots in a single-family-house neighborhood, Freedman found, many Jewish families also formally affiliated with a Jewish community institution for the first time. While he counted this fact as one hopeful sign, his overall reaction was one of concern. For many, it seemed the Jewish Center had little to do with religion. The subtitle of Freedman's article, "A Conservative Center Catering to Present-Day Needs," was a carefully chosen double entendre. Catering, in the sense of providing for social occasions, was what most characterized the life of the modern suburban Jewish Center, Freedman believed. The best Freedman could hope for from the example of the Hillcrest Jewish Center was that because it was new and its patterns for the future were not yet fixed, "a close and sober look now may offer an opportunity for those deeply concerned to help shape those patterns before the mold hardens."[9] Freedman's worries were paralleled by those of Marshall Sklare, who concluded that while the congregation had become increasingly influential in Jewish life as the congregation broadened its range of activities in the postwar era, the attitudes and life patterns of Jews in all three major branches of Judaism "depart[ed] markedly from ideal norms."[10]

These criticisms from religious journalists and commentators did not stop suburbanites from founding churches and synagogues, nor prevent those institutions from being tremendously popular. Suburbanization resulted in homogeneous communities that, far from being the sterile wastelands their worst critics feared, became the locus of incredible vitality. The suburban churches shared in this vitality, for they too were settings in which nearly all participants were between the ages of zero to ten, or twenty-three to thirty-five. These were times and places when and where everything was possible; veritable utopias in which death, cancer, and poverty appeared to have been banished. A typical suburban church or synagogue could go years without a funeral or memorial service. On the other hand, the joyful, life-affirming rituals of baptism, first communion, confirmation, bar mitzvah, and now bas mitzvah were frequently celebrated in the local houses of worship. Moreover, though the suburban family of faith might hold its meetings in an elementary school gymnasium and listen to the reading of scripture while sitting on metal folding chairs, the prospects for the future were bright: ecclesiastical budgets were ever on the rise, never in descent or tied to the declining incomes of aging and retiring members; building programs were underway (the family proud of their new split-level home would soon be attending a church equally new and worthy of pride); and the typical suburban church or synagogue had exactly what most prospective members were looking for in a religious home—people exactly like themselves.

Scientism

An unwarranted tendency to place faith in science for absolute answers to every human problem has characterized most Western thinking throughout the twentieth century. The disease of scientism reached its most acute phase, however, in American popular culture in the 1950s. During this brief era, scientism expressed itself most potently in a confidence in the power of psychology and in a fascination with atomic energy. As an ideology in competition with other worldviews, scientism posed challenges to religious thinking that far outstripped the abilities of most individuals to critically evaluate what they believed, the consistency of their beliefs, and the reasons for their beliefs.

By any measure, the 1950s deserve the title of the "Psychological Decade" of the twentieth century. Brooks Holifield has pointed out that popular interest in psychology and mental health rose during each period of war and subsequent periods of prosperity in the present century.[11] But what was true of World War I and the 1920s was certain ten times over for the years following the Second World War. During the war itself, the army alone employed more than 1,500 psychologists who were engaged in treating troops, interrogating prisoners, advising on morale, analyzing Hitler and Tojo from a distance, and planning "psychological warfare." Most importantly, the war, together with experiments in industrial psychology in the workplace, had exposed millions of Americans to professional psychologists and psychiatrists. After the war, the demand for psychologists from the business sector soared. It was common practice in the nation's largest corporations to use personality tests to screen managers for the purposes of hiring and promotion.[12]

The call for psychologists and psychiatrists was not confined to businesses alone. The study and treatment of mental illness had developed very little since the nineteenth century. Education, underfunded and understaffed as it was in the immediate postwar period, also cried out for the talents of developmental psychologists to test, track, and evaluate the progress of child and school alike. The whole culture presented problems that seemed to require the proficiency of mental health experts. Americans were anxious to hear the wisdom of psychologists on every conceivable subject from nuclear defense policy to popular music, from women's dress styles to partisan politics. The experts, for their part, were more than happy to oblige these requests.

The vocabulary of psychology could be found on the lips of Americans from coast to coast. Bus drivers pointed out neurotic riders and department store clerks discussed their complexes. By 1957, *Life* magazine was happy to report that the nation had "more psychologists and psychiatrists, engaged in more types of inquiry and activity, than all the rest of the world together."[13] Meanwhile, Hollywood had discovered psychology, and dozens of movies came out each year in the late forties and the fifties exploring psychological themes. Among the most famous were *The Lost Weekend* (1945), *The Snakepit* (1948), *All About Eve* (1950), *Marty* (1955), and anything directed by Alfred Hitchcock.

As the postwar years went on, the public's fascination with psychology led to an increased interest in personal counseling and therapeutic psychology for the individual. This interest was picked up by religious writers, and *The Basic Writings of Sigmund Freud* and Dale Carnegie's *How to Stop Worrying and Start Living* were soon joined on the best-seller's list by Joshua Loth Leibman's *Peace of Mind* and Norman Vincent Peale's *A Guide to Confident Living*. Polls of Protestant ministers indicated that they believed that church members expected them to make counseling a high priority in their ministries. Polls of the population at large confirmed this, and also showed, according to one study by the National Institute of Mental Health, that 42 percent of all persons seeking help with emotional problems turned first to a member of the clergy. The 8,000 rabbis, priests, and ministers that had become chaplains for the Armed Forces in the war found when they were decommissioned that in their absence civilian congregations had become like their army and navy counterparts: full of individuals who wanted to be listened to, not lectured to.

The demand for ministers with counseling skills led to an explosion of programs for the clinical training of clergy, the most famous of which was C.P.E., or Clinical Pastoral Education. By the end of the 1950s, there were 117 C.P.E. centers, which had formed alliances with over forty theological institutions.[14] The seminaries and divinity schools themselves responded by introducing new programs with titles like "pastoral theology," "personality and theology," "psychiatry and religion," and "pastoral counseling." The programs reflected different approaches to the popularity of psychology in the churches and culture, but nearly all theological schools offered some approach to this now-essential feature of clerical preparation. The phenomena was not limited to Protestant institutions, either. Catholic seminaries quickly expanded their curriculums, and Yeshiva University, Hebrew Union College, and the Jewish Theological Seminary developed programs of their own to meet the changing requirements of the rabbinate.

Regardless of religious affiliation, the religious leader's model of the day was Carl Rogers, whose nondirective or "client-centered" counseling quickly became the dominant mode of clerical counseling in the postwar era. Rogerian therapy was designed to draw out the person being counseled into a full realization of his or her personality and options. As such, it represented a rejection of an older style of counseling in which persons were shown their moral duties and failings and admonished to make improvement in their characters and conduct. This older style of pastoral care held a great affinity to the religious mood of the nineteenth century and to that era's clerical insistence on correctness in doctrine, but it had become both theologically and socially outdated by the end of World War II. In 1950, the prominent pastoral theologian Seward Hiltner wrote, "Most of the leading Protestant and Jewish theologians are as anti-moralistic or anti-legalistic as any psychoanalyst, and equally cognizant that such a view runs against the mores of American society."[15] Moral absolutism was dismissed as legalism and set in opposition to the Christian ethic of love by Christian theologians as widely separated as Paul Tillich and Karl Barth. Meanwhile, the Jewish thinker Martin Buber was still advocating reducing the objectification of others and stressing the importance of the relationship for honoring the integrity of the other, a case he had been making to a growing readership since the 1937 publication of the English-language edition of *I and Thou*.[16] The antilegalistic emphasis in theology suited the mood of the times well. The typical church member did not want to be "told what to do," but rather sought guidance in "making up his (or her) own mind." Meanwhile, Rogers's counseling model, built on a foundation of liberal assumptions about the goodness within each personality only waiting to be realized, allowed the counselor and the client both to have their own ways. No absolute answers were required or prescribed and no advice had to be taken.

The popularity of psychology in the postwar period made its impact felt in religious circles. But as Simeon Stylites, the *Christian Century*'s resident humorist, was quick to point out, things could go too far. "Let's keep our directions straight," he wrote. "The road to Vienna is not the road to Damascus. Psychology is a help to religious experience, but a poor substitute for it." H. Richard Niebuhr, noticing the tremendous growth in popularity of programs of pastoral counseling in theological seminaries, worried out loud that these programs were in danger of developing into a specious form of theological education, sufficient unto themselves.[17] Meanwhile, Gaius Glenn Atkins suggested that part of the General Confession might be recast to read, "We have followed too much the inhibitions and self-expressions of our own complexes. We have not sublimated our libidos, nor considered our neuroses."[18] In the minds of many others, however, "How can I be happy?" was a much more attractive question to ask of religion than "What must I do to be saved?"

The possibilities for a happier life held out by the science of psychology were paralleled by the more ominous life options posed by the power of the atom. Americans reacted to the fact of the dawning of the nuclear age with a mixture of gratitude, fear, awe, and wonder—gratitude, because for many who were in or had loved ones in the Armed Forces, it meant American lives were spared from the sacrifice of an invasion of the Japanese mainland; fear, because the existence of such a terrible weapon that could destroy a Hiroshima or a Nagasaki implied a weapon that could destroy an Indianapolis or a Boston; and awe and wonder, for at a purely technological level the revelation of the power of the atom was both magnificent and ghastly, prompting questions on the ultimate capabilities of science. Viewing the test of the first atomic bomb at Los Alamos, New Mexico, the first thing to come into the mind of J. Robert Oppenheimer were words from the *Bhagavad gita*: "I am become Death, the shatterer of worlds." But Oppenheimer was later to remark that physicists, by making the bomb, had for the first time "known sin."[19]

The atom quickly came to represent more than just the source of the ultimate in weaponry. The word "atomic" captured the popular imagination of fifties America, and the consumer of the fifties could eat Atomicburgers with Atomicshakes, bowl at the Atomic Bowling Alley, see a movie at the Atomic Theatre, and shave with a Ronson electric razor emblazoned with the symbol of electrons racing along their atomic orbit. No matter where one turned, the reminders of the atom were present in the objects of material culture. Closely related to the atomic imagery were designs and names that evoked the rocket, the satellite, and the promise of space travel. All these advertising and design choices sought to domesticate the vast and frightening powers that science was unlocking and to make the new technology friendly and hopeful. Sometimes these efforts extended beyond appropriation of the atomic as a metaphor. The wonders of radiation, after all, included glow-in-the-dark wall clocks, X-ray machines in shoe shops to check where children's toes were within the shoes, and ultraviolet hygiene devices to clean hands and toilet seats alike.

Even among those opposed to the kind of destruction it produced, the Manhattan Project was the standard of progress. Pleas for more concerted efforts to solve problems in housing, race relations, hunger overseas, and to cure polio and cancer typically began, "Why can't a nation that can make an atom bomb . . . ?" As a mark of achievement, the atom could not be beaten. In the religious realm, the southern Presbyterian Church in the United States celebrated its centenary with a new logo: a cross superimposed on a larger representation of the hydrogen atom.

Still, if the atomic symbol was an emblem of progress, it was also a token of fear. The monopoly of the United States over atomic weaponry was short-lived. To the dismay of countless American citizens, scientific knowledge knew no national boundaries, and the Soviet Union developed and exploded its first atomic bomb, dubbed Joe I, in 1949. The United States followed with the development of the hydrogen bomb, which it successfully tested at Bikini Atoll on 1 March 1954. But this brought scant comfort, for the world was already an unsafe place to live. The Cold War was underway, and when nuclear weapons would be used again, and against whom, was an open question. If deterrence failed, the most either side could force on the other was massive destruction of its civilian population. But, given national pride, human propensities toward error and vengeance, the state of emerging superpower relations, and the sheer number of theaters of conflict involving the nuclear powers, the likelihood of deterrence failing soon seemed all too real.

Nuclear fear did not go away as the decade went on. It only intensified. Numerous movies in the late 1950s featured plots centered on hypothetical exposure to nuclear fallout or focused on all-out nuclear war. These included *The Incredible Shrinking Man* (1957), *On the Beach* (1959), and *The World, the Flesh, and the Devil* (1959). Dwight D. Eisenhower spent his final years as president warning the American people against militarization and about the dangers of a self-promoting, self-sustaining "military-industrial complex" of generals, bureaucrats, and defense manufacturers. Even so, few listened; too few to prevent an arms race. For while Eisenhower preached, John F. Kennedy was running for president on a promise to close a purported missile gap in which the United States was said to lag behind the Soviet Union. Eisenhower's vice president and Kennedy's opponent, Richard M. Nixon, made matters worse by agreeing that the United States had fallen behind Russia, in spite of the fact that, as the administration knew, the U.S. nuclear arsenal was superior to Soviet forces in every relevant category. Fear of things atomic thus simply grew as the fifties progressed. Every new news story seemed to signal a conspiracy to make things less safe: the development of effective intercontinental missiles, the U2 incident, the Berlin crisis, and the Sputnik satellite debacle. Significantly, the fad of home fallout shelters came at the end of the decade and not at its inception.

In the religious community, the significance of the atomic age was also ambiguous. To some, like Charles Clayton Morrison, editor of the *Christian Century* and long-time pacifist, the use of atomic weaponry in Japan was the cause for great national shame and repentance. He claimed the bomb represented a strike against Christianity itself, because it placed the American churches on the moral defensive. For Morrison, the only possible way to overcome this position was for the churches to "dissociate themselves and their faith from this inhuman and reckless act of the American government," and to give voice "to the shame the American people feel concerning the barbaric methods used in their name in this war."[20] His successor, Harold Fey, still sounded that note in 1960 when he wrote an editorial entitled, "Fifteen Years in Hell Is Enough." In it Fey presented the typical belief of liberal Protestants on the issue, writing that "fifteen years of suspension over the fires of nuclear hell is enough. It is time for a change. Let us say straight out that we are not going to destroy our enemies and menace our friends by nuclear war. Let us demonstrate our good faith by getting rid of the means for these purposes. Then we may be able to confront the central question of the nuclear age: What did God intend by permitting men to learn how to release the energy of the atom at this moment in history?"[21]

Other observers read great portents of another kind in the dawning of the nuclear age. The dispensationalist Bible scholar Wilbur Smith of the Moody Bible Institute increased his fame in the fundamentalist world with the publication of a thirty-page pamphlet, "The Atomic Bomb and the Word of God," just after the close of World War II. Though warning against "amateurish speculation," Smith found remarkable parallels between current events and the Bible's statements about the endtime. For example, the passage in 2 Peter 3 that reads, "The elements shall be dissolved with fervent heat" suggested to Smith a judgment on the human race through the instrumentality of something very much like the bomb. Peter's choice of words about dissolving the elements in fact suggested the exact principle of nuclear fission.[22]

A more moderate evangelical like Carl F. H. Henry looked at the situation less apocalyptically, reading the meaning of the bomb in terms of the end of Western civilization, but not in terms of the end of humanity. Henry, indeed, spoke of the need to "remake" the modern mind for the years ahead. In his two-sided assessment of the future, Henry probably captured the sentiment of the vast majority of religious leaders. The secret of the atom, to be sure, signaled grave times; but though the world might be poised on the edge of a precipice, it was still capable of being improved, if not perfected.

At a more practical level, the ethical question of whom you should allow into your family's fallout shelter was the cause for much religious introspection and debate. L. C. McHugh, a Jesuit priest and former moral theology teacher at Georgetown University, argued in the influential Catholic journal *America* that allowing neighbors into the family shelter was tantamount to giving away the material resources your family needed to live in peacetime—an act of irresponsible charity. But what if the neighbors were to try to force their way into your shelter? This could be construed as an unjust attack and the neighbors could be repelled by force, so long as the means of force used were proportional to the attack. For McHugh, the truly Christian response was not to overcrowd the shelter, thus threatening the lives of all, but to help one's neighbors build their own shelter before it was too late. This atomic version of the lifeboat ethics problem caught the popular imagination, and responses to the moral questions posed by the case appeared in many different venues. An Episcopal priest, Frederick E. Jesset, expressed his reservations about the intrigue with the shelter issue in a *Christian Century* article, brooding, "I really wonder if our interest is so much in survival as in the fascinating possibility we might be legitimately able to get rid of our neighbors."[23] Science, which, in the popular mind, promised to provide all answers, turned out to provoke only more vexing questions.

The Making
of a Mass Culture

For most Americans, the most striking differences between living in the prewar era and in the 1950s were those that were observable right in their own homes. Television, high-fidelity sound reproduction, four-color glossy magazines, and mass-market paperback books were all commercially introduced after the Second World War, and their impact was quickly noticeable.

In the ten years between 1949 and 1959, the number of homes in the nation with television sets increased from 940,000 to 44 million. At the same time the number of commercial TV stations grew from 69 to 566. Initially, television was a technically crude medium. When it was first introduced, television was on only a few hours a day and on some networks there was no programming at all on some days. Interruptions were frequent and patient viewers quickly became familiar with the "Please Stand By" sign without sound and the "We are experiencing technical difficulties" voiceover without picture.

Because magnetic video taping was perfected only in the late 1950s, television depended on live performances. Comedies, dramas, and variety shows were done without benefit of second takes or editing for length, and were aired complete with mistakes. Until a local affiliate was wired for transmission through coaxial ground lines, it was also the industry practice to film its programs on a highly temperamental and flammable 16mm celluloid medium called Kinescope, then send the shows out to the local station for rebroadcast. The result was horrible to watch, but the people loved it nonetheless. Still, all was not bad. The underdeveloped state of the medium brought forth numerable efforts of creative genius that resulted in the period retrospectively termed "television's golden age." In addition to the creative talents of such legendary screenwriters as Reggie Rose and Paddy Chayefsky and newscasters such as Edward R. Murrow, Americans who had never been within a thousand miles of New York City were treated to Broadway plays, visualized versions of their favorite radio shows, and public hearings of congressional committees.

As television became more successful and advertising revenues climbed and technical values improved with the introduction of three-camera filming, taping, color broadcasts, satellite linking, and a move from New York to Hollywood, the medium became blander. But the American family had already learned to eat TV dinners on TV trays, and to tune in for TV news. In short, they had learned the art, as William O'Neill has suggested, of "staying together by staring together."[24] The television had swiftly become a powerful instrument for the shaping of American culture.

Above all, the television transmitted middle-class values to the middle class. People laughed at Jackie Gleason and Audrey Meadows in "The Honeymooners," but were inwardly grateful that they had transcended the Kramdens' material condition. Indeed, Americans learned what an ideal 1950s home looked and felt like by sharing weekly in the domestic life of Ozzie and Harriet Nelson and Ricky and Lucy Ricardo. Permanently capturing much of the leisure time of Americans, TV also provided a school in what Americans believed, in what they should own, do with their time, and have in their communities. Television thus served as the medium for spreading the gospel about other new phenomena. Drive-ins (both the food and movie varieties), the hi-fi, and bowling all owed their success in part to this tool of rapid national taste formation.

Television's power lay in the attention people paid to it and its resulting ability to shape and influence millions. It created celebrity heroes out of actors, loved for their personalities as much or more than for their performances. Because it was both popular and a truly national medium, TV could, and did, serve as a culture-homogenizing influence. It worked even more effectively than radio, and the movies had to break down regional patterns of speech and opinion. Moreover, as the results of the Nixon-Kennedy debates in 1960 showed, those who understood and made good use of the new technology won the hearts and minds of the people. Television had accentuated the development of mass markets for products and a mass culture for the reception of ideas, trends, and behaviors.

Given the demonstrated potential of the mass media, religious entrepreneurs were quick to mimic the secular culture. A Seventh Day Adventist minister, George F. Rustad, came up with the idea of competing with the drive-in movies by offering a drive-in church service. After an early attempt at implementing the concept in South Dakota was stifled by a snowstorm, Rustad took the concept to the Sunbelt. There the services, featuring a movie and a slide-illustrated sermon, proved a hit. Rustad echoed the sentiment of many: "We live in a new age and the churches should keep moving with the times."[25]

As Rustad suggested, religion kept moving with the times and embraced the new techniques offered by new media. Bishop Fulton J. Sheen and Norman Vincent Peale saw their already large followings multiplied by orders of magnitude when they made the shift from radio to television. Nearly every local television station carried locally produced religious programming prepared and paid for by religious groups such as Protestant councils of churches, Roman Catholic archdioceses, and independent evangelical ministers and their congregations. Others embraced the new technologies and distribution possibilities inherent in paperback books and color magazines. The deadly dull, all black-and-white-print religious periodical was being supplanted by new magazines and newsletters that featured line graphics, photographs, and two-color reproduction at a minimum. Even Sunday and Sabbath school curricula became more exciting, as denominational education boards commissioned artists and illustrators to make their materials attractive.[26] Hollywood, accurately gauging public sentiment and religion's interest in the popular arts, returned the favor and brought out numerous movies that explored religious themes without forsaking the boy-gets-girl plots the people loved.

Through the miracle of magnetic audio recording tape, it was also the 1950s that brought Americans Dial-A-Prayer. In 1956, John Sutherland Bonnell, minister of the Fifth Avenue Presbyterian Church in New York City, began running an ad reading, "FOR A SPIRITUAL LIFT IN A BUSY DAY, DIAL-A-PRAYER. CIrcle 6–4200. One minute of inspiration in prayer."

The ad proved highly successful and the idea spread rapidly to other cities and area codes. These were also the years when juke boxes played "Big Fellow in the Sky," bookstores offered *The Power of Prayer on Plants* and *Pray Your Weight Away*, and *Modern Screen* ran a series entitled, "How the Stars Found Faith."

Religious hucksters were quick to grasp the possibilities offered by the new mass market, and to employ new techniques to their utmost advantage. But the market also offered new wares that were purchased and used by even the most circumspect local congregation. The typical church or synagogue had its choice of electric organs, hi-fi prerecorded carillons, fluorescently lighted exterior crosses and Stars of David, public address systems, and modular church furniture. National denominational bodies also offered their constituent congregations the fruit of the new technologies in religious movies, books, filmstrips, and educational curricula. No matter what the source, the new mass media changed the look and feel of American religious life.

High Ideals
and Corruption from Within

The United States entered the period after the Second World War as the richest, most unfettered, and—at least in the minds of most of its citizens—the most God-blessed nation in the world. The causes of this singular blessing were variously interpreted. In one view, the nation had fought for noble ends and had fought selflessly, seeking no territorial gains and accepting no colonies. In another interpretation, America's waging of nonaggressive war had won the hearts of former enemies (even using the atomic bomb was justified on the basis of saving Japanese lives). From yet another perspective, the cause of the United States' success was that it was simultaneously the most democratic and most religious of all nations. What all these interpretations of America's fortunes in World War II had in common was their moral idealism. They linked fortune to the behavior of human beings and nations and were further premised on the belief that righteous actions led to military triumph, as well as moral victory. The skeptic had only to look at the other belligerent parties—Britain and France and their colonialism, Germany and its death camps, Japan and its long marches, Russia and its Communism—to see that the war paid back evil with evil in greater and lesser portions.

The lessons that America took from its sudden promotion to leader among the nations of the world were several in number. The first lesson was that Woodrow Wilson had been right; there was a role for a great and good nation in international affairs dedicated to the promotion of democracy throughout the world. The next was that the dictators and aggressive nations of the globe must be opposed and that the United States must play the part of policeman in stopping international crime. The third lesson was a corollary to the first two: America's right to preeminence as a force for democracy was a result of its virtue and that right could only be maintained through vigilance to virtue.

These were tragic lessons, for in failing to acknowledge that America had benefited immeasurably from the fact that the war had been fought on other nations' soil, that the United States had entered the war late, and that the production of war materials had rehabilitated the American economy, the lessons contained the seeds of their own disappointment. The foreign affairs of the United States in the postwar period came to be dominated by attempts to apply these lessons, attempts that too often seemed only to demonstrate the difficulty of replicating American democracy.

Still, the attempts to realize the ideals of American democracy abroad went on, and it is doubtful that a less idealistic people would have undertaken some of the projects of the immediate postwar years that did, in fact, better the lives of people they were meant to help. These included the Marshall Plan (1948–51), which assisted the rebuilding of Europe's economy, the Berlin Airlift (1948–49), in which the United States provided food, medicine, and clothing to the people of West Berlin lest they be overtaken by Soviet aggressors, and Point Four (1949), the American people's first government-sponsored attempt to offer technical assistance to what came to be called the Third World. To be sure, the American government ventured forth on these enterprises prodded by the specter of expanding Soviet influence in the world. Yet to a remarkable extent, the American people supported such policies because it suited their image of themselves as a generous and charitable people, always ready to provide assistance to others in times of crisis.

While idealism led to programs of international charity, it also led to postwar foreign policies built upon unrealizable hopes. Each new day during the late 1940s and early 1950s brought news that should have forced a reexamination of the myth that American know-how and virtue, having already saved the world, would soon guarantee both world peace and world freedom. In 1945, it became apparent that neither Poland nor Czechoslovakia would be free of Soviet control. In 1946, Winston Churchill spoke of an "Iron Curtain" while Bernard Baruch talked of a new kind of war, "Cold War." In 1947, there was a near Communist takeover in Greece. In 1948, it was the Berlin Crisis. In 1949 came the discovery that the Soviet Union also had atomic weapons. Dreams of a Pax Americana were undermined by nightmares of nuclear confrontation. Then, as the nation watched China come under the domination of the Communist forces of Mao Zedong, the cry went up to find out "who lost China." When, in addition, spies operating in America were discovered to have given atomic secrets to the Soviet Union, the search for America's traitors began in earnest.

The witch-hunt for Communists and other subversives began with loyalty oaths ordered of federal employees by President Truman. Taking things a step further, the House Un-American Activities Committee (HUAC) turned anticommunism into a virtual crusade. The committee held celebrated hearings into Communism in the State Department, the motion picture industry, and organized labor. Finally, where HUAC left off in its search for Communists, a freshman Republican senator from Wisconsin, desperate for a cause to improve his chances of reelection, took over. The senator was Joseph McCarthy, an opportunistic man who built a modest wartime service record into a career as a war hero, an up-and-coming politician, and a federal circuit court judge. McCarthy was also a Roman Catholic layman, and he combined a traditional Catholic hostility toward atheistic-totalitarian schemes of government, an equally traditional American nativism, and a vicious disregard for democratic rules of evidence and due process into a potent, though short-lived, political power base. McCarthy's repeated refrain was the anxious cry that after over five years of rooting out Communists from high places, they were still at work undermining the very foundations of the nation.

America's religious communities were deeply involved in the political thought and activity of the day. They were in no small way responsible for creating and maintaining the moral idealism that directed the course of postwar foreign policy. Yet they also became caught up in the charges and countercharges concerning who, and what, was subverting the American mission to the world.

Mainline Protestants, in particular, played an important role in planning for a world after the war. The most notable arena for this activity was the Federal Council of Churches' Commission on a Just and Durable Peace. The commission was chaired by John Foster Dulles, then a prominent Wall Street lawyer. The Federal Council's commission gave him an outlet for his moralistic political views, and he was joined in his efforts by prominent churchmen such as Henry P. Van Dusen, John C. Bennett, and Reinhold Niebuhr. The report of the commission was a blend of world-order utopianism and Christian realism; yet it had one feature rare in ecclesiastical commissions presuming to advise politicians, namely, it was in large part adopted—as the plan for what became the United Nations.

The idealistic confidence of the era also enabled the creation of the National Council of Churches of Christ in the U.S.A. (NCC), which brought together the Federal Council of Churches and several other interdenominational boards. The NCC's founding message, entitled "To the People of the Nation," spoke on behalf of Christianity to the body politic from a position of assumed strength: "The Council has nothing to fear from the times, though it has much to desire of them. . . . The Council stands as a guardian of democratic freedom. The revolutionary truth that men are created free follows from the revelation of God in Jesus Christ, and no person who knows that God as Father has given him all the rights of sonship is likely to remain content under a government which deprives him of basic human rights and fundamental freedoms. The nation may expect in the National Council a sturdy ally of the forces of liberty."[27] The message's language was forceful and muscular, and betrayed no sense that there was anything that the American people could not do if properly and spiritually motivated. It also conveys the enthusiasm of Christians in the 1950s for the newly rediscovered concept of human rights. For the religious liberal of the postwar years, *the* essential problem in the world was the failure of other countries to honor what Americans had known for 175 years, that all people were endowed by their creator with "certain inalienable rights." Both the Bible and the American Constitution agreed on this proposition, and what remained was for America to bring these facts to the attention of the rest of the world.

In view of the tendency to view faith as the necessary bulwark of democracy and the American mission, it is not surprising that religion and the Communist subversion scandals became hopelessly entangled. It was widely reported, for instance, that Donald Hiss, the brother of the supposed State Department traitor Alger Hiss, was receiving instruction prior to baptism in the Roman Catholic Church from none other than Fulton J. Sheen. Donald Hiss, a former State Department officer who, like his brother, had been accused of Communist sympathies, joined his brother's chief accuser, Whittaker Chambers, in professing a conversion to Christianity from the errors of his past life.[28] Meanwhile, organized Protestantism came under attack from the muckraking pamphleteer John T. Flynn, who charged in his book, *The Road Ahead*, that the United States was being slowly pushed toward socialism and ultimately toward Communism or fascism. One of the chief agents identified by Flynn in the conspiracy to deprive Americans of their democratic liberties was the Federal Council of Churches, the chief expression of ecumenical Protestantism at the time. Three Federal Council leaders were particularly singled out as responsible for leading the American people into a Communist booby-trap under the name of religion: Methodist Bishop G. Bromley Oxnam, popular author and preacher E. Stanley Jones, and Union Seminary professor John C. Bennett. The charges would continue to haunt these men and the Council's successor, the National Council of Churches, for years to come. Previously, in testimony before the House Un-American Activities Committee on 26 March 1947, J. Edgar Hoover said: "I confess to a real apprehension so long as Communists are able to secure ministers of the Gospel to promote their evil work and espouse a cause that is alien to the religion of Christ and Judaism."[29] The long-term effect of these charges from the right wing of American political life was to create an enduring suspicion among many laypersons that religious leaders were blind to the dangers of godless Communism. Throughout the fifties, any statement by religious leaders on issues of the day that was the least bit critical of the American economy or way of life was greeted with scorn and derision. In a climate of fear, the idea that even in the churches subversives were already at work easily found many followers.

There was also a religious dimension to the narrower category of McCarthyism. Catholics—whose loyalty had long been questioned by nativists who believed that Catholics' ultimate political allegiance was to Rome—demonstrated, once and for all, their opposition to Communism. Unfortunately, not all religious and ethnic groups were as lucky. The victims and targets of anticommunist witch-hunters were often Jews. In investigations of trade unions, the motion picture industry, and writers, many socialists and former Communists were named by friends and government informants. Partly because many Jews worked in the industries investigated, partly because of the interest of Jewish immigrants from Russia in the revolutionary movement that had toppled the tsarist system, and partly because the traditional Jewish interest in prophetic social justice led them to create or join organizations for radical social change, Jews were disproportionately represented among those named and blacklisted.

For Protestants, the long-range effect of the religious confrontation with Communism and anticommunism in the late 1940s and early 1950s resulted in an abiding polarization of Protestantism into two schools of thought that divided denominations, seminaries, and even local congregations. These might be called "politically liberal Protestantism" and "politically conservative Protestantism." The politically liberal Protestants tended to support their leaders' right to speak out on public issues. For them, every political issue was a moral issue, and thus a religious issue. On the other hand, the politically conservative Protestants maintained that the church needed to attend to spiritual matters and believed that political issues were best left to the consciences of individuals and to the experts in government who could be expected to "know what is best." Even so, the conservatives and liberals shared the same basic assumptions about the American role in the postwar world. The conservatives accused the liberally oriented of being insufficiently attuned to the blessings of liberty and to the fragility of democracy. Politically liberal Protestants responded that the test of a democracy was how well it tolerated dissent directed toward its perfection, and they produced a whole host of literature arguing this point.[30] Fundamentally, however, both parties agreed that the American tree was ready for transplantation and would easily take root when planted in new soil, in lands where others were hungry for its fruits.

For all the expressions of fear about Communism, there was little articulation of national self-doubt. These were confident times and few Americans were prepared to hear the somber realism of Reinhold Niebuhr. In his 1952 book, *The Irony of American History*, Niebuhr pointed out the distance between the desires and possibilities of the hour in one broad stroke. "Our age," he wrote, "is involved in irony because so many dreams of our nation have been so cruelly refuted by history. Our dreams of a pure virtue are dissolved in a situation in which it is possible to exercise the virtue of responsibility toward a community of nations only by courting the prospective guilt of the atomic bomb. And the irony is increased by the frantic efforts of some of our idealists to escape this hard reality by dreaming up schemes of an ideal world order which have no relevance to either our present dangers or our urgent duties."[31] In the America of 1952 both dreams of pure virtue and schemes for an ideal world were alive and well.

The greatest irony of American history in the fifties was, as it had been throughout the nation's history, that the rights and liberties Americans recommended to others were denied to some at home on the basis of race and color. The Communist crisis drew undue public attention during the fifties. Meanwhile, issues of race quietly ate at the soul of the American Dream.

America at the end of World War II was a country where only 250,000 black Americans were registered to vote in the states of the former Confederacy, and where blacks could not obtain hotel and restaurant accommodations in many cities in the northern states as well as in the South. It was a country whose national pastime, baseball, had no black athletes in the major leagues, and a country whose armed forces had regular companies and "Negro units"—units often not trained in combat but only in servicing the domestic requirements of white officers. It was a land in which blacks rode at the back of the bus in urban areas and in segregated railcars when traveling cross-country. Public schools, South and North, were segregated by custom and, in some places, by law—law that was protected by the Constitution of the United States under the judicial doctrine of "separate but equal." It was a country where a black man could still be lynched for looking at a white woman with "too much familiarity" and where police authorities would defend the action of the lynch mob.[32]

Progress toward racial equality came from diverse sources in the postwar years. Gains were made through the Truman administration's use of executive orders, through the efforts of the National Association for the Advancement of Colored Persons (NAACP) to obtain equality under the law through court challenges to the institution of Jim Crow, and through the initiative of religious and civically minded groups of citizens determined to counter racism through direct action. Cultural events pointed up the contradictions of institutionalized racism in the "land of the free." Jackie Robinson joined the Brooklyn Dodgers in 1947 and encountered racist hatred on a personal basis almost daily in his first years with the team, but there was no denying he was a superb athlete. The constant reporting of the indignities he was forced to suffer because of his race caused many white Americans to reexamine the racial climate of their country. The experience of black Americans was also interpreted to the wider culture in two highly explosive and much-read autobiographical novels, Richard Wright's *Black Boy* and Ralph Ellison's *Invisible Man*. Together the Wright and Ellison books painted a picture of a brutal and brutalizing America that was not confined to the deep South, but could be found in northern ghettos, too.[33]

Good feelings of fairness, feelings of shame, and even potent portrayals of growing up black in America, while stirring the emotions of people disposed to see the world differently, did not in and of themselves secure the blessings of liberty for blacks. And so it was that the NAACP's strategy of supporting legal challenges to racial injustice became important in translating changing racial attitudes into public policy protected by the Constitution. In 1954, the NAACP realized a crowning achievement in its struggle against segregated public education, when in its decision in the four cases collectively known as *Brown v. Board of Education* the Supreme Court unanimously declared: "We conclude that in the field of public education the doctrine of 'separate but equal' has no place." [34]

Legal rights also have their limits, and many of the white citizens of the southern states vowed a policy of "massive resistance" against the enforcement of the Court's school integration order. The NAACP continued to pursue legal redress through the courts, but the pattern of subtle and not so subtle resistance to the law by the states, Congress, and even the Eisenhower administration made clear the need for additional tactics on behalf of the goal of racial justice.[35] For the balance of the decade, the most important new tactic was nonviolent direct action.

The direct-action approach to the modern quest for civil rights dated to 1941 and labor leader A. Philip Randolph's March on Washington movement. Though short-lived, the mass organization of African Americans poised to march on the District of Columbia posed a substantial enough threat to Franklin D. Roosevelt to cause him to create the Fair Employment Practices Committee. Soon after, in 1942, a group with roots in the Quaker organization, the Fellowship of Reconciliation, formed the Congress of Racial Equality (CORE). CORE's religious pacifist founders were interested in applying nonviolent, direct-action techniques to racial problems. CORE combined lessons learned from the Indian leader Mahatma Gandhi with a more indigenous new protest instrument—the sit-in— which was apparently derived from the famous 1930s sit-down strikes in Detroit's automobile factories. CORE, a mostly white organization at its inception, used the technique of placing its members' bodies where segregationists found them obstructive and succeeded in opening up Chicago pools and restaurants to people of both races shortly after the end of the war. It also pioneered what would later be called the "Freedom Ride," in which black and white members would ride interstate buses to test compliance with the Supreme Court's *Morgan v. Virginia* decision of 1946, in which the court held that states' requirements of segregation on such buses constituted an undue restraint of interstate commerce.[36]

Not all religious groups acted like CORE and campaigned for fairness and justice. Religious bodies were also deeply involved in the perpetuation of the racial status quo. The *Christian Century*'s Memphis correspondent reported in March 1950 that his city's Brotherhood Week had been a great success. Nearly all civic organizations holding meetings that week had requested a speaker from the observance's sponsor, the local chapter of the National Conference of Christians and Jews. Yet the NCCJ itself was hostile to inclusion of blacks in Brotherhood Week events, explaining that the NCCJ was, after all, "not an interracial organization."[37] In the end it was not CORE, but a young Baptist minister, Martin Luther King, Jr., who seized the attention of the nation and provided the inspiration necessary to galvanize a considerable portion of the religious community to throw its weight behind the cause of racial justice.

King was pastor of the Dexter Avenue Baptist Church in Montgomery, Alabama, when Rosa Parks was arrested for refusing to give up her seat on a city bus on 1 December 1955. A prominent citizen, E. D. Nixon, proposed that King head an association that would end busing segregation. King was ready to join such an effort, but he was not prepared to be its president. Nevertheless, as Lerone Bennett wrote of him: "King did not seek leadership in Montgomery; leadership sought him."[38] King soon found himself not only the president of a local group, but the spiritual leader of a national movement.

King's leadership quickly placed him in the path of enacted hatred. First came threats, then violence. When King's home was bombed on 30 January 1956, his commitment to nonviolence was sorely tested. Yet when he was faced with a racial confrontation in his front yard that night, King was able to calm the crowd, saying: "We must love our white brothers, no matter what they do to us. We must make them know that we love them. Jesus still cries out in words that echo across the centuries. 'Love your enemies; bless them that curse you; pray for them that despitefully use you.' This is what we must live by. We must meet hate with love. *Remember, if I am stopped, this movement will not stop, because God is with the movement.* Go home with this glowing faith and this radiant assurance."[39]

King's ability to preach the gospel of nonviolence in this way proved the decisive catalyst for inspiring thousands of clergy and millions of Christians and Jews to see things King's way and join the struggle. These people, impressed by King's display of faithfulness, took their cues for action from King himself as communicated to them by influential magazines such as *Life* and *Time*. In 1957, after the success of the Montgomery bus boycott had propelled him to national recognition, the *Christian Cen-*

tury asked King to write an article on the crisis in race relations. King took the opportunity to set the terms of protest for the religious civil rights movement. The methods would be nonviolent and they would be directed at positive ends. He began by rooting the need for nonviolence in the words of Jesus, asking, "How is the struggle against the forces of injustice to be waged? There are two possible answers. One is resort to the all-too-prevalent method of physical violence and corroding hatred. The danger of this method is its futility. Violence solves no social problems; it merely creates new and more complicated ones. Through the vistas of time a voice still cries to every potential Peter, 'Put up your sword!'"[40] King went on to make five points about nonviolence: it was not a method for cowards, it did resist evil; its objective was not to humiliate the opponent, but to win the opponent over; its methods were directed against evil, not against people; it avoided not only "external physical violence but also internal violence of the spirit"; and it was based on the conviction that the universe was on the side of justice. King elaborated his final point: "There is something at the very center of our faith which reminds us that Good Friday may reign for a day, but ultimately it must give way to the triumphant beat of the Easter drums. Evil may so shape events that Caesar will occupy a palace and Christ a cross, but one day that same Christ will rise up and split history into A.D. and B.C., so that even the life of Caesar must be dated by his name. So in Montgomery we can walk and never get weary, because we know that there will be a great camp meeting in the promised land of freedom and justice."[41]

In retrospect, with such a clear linking of racial justice to the essential features of the gospel, the emergence of a successful civil rights movement out of the ranks of people inspired by King's message and example is not surprising. Yet this was still a time when segregation also had its Christian apologists. As of 21 March 1956, there were reportedly no voluntary organizations supporting the Supreme Court's decisions, but more than forty anti-Court organizations had been formed. These included the infamous "White Citizens Councils," some of which went so far as to specifically exclude those who did not ascribe to "the divinity of Jesus Christ."[42]

More telling, perhaps, of the enormity of the resistance to racial justice among white Christians were the kinds of letters that were regularly sent to the editors of major religious periodicals after they had run articles suggesting even moderation in solving the problems of segregation. A typically bad example appeared in the February 1, 1956, issue of the *Christian Century*: "Sir: I am shocked to learn that a preacher of the

Gospel of Christ does not seem to know that almighty God was the author of segregation of the races. . . . The main cause of his sending the judgment of the flood was the sons of God (the righteous line of Seth) intermarrying with the unrighteous line of Cain." The author, Arnold Z. Mathews of Columbus, Georgia, combined his religious/racial interpretation of the so-called "curse of Ham" (an interpretation that had long supported slavery before it was used to prop up segregation) with a view of current events that was exceedingly common, further voicing his opinion that "the Supreme Court patterned after the Communist platform when they handed down their diabolical decision, in fact they got it from the Russian Reds, who got integration of the races directly from his satanic majesty." After wishing a Negro son-in-law on each and every supporter of school integration, he closed his letter by saying, "I hope you see your mistake and repent. If you don't, it will not be good for you when you are called to meet the Author of segregation."[43] The racial invective in this example was remarkable for its degree, but not for its presence. The American racial situation was an underlying problem for Christians and Jews throughout the fifties and one of the factors that most worked to curb the triumphalism of the period.

The blossoming of a civil rights movement in the last years of the 1950s may appear to argue against our central thesis about the period, namely, that fueled by the realization of dreams long deferred, and driven by optimistic hopes for the future, the American people approached their world, their work, and their lives with a conviction that their civilization was the greatest ever achieved and that continued progress was guaranteed. Painted against this background, the civil rights movement appears as a stark contrasting image; an admission that the civilization had a long way to go. And yet, looking at the writings and speeches of Martin Luther King and the actions of the protesters, boycotters, and riders, it is impossible to fail to detect that same note of optimism so characteristic of other aspects of postwar American culture. Here, too, things were getting better. Racial justice, television, American democracy, space exploration, domestic housing, and automobile production were all boats set in a flowing river of progress. Some moved more slowly, perhaps, while some needed human help to keep from foundering, but all crafts moved forward in the swift stream of postwar advance. To the dominant way of thinking, the reason for that river of progress had much to do with the subject of our next chapter: the return to religion.

2

The
Return to Religion

■

In the late 1920s and early 1930s, it appeared to many observers that the age of religion was quickly passing. Only a generation before, a great evangelical consensus had seemed to rule the nation. Now people were tired of fundamentalist and modernist alike, with their claims that respectively either violated common sense or evacuated the traditional rewards and values of religion. Instead of joining in the fray, the public wished a plague on both their houses and expressed its own sentiments about organized religion by voting with its feet and, in the words of one wag, "staying away in droves." The American public ignored or defied Protestantism's great contribution to national morality—prohibition—and readily embraced a wealth of new entertainments that organized religion looked askance at: card playing, public dancing, the fashion of short skirts and "immodest" swimwear, motion pictures, motoring trips on Sundays, and unchaperoned dating for single adults all became popular during the twenties. Meanwhile, church attendance declined, not only in the economically depressed rural areas, but also throughout the country generally. At the same time, in 1928 the Foreign Missionary Conference of North America reported that only 252 students had offered themselves for foreign missionary work, as compared to 2,700 students eight years earlier. Clearly, the vital signs of organized religion had taken a turn for the worse.[1]

Intellectuals also turned on religion. Sinclair Lewis's books, *Elmer Gantry*, *Dodsworth*, *Babbitt*, *Arrowsmith*, and *Mainstreet*, all appearing in the

1920s, left no doubt where he stood on the subject of religion, and earned him the Nobel Prize for literature, the first American to win the award. Pearl Buck's *The Good Earth* was as hard on missionaries as Lewis had been on domestic evangelists and ministers, but caught the public's attention and garnered the critics' praises. For her efforts, Buck won the Pulitzer Prize in 1932 and received the Nobel Prize in 1938. But it was the Baltimore newspaper writer H. L. Mencken who most regularly and—for his generation—memorably excoriated religion:

Any literate plowhand, if the Holy Spirit inflames him, is thought to be fit to preach. Is he commonly sent, as preliminary, to a training camp, to college? But what a college! You will find one in every mountain valley of the land, with its single buildings in its bare pasture lot, and its faculty of half-idiot pedagogues and brokendown preachers. One man, in such a college, teaches oratory, ancient history, arithmetic and Old Testament exegesis. This aspirant comes in from the barnyard, and goes back in a year or two to the village. His body of knowledge is that of a street-car motorman or a vaudeville actor. But he has learned the clichés of his craft, and he has got him a long-tailed coat, and so he has made his escape from the harsh labors of his ancestors, and is set up as a fountain of light and learning.[2]

Was it any wonder that the ministry was seen as an unattractive profession, and that churches had difficulty filling their pulpits in this time that Robert T. Handy has rightly labeled, "The American Religious Depression," or that a group of prominent thinkers in New York should issue a Humanist Manifesto in 1936? Unquestionably the time had come to abandon faith in all such outmoded, otherworldly schemes of religion that had repeatedly demonstrated their all-too-human origins and weaknesses. Or so it seemed.[3] During the course of World War II, however, religion's fortunes began to perceptively improve. Over the course of the next fifteen years the increasing interest in religion would prove to be an enduring and multifaceted phenomena. The return to religion would come to have popular and intellectual dimensions, to have a close affinity with the psychological outlook of the day, though first of all the return was evidenced in the increased membership and attendance at the nation's houses of worship. It is therefore appropriate that we consider first the ecclesiastical dimension of the return to religion.

Rebound from the American Religious Depression

At the beginning of the 1950s, postwar church growth had already been noted and an explanation advanced by Benson Y. Landis, editor of the *Yearbook of American Churches*: "The people of the United States turned to churches in a period of war, international crisis and the atomic age—1940–1950—to a much greater extent than during the depression years of the '30s or the relatively prosperous years of the '20s."[4] Yet at this point, in 1950, it remained to be seen whether once the crisis disappeared the church members would as well. In fact, the churchgoers did not disappear. Even so, as the American people settled into the fifties, they continued to watch the figures on church membership and attendance with intense interest.

In a culture where the past year's batting averages of famous baseball players could be used as a wartime sign of whether a stranger was an American or an enemy spy, it is not surprising that Americans recorded and consumed statistics about their religious life. Fascinated by figures and percentages, Americans read not only their past but, they hoped, also their national destiny in new reports of the growth in the numbers of churches, in religious giving, in new church building starts, in the numbers of people professing a belief in God, and in the level of those who engaged in prayer. In a culture locked into growth as a way of life, Americans sought proof of their progress—material and moral—in statistics. The major newsweeklies, newspapers, and radio and television stations all regularly obliged the thirst for these signs of progress; so too did a popular annual book entitled *The Yearbook of American Churches*. Even at the level of the local congregation, the figures were hard to miss. From the pew in many a church, worshippers could look up to signs on the wall not only for the numbers of the day's hymn selections, but also for the Sunday school and church attendance, with figures in two columns labeled "One Year Ago" and "Last Week." It was a rare church in the 1950s where the figures under "Last Week" were not the larger ones.

The newsweeklies never tired of running the church statistics stories. Year after year in the fifties they appeared with titles such as "High Tide of Faith," "88,000,000 Strong," "Emphasis on Religion," "Many Mansions," "Numbering the Faithful," "New High," and "Those Church Statistics." Throughout the decade the story was always the same: the trends

TABLE 2.1

Religious Affiliation by Group, 1951–1961

Year	Membership	Buddhist	Old Catholics	Eastern Orthodox	Jews	Catholics	Protestants	Total U.S. Population
1951	88,673,005	73,000	337,408	1,858,585	5,000,000	29,241,580	52,162,432	150,697,361
1952	92,277,129	73,000	366,956	2,353,783	5,000,000	30,253,427	54,229,963	
1953	94,842,845	63,000	366,088	2,100,171	5,000,000	31,476,261	55,837,325	
1954	97,482,611	63,000	367,370	2,024,219	5,500,000	32,403,332	57,124,142	
1955	100,162,529	63,000	367,918	2,386,945	5,500,000	33,396,647	58,448,567	
1956	103,224,954	63,000	351,068	2,598,055	5,500,000	34,563,851	60,148,980	
1957	104,189,678	10,000	468,978	2,540,446	5,500,000	35,846,477	59,823,777	
1958	109,557,741	10,000	488,246	2,545,318	5,500,000	39,509,508	61,504,669	
1959	112,226,905	20,000	484,489	2,807,612	5,500,000	40,871,302	62,543,502	
1960	114,449,217	20,000	589,819	2,698,663	5,367,000	42,104,900	63,668,835	
1961	116,109,929	60,000	572,897	2,800,401	5,365,000	42,876,665	64,434,966	179,323,175

Percentage increase from 1951–1961:

	30.94	−17.81	69.79	50.67	7.30	46.63	23.53	19.00

SOURCE: G.F. Ketcham and B.Y. Landis, eds., *Yearbook of American Churches* (Nashville: Abingdon, 1951–1961).

NOTE: The category "Old Catholics" includes all Western Rite, non-Roman Catholics. The figures reported for Buddhists and Jews are round figures since the editors of the *Yearbook of American Churches* simply reported the figures given by the institutional representatives of religious groups, which for these groups were estimates and not the results of a census. The estimate of 5.5 million Jews throughout the 1950s, for instance, came from the *American Jewish Yearbook*, where the figures themselves were the result of compromises between the branches of American Judaism, some of which did not want to count Jews at all.

were up and up, and more Americans belonged to a church or synagogue than ever before in history. (A summary of these statistics appears in Table 2.1.)

The statistics indicated that people were formally affiliating with churches at rates faster than the growth in population alone might provide. Thus, while the U.S. population grew at a rate of 19 percent in the 1950s, the overall number of persons in a church or synagogue grew by more than 30 percent. The proportion of the population that was institutionally religiously affiliated thus rose in ten years from 59 to 65 percent. At first glance, this does not appear to be a large shift. But seen from the perspective of the religious groups themselves, the numbers were quite striking: given the sizable increase in population, and the fact that the religious groups were enjoying an ever-increasing market share of the population, a typical denomination might see its ranks increase by as much as half in the course of the 1950s.

Viewed over a longer period of time, the change that the postwar period represented over that of the "religious depression" was even more dramatic. At the beginning of the decade, even before the 1950s increases were factored in, a National Council of Churches report noted that over the years 1926–1949 the percentage of the population who were church members had increased 51.6 percent, while the population itself grew less than 30 percent, this church growth being concentrated mostly in the 1940s. The report also noted, however, that among the fastest growing churches were some of the evangelistic sects such as the Church of God in Christ (1,025 percent) and the Assemblies of God (474 percent). "Once thought of as appealing especially to the socially disadvantaged," the report remarked, these churches were "now bringing into their ranks large numbers of the 'comfortable' portion of the population."[5]

A second way to measure the popularity of organized religion in the 1950s was to go right to the people and ask them with what religious tradition they identified themselves. This was the approach favored by the Bureau of the Census, which in 1957 made its first test of the religious waters in twenty-one years (see Table 2.2.). Here again, the indications were that religion was more popular than ever. The census's conclusion that 96.39 percent of the adult public identified itself with a religious tradition was paralleled by findings of Gallup Opinion Surveys administered in adjacent years. The total percentage of adults expressing some religious preference in these surveys was found to be 94, 98, and 98 percent for the years 1947, 1952, and 1962, respectively. This meant that

TABLE 2.2

Religions Reported by American Civilians

Religion	Persons 14 years of age and over	Percentage Distribution
Protestant	78,952,000	66.16
Catholic	30,669,000	25.70
Jewish	3,868,000	3.24
Other Religion	1,545,000	1.29
No Religion	3,195,000	2.68
Not Reported	1,104,000	0.93
Total	119,333,000	100.00

SOURCE: *Current Population Reports* (Washington, D.C.: Bureau of the Census, Series P-20, No. 79, 2 February 1958).

a high percentage of Americans classified themselves as Protestant, Catholic, or Jewish, whether or not they were claimed as members of particular religious bodies representing those traditions. Moreover, the statistics show a small increase in the 1950s in the percentage of people identifying themselves as religious, and a tremendous decrease in the number of persons professing no religion: in 1947 6 percent of all adult Americans expressed no religious connection or preference, a figure that was to drop by two-thirds throughout the 1950s and was not to be equaled again until 1975.

Comparing these figures for religious identification with the church membership statistics for the 1950s, several things become clear. People considered themselves Protestants without actually belonging to a church, so that no particular church could claim them as a member. Protestantism appeared to be the basic default option for many Americans in this period, and if organized Protestantism claimed only 59,823,777 actual members, it represented the psychological home of a far larger number of Americans. Indeed, in retrospect it can be argued that this was the last era in which Protestantism was truly hegemonic in American culture.

As for Roman Catholics, the number of adults identifying themselves as Catholics corresponded much more closely to the number of members the Roman Catholic Church reported in its *Official Catholic Directory*. Allowing for the 27 percent of the nearly 36 million Roman Catholics reported in the *Directory* in 1957 as being below the age of fourteen, we can calculate that approximately 26.2 million persons over the age of fourteen were counted by the Church as members, leaving another 4.4 million expressing a preference for Catholicism without actually being counted as a member by the Church. This is, however, deceptive, because the Census Bureau did not provide a separate category for the more than three million Catholics of Polish, Armenian, Ukrainian, Greek, and Russian origins, among others. Thus, the proportion of Catholics who were not associated with an actual parish was much lower than the proportion of Protestants similarly situated. Indeed, these years were ones in which the typical Roman Catholic was almost twice as likely as a Protestant and more than three times as likely as a Jew to attend a religious service in an average week. Of the three major American religious traditions, Catholics were thus bound most closely to a regular congregational expression of their religion; yet both of these other traditions experienced substantial increases in service attendance.

When we turn to the statistics for Jewish identification, we see that the census found that 4,975,000 persons of all ages identified their religious preference as Jewish. This contrasts with the *American Jewish Yearbook's* estimate that there were five and a half million Jews in the United States. Thus it would appear that of the three major American religious traditions, only Judaism had fewer people claiming to be adherents than official estimates provided for. But this comparison would be misleading, for the official estimates of how many Jews lived in the United States were not based on the number of synagogue members, but rather on sociologists' and demographers' estimates of the number of living persons of Jewish descent. Looming large behind these statistics was the debate over what should be reported. Nathan Glazer called attention to the split between "Judaism, the historic religion, and Jewishness—namely, all the activities which Jews came together to carry on without the auspices of religion."[6] This split found a parallel in the ranks of those called on to count the Jewish population: some demographers favored reporting based on a more religious definition of who was a Jew than others did. Meanwhile, with the exception of the Union of American Hebrew Congregations—the Reform branch of American Judaism—the national Jewish denominational bodies kept no reliable counts of the number of congregations associated with them. To obtain figures exactly corresponding to the membership statistics of Christian churches is therefore impossible. However, even from the fragmentary evidence that is available, a case can be made that there was a revival of interest in Judaism and a return to its formal institutions in the 1950s. The Union of American Hebrew

TABLE 2.3

Per Capita Giving by Full or Confirmed Members to Selected Protestant Churches and Growth in Religious Giving in Relation to Per Capita Disposable Income, 1950–1960 (All Figures Adjusted to 1967 Constant Dollars)

Denomination	1950 ($)	1955 ($)	Change 1950–1955 (%)	1960 ($)	Change 1950–1955 (%)	Increase in Giving above Income Growth (%)	
						1950–1955	1955–1960
Church of God (Anderson, Ind.)	—	135.92	—	148.76	9.4	—	4.3
Church of the Nazarene	145.14	156.61	7.9	160.41	2.4	3.1	-2.7
Episcopal Church	58.87	60.52	2.8	72.7	20.1	-2.0	15
Lutheran Church in America	49.26	68.08	38.2	82.23	20.8	33.4	15.7
Lutheran Church–Missouri Synod	68.75	95.18	38.4	108.39	13.9	33.6	8.8
Southern Baptist Convention	39.58	55.54	40.3	62.75	13.0	35.5	7.9
United Church of Christ	51.52	71.48	38.7	83.88	17.3	33.9	12.2
United Methodist Church	37.25	53.45	43.5	62.93	17.7	38.7	12.6
United Presbyterian Church	55.3	84.63	53.0	95.03	12.3	48.2	7.2
Per Capita Disposable Income	1,982	2,077	4.8	2,183	5.1		

Source: Jackson W. Carroll, Douglas W. Johnson, and Martin E. Marty, *Religion in American: 1950 to the Present* (San Francisco: Harper and Row, 1979), 23.

Congregations had roughly 300 synagogues in the early 1940s and about 500 in 1955. In the same period, the estimated number of Conservative synagogues increased from 200 to 500. In both cases, the average size of the congregations rose. Another way to gauge the institutional vitality of Judaism in the postwar period is to note that the number of children getting any kind of Jewish religious education rose from approximately 230,000 in 1946 to about 400,000 in 1954. Despite the much heralded baby boom, it was hardly likely, as Nathan Glazer observed, that the school age Jewish population rose by more than 73 percent.[7] Thus, here too, the indications were that ecclesiastical affiliation was on the rise.

A third way to measure the popularity of institutional religion is to examine financial data. The 1950s witnessed the greatest church-building boom in American history, in which three billion dollars was spent on new church construction from the end of the war through the summer of 1955. By then a pattern had been established. One out of four of the new buildings was thoroughly modern in architecture. Redwood, abstract stained glass, windows composed of rectangles, a resemblance to Noah's ark, movable seating, and the parabola all came to stay.[8] Though some of this new construction was financed through long-term mortgages, it reflected in the main a tremendous increase in giving to religious organizations, as illustrated in Table 2.3.

What Table 2.3 indicates is that, for a wide range of denominations, the 1950s were a time of increasing financial commitment to churches. Since these figures are adjusted for 1967 constant dollars and are per capita levels of giving, the information reported does not merely reflect increased memberships or wage price levels. Instead, the figures indicate that individuals in these years were willing to give an increasing proportion of their total disposable incomes to a religious organization. Thus it can be empirically stated that on average individuals were finding organized religion to be of increasing value relative to other goods and services in the 1950s. The impact of this increased valuation was compounded by the religious bodies' membership growth already noted and by real increases in the average American's disposable income. The net result was that religious bodies found themselves rich beyond their dreams as the dollars available for new buildings, for increased educational services and bureaucracy, and for mission and relief activities grew in rates well in excess of the already tremendous rate of growth of real national income.

We have established that people in the 1950s joined religious organizations in increasing numbers, that they sought to identify themselves with the major religions of their country, and that they contributed monetarily to the support of organized religion at a level that had no prior parallel. But to get at how they felt and what they thought about their churches and synagogues, we must turn from statistics to more literary evidence. In reading the magazines and newspapers of the era, we find that in the 1950s the church was popular in its own right.

Beginning in 1954, *Good Housekeeping* ran a series of articles under the name "I Remember a Church" about different churches "by different people who love them."[9] For its part, *Holiday* magazine had a regular feature entitled "Place of the Month" in which a covered bridge, or a museum, or the Grand Canyon might be spotlighted as a place for Americans to visit on vacation. For the December 1952 issue, the Place of the Month was the church. Alongside a photograph of a quintessential New England congregational church, an essay appeared extolling the virtues of the church and recommending it to one and all: "Throughout the entire world, to those who sense the immemorial voices of herald angels proclaiming Glory to God in the Highest, and on earth peace, good will toward men, there is only one fortress of the human spirit. It is the church in all its forms. Wherever it exists among the uncertainties of an uncertain world in 1952, it is the place to be as often as possible during this birth month of Christianity, for within its walls there are no destroying confusions, only one great truth: God is a friend." After this theological affirmation, *Holiday* proceeded to celebrate the United States' foundation of national greatness based on faith and freedom and to demonstrate the proposition that despite the many variations of form—from converted Bowery pool hall to Indian Reservation Quonset hut to towering Gothic cathedral, and locales from Korean battlefields to suburbia—there was but one essential church, concluding: "The church is ubiquitous and within it at this time of the year, as at all times there is room for every traveler. Who will say, in 1952, no matter how seemingly snug and self-contained, that he is not a traveler and the church not a sanctuary?"[10] Clearly, in *Holiday* magazine's view at least, the church had arrived.

More common than *Holiday*'s open endorsement of the church as a place to be were articles reporting the religious building boom. Here the churches were popular as objects of art and architectural endeavor. *McCall's* adoring coverage of the new churches was typical. Under the title, "The Churches Rise Again," McCall's proclaimed proudly, "Not since Solomon have people lavished so much on housing for God and those who would worship Him."[11] And what marvelous housing it was. It displayed all the features of modern design and employed a great proportion of the creative energies of the era's architectural innovators, for after all, commissions for church building in dollar volume in the 1950s were second only to hospital construction. And of all kinds of construction, perhaps only art museums offered more symbolic possibilities and freedom from functional concerns. Pietro Belluschi, Dean of Architecture at the Massachusetts Institute of Technology, sang the praises of the new forms for religious architecture over the old: "It is easy to prove by any standard that imitative forms have no power to move, and that only the joyous excitement of new ideas, surging from a deeply felt experience and expressed with poetic clarity in structural honesty, can succeed in giving spiritual and emotional nourishment."[12] It was estimated that 25 percent of all new Christian houses of worship were of completely contemporary design. For synagogues, estimates were as high as 85 percent.[13] But one did not need Frank Lloyd Wright or Marcel Breuer to build a church appropriate to the spirit of the age.[14] For those many Americans who were so inclined, the *Saturday Evening Post* carried an article entitled, "How to Build Your Own Church," neatly allowing them to combine two of the most popular activities of the 1950s in a single experience.[15]

The new style in ecclesiastical building also had its disciples among churchgoers. As one man put it upon coming out of services at a thoroughly modern church, "For the first time I feel that in going to church I haven't left life!"[16] Indeed, the easy functionality of the spaces outside the sanctuary bore a striking similarity to that found in the modern suburban tract home. The Sunday school had moved out from a dank basement underneath an urban sanctuary into a wing of its own with lots of light; little fiberglass and plywood-laminated tables and chairs—even tiny toilets—made especially for God's smaller children reinforced the impression that here, too, the prevailing culture was child-centered. Boy Scouts, Girl Scouts, teen clubs, square dances, B'nai Brith, meetings of the temple sisterhood, pancake dinners, potluck suppers, hobby clubs, and choirs for all ages filled out the activity calendar and physical space of the typical suburban church or synagogue. All this activity seemed to be fueled by refreshments. As David Siegel, the Executive Director of Long Island's Hillcrest Jewish Center, remarked: "There's no gathering that can take place without danish and coffee."[17] Indeed, while older rural and urban churches were still debating the morality of the trend toward the "coffee hour" held for socializing between members before or after worship services, suburban congregations led the way and almost universally adopted this greatest innovation in American church life since Charles G. Finney's "New Measures" had been introduced in the revivals of the early nineteenth century. The coffee hour, the new member's group, the emphasis on children, and the endless round of social activities all indicated that the church or synagogue of the 1950s was serving a great variety of felt needs. The religious center's popularity derived from multiple sources, but not to be discounted was the role it played as a de facto community center.

This newfound popularity of the church and synagogue did not escape critical observers. Canon Bernard Iddings Bell, of the Episcopal Church, warned that "Churchianity" was a clear and present danger for both his own church and the other Protestant mainline churches, for in mixing devotion to a church with the power of faith it was quite conceivable that men and women could be good church members with no knowledge of Christianity or commitment to Christ. The popularity of the church or synagogue in the 1950s was beyond question, but as Bell pointed out, the reasons why Americans were seeking out the church were far from clear. An interpretation of the causes of the return to institutional religion will be offered later in the chapter, but for now it may do to ponder one answer the phenomenon's contemporaries offered. Regularly during the 1950s an advertisement appeared on the church page of the *Dallas Times Herald* that proclaimed reasons for going to church: "The Church for All, All for the Church. The Church is the greatest factor on earth for the building of character and good citizenship. It is a storehouse of spiritual values. Without a strong Church, neither democracy nor civilization can survive. There are four sound reasons why every person should attend services regularly and support the Church. They are: (1) For his own sake. (2) For his children's sake. (3) For the sake of his community and nation. (4) For the sake of the Church itself, which needs his moral and material support. Plan to go to Church regularly and read your Bible daily."[18]

The Popular Return of Religion

As popular as the church and the synagogue were in the America of the 1950s, they were not the sum total of the popular return to religion. The massive popularity of religion in the 1950s was also manifested in an increasingly expressed public belief in God, in interest in prayer, and in devotion to religion itself.

God

In an opinion research survey by Ben Gaffin & Associates in 1952, 99 percent of Americans over eighteen years of age professed belief in God. Nearly 100 percent of the women surveyed counted themselves sure of a God, while 98 percent of men expressed this same belief. Out of every 100 persons, however, 87 were "absolutely certain" there was a God. By religious affiliation the percentage of "absolutely sure" respondents was Catholics, 92; Protestants, 87; and Jews, 70. Of those with no religious affiliation, 55 percent were completely certain of the existence of God, while 12 percent did not believe in God. One of the things the survey demonstrated without explicitly trying to do so was that the percentage of the population that identified itself with no religious tradition was very small indeed.[19] Here too, in counting believers as with counting church members, there was a tendency to judge the faithfulness of the nation on the basis of statistics. *Time* and *Newsweek* both ran, on average, a story a year on the results of "Do you believe in God?" surveys. The interpretation given to the results is indicated by the headlines under which the stories appeared: "99 to 1," "Proof of God," "I Believe in God," "Glory, Glory, Glory."[20]

The respondents to the 1954 Gallup Poll's survey of religious belief who confessed to a belief in God—96 percent—were asked what they thought was the most convincing argument for God's existence. Their replies, in order of frequency, were as follows: "(1) The order and majesty of the world around us, (2) There must be a Creator to explain the origin of man and the world, (3) There is proof of God in the Bible (or other church authority), (4) Past experience in life give me faith that there is a God, (5) Believing in God gives me much comfort."[21] The reliance on design and first causes as arguments for the existence of God represented a departure from the nineteenth-century view, which, chastened by the criticisms of David Hume, tended to favor arguments from the emotional experience of the individual believer. John Wesley's argument, that the "heart strangely warmed" provided a believer with the best available evidence of the reality of God, had been readily accepted by generations of Americans who came to faith by means of the great evangelical revivals. But the generation that joined the revival of religion in the 1950s desired something more universal to stake their newfound faith upon, and so not surprisingly they returned to the arguments of the existence of God that had undergirded the faith of the middle ages. They also tended not to trust in the subjective nature of individual experience and—as much or more than other generations—wanted to believe with assurance in the existence of God without themselves actually having to have "a religious experience." This fact, however, did not mean that people of the fifties were not interested in the religious experiences of others. On the contrary, stories of personal experiences of God were popular features in many mass-market magazines.

Howard Whitman, a reporter on assignment for *Collier's*, went "in search of God" in a multipart series for the magazine. Two of the places he visited in his search—Fort Sam Houston, where Korean War evacuees came for medical treatment, and the scientist's laboratory—were significant sites for disclosing his contemporaries' conceptions of God. The battle-scarred soldiers at Fort Sam Houston discussed fate, luck, destiny, and the deity and faced the problem of theodicy in a variety of ways. Some were fatalistic: "When the old man swings that scythe," said one master sergeant, "there's no use ducking." A member of a bomber crew that survived a particularly heavy engagement stated his belief that they survived because they believed they would survive. The power of positive thinking was championed by other soldiers as well. But where was God in all of this? The bomber crew member opined, "You don't suppose God put His finger down and said, 'These men will come through.' Naw, He had more important things to do." But Lieutenant Colonel William F. Kernan thought otherwise. "It *must* be God," he insisted. "Men were killed beside me, in front of me, all around me—and me with just this," he said holding up a nicked finger. "God must decide these things." Just as much diversity of opinion could be found on whether God willed war. A master sergeant declared, "God plans these wars. He has a purpose— maybe to cut down the population. Even famine and the bombing of women and children have a purpose." But a new draftee disagreed: "Don't hang it all on God. The only place God comes in is: He forgives us. God forgives us. God forgives us for killing simply because He makes allowances for the stupidity of man."[22] Thus, even in the Korean conflict, theological discussion was present and intense, even if it did not proceed along the lines envisioned by the church.

When he turned to the scientists two months later, Whitman found several of the kind that were most common in the 1930s and would be again in the decades to come—scientists with no belief in God and no use for religion. When he asked one physicist, "Do you think there is any ultimate purpose in life itself?," the physicist responded, "That's meaningless because there is no way of checking. Anybody's answer is as good as anybody else's." After an uncomfortable pause he added, "I was always told as a child that I should have faith, and all that. But I examined those things and found they didn't hold water. So I threw them out. I feel better now."[23] On the whole, however, most of the scientists Whitman found had moved in the other direction, becoming more convinced of the existence of God as a result of their scientific inquiries. Mineralogist Paul Francis Kerr of Columbia University was typical of this latter type of scientist. Because of all he and his generation knew about the earth, Kerr maintained, they were in the fortunate position of being able to say something more definite about God than the ancient philosophers who had merely "guessed" there was a God: "All they could say was, 'God is.' But we have so much more evidence to go on. We have seen so much more of His handiwork. We can say 'God *must be*.'"[24]

Other scientists expressed their reasons for belief in other ways. An astronomer, Jason John Nassau, found the mystery of life contained in the ability of a human mind to observe and comprehend the universe. The discoverer of Aureomycin, Benjamin Duggar, said "I can't conceive of nothing. I can of something." The reactor research coordinator at Brookhaven National Laboratories, John J. Floyd, declared his belief that, as he worked at the atomic pile, "I feel God is there." The weight of the opinions of scientists, if not scientific opinion, seemed to be coming down on the side of the existence of God. But the scientists did not simply affirm the kind of God represented in traditional Judaism or Christianity. The scientist of the 1950s who agreed with Kerr that science had made him more, not less, of a believer in a "Supreme Power" was also likely to agree with his proposition that "we are just stripping away some of the superstition and mythology. We are getting closer to the essence."[25] Here again, as at Fort Sam Houston, there was evidence that the great upswing in belief in God was, at best, proceeding along a parallel path with the faith of the church.

Prayer

The quantity of public discourse affirming the existence of God in the postwar years was certainly impressive as a sign of the popularity of religion in the 1950s. But even more revealing of the nature of the revival of religion was the tremendous interest in the subject of prayer.

Prayer in the 1950s was often portrayed as a source of power; a way of harnessing the divine to one's own purposes. At a time when nearly everyone wanted to be more popular, more secure, and more successful, prayer held out the promise of delivering all three objectives. James Bender and Lee Graham, coauthors of *Your Way to Popularity and Personal Power*,[26] suggested one way in which this was possible. "People who believe in God and ask him for help," they wrote, "seem to have the greatest share of popularity and personal power. Why? Because their faith makes them the sort of individuals whom other folks instinctively like. Their inner strength attracts friendship and love like an irresistible magnet."[27] Thus prayer worked all kinds of wonderful effects on the exterior life of the supplicant. Despite protests to the contrary and attempts to redirect the attention on prayer to other aspects of prayer, such as conforming the will of the prayer to that of God or unity with God, a sense lingered throughout the fifties that prayer was a way of getting God to intervene on one's behalf; a kind of adult's version of the child praying for and receiving a bicycle. Peace of mind, personal magnetism, a new job could all be had—according to some prayer authorities—with "just a talk to the man upstairs."

Everybody who was anybody seemed to want to get on the prayer bandwagon. Singer Eddie Cantor, writer Fulton Oursler, and Madame Chiang Kai-shek were just some of the celebrities that vaunted the power of prayer for the *Reader's Digest*'s loyal millions.[28] The *Digest* was not the only magazine carrying articles on prayer in the 1950s, either. Next to an advertisement with practical advice on making "something golden happen" with Fluffo brand shortening, McCall's magazine featured an article giving equally practical advice on "How to Pray . . . and What to Pray For." In it, ten experts answered everyone's burning questions about prayer, the underlying tone of which was "How can I get something out of prayer?" The preponderance of the questions focused on the morality and efficacy of prayers for material success. Reinhold Niebuhr expressed his belief that "it is wrong to pray for success in a business enterprise. It is selfish to pray for yourself." But Norman Vincent Peale, when asked

"Should I ask for specific things?" replied, "Yes. Tell God what you want, as a child would talk to his earthly father. . . . Even tell him about the material things you feel essential to happy living."[29] Julius Mark, Rabbi of New York's Temple Emanu-El, steered a middle course, noting that poverty was not to be wished for and arguing that "prayer is not meant to be a short cut to material results. . . . It is naive to expect an interference with the laws of nature."[30]

If people did not like the answers the religious leaders offered to questions on prayer, they could get their prayer information from leaders in other fields. Newspaperman Jim Bishop wrote a book on his own personal experiences of prayer, *Go with God*, in which he included prayers for all occasions and the favorite prayers of celebrities. Motion picture producer Cecil B. DeMille was represented, as were baseball player Mickey Mantle, *New York Times* publisher Arthur Hays Sulzberger, Clare Boothe Luce, John D. Rockefeller, Jr., industrialist Henry J. Kaiser, and General Douglas MacArthur. From MacArthur came "A Father's Prayer," which read, in part, "Build me a son, O Lord, who will be strong enough to know when he is weak and brave enough to face himself when he is afraid; one who will be proud and unbending in honest defeat, and humble and gentle in victory." If this pious request was granted then his father could "dare to whisper: 'I have not lived in vain.'"[31]

As the decade progressed, Americans sought to harness the "power of prayer" to accomplish all kinds of objectives. In January 1952 *Newsweek* reported on all the winning athletes who had prayed before significant sports victories. Heavyweight boxer Jersey Joe Walcott also added the power of Bible reading to his prechampionship fight warmup routine.[32] In April, the magazine reported the plan of the promotion director of the Episcopal Church's National Council to hasten the liberation of people in Communist countries through the power of prayer. The director's plan to unite people on both sides of the Iron Curtain was undertaken through a "Crusade for Freedom" that enlisted the support of ministers, priests, and rabbis across the nation. Soon the Voice of America and Radio Free Europe were able to inform the "Iron Curtain peoples that the crusade of prayer was on."[33]

The power-of-prayer craze reached its zenith (or nadir, depending on one's perspective) in the late 1950s with the publication of two books. In 1957, Charlie W. Shedd's *Pray Your Weight Away* appeared on the bestsellers' list as an instant hit in two well-established categories—it was a dietbook and an inspirational classic simultaneously. Equating sin and fatness, Shedd provided techniques whereby fat bodies could be returned to the thin temples of the Holy Spirit that God originally "dreamed" them to be.[34]

In 1959, there appeared the results of six years of intensive research by Franklin Loehr, a Presbyterian minister with a college background in chemistry. His subject, and the title of his book, was *The Power of Prayer on Plants*, and his experimental findings were dramatic. Loehr told of an experiment in which a ten-inch cake pan filled with dirt and divided in half was planted with twenty-three kernels of corn on each side and subjected to prayer for eight days. One side received positive prayers for growth, the other prayer against growth. The result was that sixteen sturdy seedlings emerged on the prayed-for side of the pan, while only one weak seedling grew on the negative side. A few "brief 'bursts' of negation" and the weak seedling darkened, withered, and grew no more. When asked to give such negative prayers, one woman called her seedlings "Communists." Loehr reported that this ideological labeling worked, for "those poor seeds seemed to twist and writhe under the negative power showered on them." The payoff for such research was, as Loehr saw it, the demonstration of two things: "(1) That prayer is fact, and (2) That scientific laboratory research can be done in basic religious fields."[35] It also suggested that prayer could be placed at the control of ordinary human beings for various purposes of their choosing. There was additionally a sense of evidence of God in any paranormal experience. That is, in any unusual event such as the growing of the corn seeds on one side of a cake pan and not the other, or the many sightings of flying saucers, the religiously disposed mind of the fifties could find confirmation of its religious convictions by using the simple rule that what could not be explained by science was obviously spirit.

It was also the 1950s that brought American culture Dial-A-Prayer, whereby those who could not think of a prayer on their own, or those who preferred to have their prayers produced professionally, could get one over the ubiquitous telephone. Sponsored by local churches or councils of churches, the typical Dial-A-Prayer was uplifting enough not to increase the guilt of any caller. And like its close cousin, the newspaper horoscope, any Dial-A-Prayer was general enough to be applicable to any given caller. A representative example of the genre went as follows: "Eternal Father of us all, without the assurance of Thy love, we are without hope. Draw near unto us as we draw near unto Thee. Even as we bow down in humble confession, cause us to rise up with faith and courage to meet the temptations and trials which beset us. Lighten our darkness, O Lord, and grant us Thy salvation. Amen."[36]

In 1955 the Dial-A-Prayer program started by Rev. Robert W. Younge, pastor of the Hitchcock Memorial Church of Scarsdale, New York, proved to be an immediate success. *Newsweek* reported that "it caught on like Davy Crockett. From 25 to 30 calls a day it mushroomed to 425. Gagsters didn't miss the obvious opportunity—an insurance man back from lunch found a message to return a phone call. Hoping a prospect had sought him out, he dialed the number and heard a voice exhorting him to have courage." This kind of use did not dismay the service's founder. Dr. Younge looked at the backlog of phone calls and read the signs of the time, saying, "A few people used it for practical joking. But I believe that most of the callers are sincerely seeking comfort and inspiration. This is another evidence that there is a genuine resurgence of religious faith in our country."[37] The Atlanta Dial-A-Prayer sponsor, the Rev. Wendell H. Mixson, explained the success of his service this way: "People are seeking God free from all the trappings and ceremonies." Someday, he hoped, "it will be as much a habit to dial for prayer as to dial for time."[38]

Wendell Mixson's hope that dialing for prayer would become a lasting habit for the American people was not to be fulfilled, but his analysis of the cause of Dial-A-Prayer's popularity proved to be on target. For in addition to filling the churches, Americans were celebrating religion as a positive good, regardless of its content, trappings, and ceremonies.

Religion

In the age when Madison Avenue came into its own and advertising reached a new plateau, religion was aggressively marketed—alongside Super DeLuxe automobiles and new brands of soap—in the Religion in American Life campaign conducted by the United Church Canvas in co-operation with the Advertising Council. American industry, led by General Electric president Charles E. Wilson, contributed millions of dollars worth of radio time and magazine, billboard, and bus-card space in order to publicize the importance of religious institutions in American life.

Magazine articles on religion appeared everywhere, even in the most unlikely places. These articles were featured in *Popular Mechanics* ("Pre-fab Church Seats 180") and *Popular Science* ("New Look for Churches: Modern Design Takes Over").[39] Even *Mademoiselle* ran a piece on the hot topic of the day, an article on "Religion's Root Meaning." In that contribution to the revival, Nancy Wilson Ross wrote that, in spite of troubles in the Far East, perhaps religion could serve as a bond in a world where the West was no longer on its pedestal, but "down on an equal level looking eye to eye at its Eastern brother." Surely, Ross argued, there had never been a time in which it was more important to search for the common elements that bind human beings together: "And it is here that religion, in the old Latin root meaning of the word 'to bind,' may serve us as a tool; for the East, with the possible exception of China, is profoundly concerned with all the values that we somewhat vaguely group around the word 'religious.' It does not matter what our opinion of the Easterner's form of religion may be. It is for him a faith that deeply and personally absorbs him. He lives his religion—*whatever* it may be. It lies intimately, inseparably, at the heart of his everyday existence."[40] Thus religion, "whatever" it might be in any particular case, was good in so far as it inevitably served as a tool for human cohesion. Such a statement might be expected to bother the devotees of any one of those particular traditions, for whom religion was not a means toward anything, but rather truth itself. Yet in the 1950s the practical utility of religion had champions from many quarters; mass-market magazines were only the beginning.

Religious books in the 1950s came in all kinds, but they shared one common feature: incredible popularity. A fictionalized life of Christ by Fulton Oursler, *The Greatest Story Ever Told*, was first published in February 1949. By September 1951, the book was in its forty-eighth printing. The rise to power of Francis Cardinal Spellman was fictionalized by Henry Morton Robinson in 1950.[41] Halfway through the decade, Alice Payne Hackett gave sales figures for best-sellers over the previous sixty years and among them were a sizable number of recent religious titles. Fulton J. Sheen's *Life Is Worth Living* and *Peace of Soul* both sold in the hundreds of thousands. Rabbi Joshua Loth Liebman's *Peace of Mind* sold more than a million copies. Peter Marshall's book of down-to-earth sermons, *Mr. Jones, Meet the Master*, sold half a million copies, and Catherine Marshall's adoring inspirational biography written after her husband's sudden death, *A Man Called Peter*, sold nearly three times that many copies. In comparison to other books, religious books tended to remain on the best-seller lists longer. Norman Vincent Peale's *The Power of Positive Thinking* stayed on the list of top-selling books of all types for the entire period of 1952–55.[42] In terms of tone and content, these religious books had in common something else: they all appealed to a broad spectrum of the population and required no prior faith commitment to enjoy the fruits they had to offer.

Throughout the 1950s celebrity conversions were widely reported and were taken as a sign that the religious reawakening was making itself felt even in places like Hollywood, previously considered to be beyond hope. These conversion accounts typically illustrated that the starting place for much of the return to religion was the felt need of the individual. Bishop Fulton Sheen, who presented his appeal for conversion to the masses over the radio and television, insisted that "every conversion begins with a crisis." The crisis could be a loss of a loved one, a sudden illness, or even the inability to go on cheating on a spouse, but no matter what the cause, the crisis worked by forcing the soul inward. When the soul saw and admitted "its emptiness," Sheen believed, "God fill[ed] it with a rush of treasure."[43] Sheen surely had the credentials to describe conversion, for among the many celebrity converts he made were Clare Boothe Luce, violinist Fritz Kreisler, Henry Ford II, Broadway stage designer Jo Mielziner, and columnist Heywood Broun. The interest in religion claimed even Mickey Spillane, the scandalous and popular detective fiction writer, who joined the Jehovah's Witness fold in 1952.[44]

Besides celebrity conversions and the flood of books and magazine articles on religion, there were other signs of interest in religion in the popular arts. By 1955 there had been a spate of movies about early church history where the hero, faced with a choice between "a lightly clad pagan wench and allegiance to the new truth, succumbs to the latter." As for popular music, it was not to be left out. One songwriter produced these lyrics:

> Faith, hope and charity
> That's the way to live successfully.
> How do I know?
> The Bible told me so.

Not everyone was impressed by such displays of religious vitality in the popular arts. *Commonweal*, the voice of the Catholic intellectual, noted the progress of religion in the popular media and commented on the revival: "We remain somewhat jaundiced concerning such manifestations of 'religious' interest."[45]

Even so, if *Commonweal*'s editors remained "jaundiced" about the revival, they also remained in the minority. In these years politicians in Washington attended prayer breakfasts by the dozen. These meals were typically presided over by a rabbi, a priest, and a Protestant minister who together provided what New Testament scholar Martin Franzmann described as "a sort of ecclesiastical garnish to all manner of secular dishes."[46]

Those same years saw Congress seeking a quasi-confessional validation of the nation's religious identity in three symbolic acts.

The first of these acts came in the spring of 1954 when the Eighty-third Congress voted to add the words "under God" to the Pledge of Allegiance. Homer Ferguson, the Senator most responsible for the act, neatly explained its necessity in terms of both the Cold War and the value of religion: "Spiritual values are every bit as important to the defense and safety of our Nation as are military and economic values, and I believe passage of the resolution will enable us to strike another blow against those who would enslave us."[47] His House of Representatives colleague Louis Rabaut put it even more pointedly: "You may argue from dawn to dusk about differing political, economic, and social systems but the fundamental issue which is the unbridgeable gap between America and Communist Russia is a belief in Almighty God."[48] If the only thing that separated the beloved American way of life from godless Communism was American belief in God, then to maintain their status as free men and women Americans were obliged to declare their nation's ultimate dependence on the deity. This reaffirmation of religious commitment was not simply one of conservative evangelical Protestants but rather embraced the full range of Protestants, Catholics, and Jews. Indeed, the Cold War could be seen as bringing together these groups: Senator John F. Kennedy helped to introduce Knights of Columbus resolutions in favor of amending the pledge, while the Rev. George Doherty, pastor of the New York Avenue Presbyterian Church, campaigned for the same change from his influential capital city pulpit. The only public opposition to this addition to the pledge came from the Unitarian Minister's Association of Boston.[49]

The following year brought forth the second key symbolic act. Congress passed Public Law 140, which required that the words "In God We Trust" be placed on all coins and currency of the United States. Although the Treasury had been mandated to employ the motto on certain coins since 1908, there was no legal guarantee of it on all U.S. money. Congress now erected such a guarantee and President Dwight D. Eisenhower signed the law affirming its value as a spiritual bulwark in the midst of challenge and crisis. Finally, in 1956, Congress extended its action and made "In God We Trust" the national motto, replacing "E pluribus unum." On July 27, 1956, the Senate Judiciary Committee reported favorably on the Joint Resolution (H.J. 396): "It will be of great spiritual and psychological value to our country to have a clearly designated national motto of inspirational quality in plain, popular accepted English."[50] Three days later Eisenhower endorsed the resolution and the United States had an official motto affirming national trust in God.

It was appropriate that these popular official declarations of religion's importance should come during the Eisenhower years, for in addition to being the nation's president, Dwight David Eisenhower was also the high priest of the popular return to religion. In his personal life, in his leadership, and particularly in his public speeches, Eisenhower endorsed the value and importance of religion, without ever getting overly specific about that of which it should consist.

The first clue that Eisenhower was going to cast the mantle of the presidency over religion came when it was revealed that the administration's cabinet meetings opened with a minute of silent prayer. The practice began before the inauguration, when Eisenhower asked Ezra Taft Benson, his Secretary of Agriculture and a high official of the Mormon Church, to lead the cabinet-designate in prayer in its meetings. The Catholic journal *America* applauded the practice: "The President and the Cabinet deserve the sincere congratulations of all Americans for their forthrightness in thus testifying to the realization of our dependence on God's providence."[51] Eisenhower also departed from the secular customs associated with the inauguration when he read a prayer just before the ceremony:

Almighty God, as we stand here at this moment, my future associates in the executive branch of government join me in beseeching that Thou will make full and complete our dedication to the service of the people in this throng and their fellow citizens everywhere. Give us, we pray, the power to discern clearly right from wrong, and allow all our works and actions to be governed thereby and by the laws of this land.

Especially, we pray that our concern shall be for all the people, regardless of station, race or calling. May co-operation be permitted and be the mutual aim of those who, under the concepts of our Constitution, hold to differing political faiths, so that all may work for the good of our beloved country and Thy glory. Amen.[52]

To be sure, this prayer sounded a bit like Eisenhower instructing the deity in the workings of the Constitution. Yet behind the odd turns of phrase, Eisenhower was appealing to what he believed was a religious faith common to nearly all Americans, a faith in a single God who was worshipped by all in spite of the labels Christian or Jew and despite what other "political faiths" individuals might also profess.

Eisenhower also helped make it fashionable to go to church on Sunday.

One contemporary cleric observed that Eisenhower's weekly attendance "makes it impossible for any man to say he's too busy to go to church."[53] The impact of Eisenhower's example was not merely the result of his being president. Had Adlai Stevenson been elected Chief Executive and decided to attend church every week, it is quite imaginable that the businessman's excuse of more important things to do would have been more easily and frequently offered. As soldier, statesman, war hero, college president, and small-town boy, Eisenhower embodied all that was good in America. Not since George Washington had been hailed as Cincinnatus had a president so completely encompassed the nation's virtues in his person. Furthermore, Eisenhower embraced and endorsed religion in a thoroughly American way, showing that one could be religious without being a weak sissy, an overly intellectual egghead, or a dogmatic zealot. Eisenhower demonstrated to millions that the best approach to faith was warm and pragmatic, sentimental and not overly dogmatic—all at the same time. As he de-ideologized politics in the fifties, so too was his contribution on behalf of a de-ideologized religious belief.

Eisenhower often spoke on the issue of the importance of religious faith; so often that when *Life* magazine first published a double year-end issue in December 1955 and chose as its sole subject Christianity, it was able to begin with words of the president taken from seven different major speeches on the topic given in his first three years in office.[54] These included his famous remark: "America is built on a strong religious faith and I don't care what it is." By this, Eisenhower almost certainly meant Protestantism, Catholicism, and Judaism, but he gave the impression to some that Zoroastrianism would have done just as well. In fact, while Eisenhower may have himself been close to the traditional monotheistic core, others in the fifties were actively celebrating any religion so long as it was a creed one lived by. The clearest example of this celebration was the radio series put together by Edward R. Murrow, "This I Believe."

"This I Believe" was broadcast 2,200 times a week from 196 of the United States' most powerful radio stations in the 1950s. Through this medium it reached 39 million persons a week, on an average of twice a week. Furthermore, it was broadcast in six different languages over 150 foreign stations and the Voice of America. The program was so popular that it soon became a weekly feature in eighty-five of the country's leading daily newspapers and was later published in book form.[55] The feature was also deemed to be so characteristic of what was good in American life that the State Department adopted a policy of offering it to the most important newspapers in each of the ninety-seven countries with which it then maintained diplomatic relations.

The idea for "This I Believe" was conceived by four men having a business luncheon in 1949. They began their conversation with the observation that "among people generally material values were gaining and spiritual values declining," and went on to ponder what could be done to reverse this trend. Believing that there had seldom been a time when an "inventory of one's personal beliefs and sense of values seemed to be more needed," they proposed a plan whereby people of many colors, faiths, and walks of life would be asked to unfold their personal credos on a five-minute radio program. The only criterion for selection of these guests was that they be "successful in their chosen profession and in their adjustment to life and living." It did not matter whether these personal philosophies clashed with one another or were built upon any recognizably religious doctrines, "for the individual's credo contains the seeds of the strength and happiness of the family, the community and the nation" (xviii). The underlying premise of the series then was that it did not matter what you believed, as long as it was truly your own belief that you fervently believed. A few examples from the series illustrate the range of this popular faith in the fifties.

A classics professor, Gilbert Murray, placed a caveat before his statement of faith, saying that he could not recite one of the traditional creeds, Christian, Jewish, Moslem, or Buddhist, for one was merely born into them as an accident of country and parentage. Still, he believed that "a great mystery surrounds us, in which the human mind can at best catch glimpses and express itself in metaphors." Not surprisingly, the best metaphors for Murray came from the Greeks, so that he was willing to conclude, with one of their philosophers, "The helping of man by man is God" (125).

The executive director of the International Film Foundation, Julien Bryan, came away from his globe-trotting experiences with a "deep respect for all of man's great religions." This was true to the extent that he had come to believe that "despite their differences all men can worship side by side." Bryan's belief that all religions led to the same end was a remarkably common one, both in "This I Believe" and in the culture. It represented a belief in the value of religion without any of the particularism or exclusivity that was associated with most if not all of the religions that the sophisticated traveler claimed to respect. Bryan, though, did have the self-knowledge to go on and state the substance that lay behind his respect for the great religions: "My real faith, then, is in a dream that in spite of daily headlines prophesying man's destruction, we can build a better world, a world of peace and human brotherhood. Yes, even in our lifetime!" (20).

Alongside expressions of hope and belief in humanistic progress, there were also sentimental appeals to the faith of prior generations that seemed to be absent in the present age. William O. Douglas, Associate Justice of the Supreme Court, though one of the most committed jurists to the principles of liberty, was also one of the most religious men to sit on the court during the twentieth century. His celebrated affirmation, "We are a religious people whose institutions presuppose a Supreme Being," written in the context of a majority opinion in the case of *Zorach v. Clauson*, was often repeated with approval as the decade wore on.[56] But of all the contributors to "This I Believe," Douglas was conspicuous in his proximity to Christian orthodoxy. After telling of his father's deathbed testament, "If I die it will be glory, if I live it will be grace," Douglas made his own stand. "These days I see America drifting from the Christian faith," he wrote, "acting abroad as an arrogant, selfish, greedy nation, interested only in guns and in dollars . . . not in people and their hopes and aspirations. These days the words of my father come back to me more and more. We need his faith, the faith of our fathers. We need a faith that dedicates us to something bigger and more important than ourselves or our possessions" (44).

Of the 100 radio essays chosen for inclusion in the book version of "This I Believe," many expressed the belief that "no man is an island," an opinion repeated at least as often as a belief in a conventional God recognizable to those within the Jewish and Christian traditions. The contributors' most often voiced sentiment, however, went something like this: "I believe that everyone is basically good. The key to the future of world progress is developing that which is good in each person." The next most frequently expressed belief was a version of the Shakespearean line, "to thine own self be true." Also common was a personalized argument from design for the existence of God, such as, "The fives senses and the mystery of the breath draw in the wonder of the world, and, with that, the glory of God." But above all, the note of toleration was sounded. Nearly every one of the contributors was in agreement with the poet Robert Hillyer's justification of multiple creeds: "There are other patterns for other people, and I have no quarrel with these. 'By many paths we reach the single goal'" (71).

While the people who offered their personal confessions of faith to

Edward R. Murrow and CBS radio listeners were by their very nature society's elites, the popularity of the program and the content of their creeds spoke volumes about the belief structure of the masses of Americans who contributed to the revival of religion in the 1950s. The public opinion polls showed that the bulk of Americans thought that religion was important, that its influence was on the rise, that it was not so important to go to church as to live a good life, that the soul was immortal, and that God's heaven was open to those of any creed who lived that good life.[57] This suggests that the elites represented in "This I Believe" were not unlike other citizens of the nation in their beliefs, but only in their articulateness about those beliefs. Religion, like the church, was more popular than ever in 1950s America and it was by "many paths" that Americans sought to "reach the same goal." But just what was the common goal? A clue lies in the intersection of the popular religious revival with the social psychology of the day.

The Psychological Return to Religion

The revival of popular interest in religion in the fifties, though displaying many facets, had an underlying character that had been well anticipated in a 1936 book entitled *The Return to Religion*.[58] In the book, Henry C. Link, a psychologist, told how through scientific inquiry and discovery in his professional field he was led to see the importance of religious beliefs he thought he had cast off twenty years earlier. More importantly, he believed, his recounting of his psychological findings demonstrated the scientific logic and psychological healthiness of any individual's return to religion.

Link was a practicing psychologist who had seen more than 4,000 individuals in either a therapeutic or consultative context in fifteen years of practice when he wrote his book. The genesis of the ideas in *The Return to Religion* came to him as he caught himself recommending religious organizations, membership, and activities to his patients as ways of overcoming problems they identified in other, nonreligious areas of their lives: "Although I had not attended church more than twenty times in twenty years, I found myself frequently including in my recommendations to individuals that they take a more active part in church work, or join a Y.M.C.A. or Y.M.H.A" (5). One opportunity for such a recommendation presented itself to Link in the form of a young woman who came to him complaining of difficulty in getting along with other adults, and with men more than women. She asked Link, "Do you think that I am obstructed by certain inhibitions which might be removed?" Being no Freudian, Link responded in a way that demonstrated his chosen psychological methodology: "My diagnosis was that it was not the presence of inhibitions but the absence of certain desirable habits and skills which were the root of her difficulty. The skills she lacked could be acquired only through practice, not by self-analysis or introspection. So I recommended a specific list of things she was to do, prominent among which was to join a church and to accept all opportunities to be active in its affairs. She had already admitted her belief in religion and her membership in a church in her home town. 'Oh!' she exclaimed, 'wouldn't it be terribly sordid to join a church just to help me in developing social ease?' (6). To this rudimentary theological objection to doing something religious for the sake of some nonreligious end, Link had no direct response. Still, he proceeded to lay out his understanding of the beneficial relationship between this woman's Christianity and her happiness: "With such a challenge I soon found myself explaining the psychological significance of the Christian religion as exemplified by the social aggressiveness of its Founder and its emphasis on forgetting oneself in the service of others. In her case, the explanation was particularly apt, for her conception of religion had been one merely of believing certain things rather than of works or service. She had never learned to forget herself in the heat of activity for or with others. In this incident I found myself, practically a pagan, certainly an agnostic, vigorously and with scientific conviction advocating the religious life" (6–7).

Link's own religious story was that of a young man raised in an evangelical Methodist household. He had attended Sunday School and Sunday morning and evening services, together with Wednesday prayer meetings, Christian Endeavor, and periodical revivals from an early age. He had "gone to the altar" as a revival meeting convert, became a Sunday School teacher, and taught Bible classes in the Y.M.C.A.—all before the age of eighteen. But when Link entered a small church college after high school he found the intellectual atmosphere stifling. He transferred to an east coast university where it quickly became clear to him that the brightest intellects among his colleagues were the most likely to discard their religious beliefs in the light of their new-found scientific understanding. By contrast, Link discovered that "the duller the student, the more likely it was that his religion would remain intact, in a logic-tight compartment which his studies failed to penetrate." He learned from his professors to divide fact from opinion, and to separate scientific knowledge from wishful folk mythology. Link graduated from college "convinced that religion was the refuge of weak minds" (10).

But just as science had been the path by which Link had escaped the grasp of religion, so it became also the means of his return. Through his work with individual patients and even more through his role as an advisor in the Adjustment Service of New York City, Link began to conclude that "the individuals who believed in religion or attended a church had significantly better personalities than those who did not" (13).

The religion that Link returned to in the mid-1930s was a kind of "least common denominator" Christianity; a Christianity stripped of any denominational, confessional, or controversial features. Link described the contents of his religion: "It includes the belief in God as a Supreme Being; the belief in a divine moral order expressed in the Ten Commandments and in the life of Christ, and acceptance of the Church as the chief, even though imperfect, vehicle of religious truths that are greater than science, and values that are higher than reason." Even this minimalist conception of faith might be too restrictive for people of religions outside Christianity, Link admitted, adding, "It probably is, and I frankly admit the accident of birth which makes it so." The content of one's religion was unimportant, compared to the bare fact that one had religion. In practice, Link revealed, "I often encouraged Roman Catholics to be better Roman Catholics, . . . I have encouraged many Hebrews to identify themselves more fully with the institutions expressing their religion." In all cases, Link wrote, "I have been governed by the background and the needs of the individual, and the necessity of utilizing whatever good materials were available" (14). Later on, Link made his point even more clearly. "Agnosticism," he wrote, "is an intellectual disease, and faith in fallacies is better than no faith at all. . . . The belief in palmistry leads, at least, to the holding of hands; phrenology to the study of others people's heads; numerology and astrology to an interest in people's birthdays; spiritualism to the joining of knees under a common table" (63).

Thus, what even the most fallacious religious group had to offer was that it brought people together. Christianity did not do something essentially different from New Thought or Couéism, it just did it better. What

Christianity had to offer was the great example of its founder. Jesus was the very model of "social aggressiveness."

Describing Jesus has often proven to be a kind of Rorschach test for the people who attempt it. What people have seen in this dimly known historical figure tells much about what they think is important in the religion of his followers. In his portrayal of Jesus, Link revealed himself as one who valued extroversion above all other things: "Jesus Christ, the ideal of unselfishness and the great exponent of the unselfish life, was an extrovert. He was extrovert to a degree which few can hope to achieve. He was highly aggressive in making social contacts. He did not hesitate to accept water from the woman at the well because she was a Samaritan, nor did he confine his attentions to those who were worthy of him but devoted himself to Zaccheus, the tax-collector, Nicodemus, the Pharisee, to the halt, the maimed, and the blind, the publicans, and the sinners. He did not wait for people to invite him, he invited them" (49).

Indeed, Link valued extroversion so much that he reserved his greatest praise and moral indignation for the categories of extroversion and introversion. Using the example of artists and musicians, he said that those "who remain introverts are usually those who fail to sacrifice their pleasures and impulses to the strenuous demands of practice and competition. Their aspirations remain dreams and fantasies and as such benefit neither themselves nor humanity" (42). The word for such people was simply "selfish." For Link, Christ was above all the model of unselfishness, and the central teaching of the Christian church was selfless activity. Scripture merely bore this out, as all four gospels agreed, "for whosoever will save his life shall lose it: and whosoever will lose his life for my sake shall find it."[59] The wisdom of Christianity could thus be reduced to an iron-clad religious law which guaranteed that selfless commitment would result in a successful self (32).

The introvert could always come up with a thousand good reasons not to become involved with others: the insincerity and hypocrisy of church members; the low intelligence and uncultured nature of many believers; the unbelievable dogmas of the church; the multiplicity of sects; the personality of the local religious leader. These excuses were to be expected from those whom Link called "Fools of Reason." But salvation did not always lie in the direction of reason. Often it lay in the practice of adjustment.

The psychology of adjustment counseled people to adjust themselves and their expectations to the personalities, expectations, and needs of others. Thus a woman who sought out Link for help in making friends was told to accept each and every invitation offered to social activity. Three days later, she called Link in a panic: "Did you really mean that I should accept *any* invitation?" Link replied that he did, and asked what the problem was. It turned out that she had been asked to dinner and the movies by an auto mechanic whose English was defective and whose manner was uncouth. Link's advice was direct. "Suppose," he said, "you try to make this young man's evening as pleasant for him as you can. Since you have nothing to lose, it should be easier for you to practice being a good companion. You are bound to learn something from this experience which will help you to be a better friend in the next. Call it self-sacrifice if you will, but the ability to make and to hold friends comes in no other way" (25). The road to happiness was paved by action, by work, by accommodation, not by introspection or self-analysis. Modern psychology had replaced the Socratic maxim "Know thyself" with a new slogan: "Behave yourself" (20–21).

In the end, Link was absorbed in demonstrating that his early belief that religion was for weak intellects was wrong. For the reconstructed Link, religion, insofar as it was understood as connected to other people and not just beliefs, was the best possible source of individual health. "The religion I speak of," he insisted, "is not the refuge of the weak but the weapon of those who would be strong. I see religion as an aggressive mode of life, by which the individual becomes the master of his environment, not its complacent victim" (15–16).

In its reliance on science for the validation of faith, Link's book was both a part of his times and ahead of them as well. He simultaneously countered his own era's views about the unscientific nature of religious ideas, and presented a case for a pragmatic involvement in religion that was to prove attractive for the next generation. By providing a basis for begging the sticky question of the validity of religious beliefs through appeal to the beneficial psychological results of religious affiliation, Link was able to arm those who wished to associate themselves with religion with powerful reasons to maintain their association. Those unable to confront conventional doubt—in others or themselves—need no longer feel defeated or even required to face the troubling questions about doctrine and beliefs or even the existence of a god, for religion was defensible if on no other grounds than because it worked. The religious individual's adjustment to life was improved, and he or she lived longer, had more friends, and was happy even in times of adversity.

Without attributing any direct influence to Link, it is possible to credit him with prefiguring the religious mood of the fifties in so many of its aspects: the personal happiness argument for the existence of God; the hostility to particulars of denominational doctrine; the turning to religion to provide children the moral foundations of society; the expectation that meaning in life will be found in adjustment and sociability with a religious group; and the connection of the religion of Jesus to a conservative political agenda. All of these characteristics of the popular conception of the place and value of religion associated with the 1950s are present, to a remarkable degree, in *The Return to Religion*. Indeed, one testimony to the power of Link's arguments for religious faith and affiliation for postwar Americans is the fact that the book remained a top-selling inspirational book throughout the 1950s. By 1959, *The Return to Religion* had been through forty-seven printings.

In the 1950s, the foremost representative of this psychological faith was Norman Vincent Peale. Peale was known to the American public through his radio and television programs, through *Guideposts* magazine, through his books *Faith Is the Answer* and *The Art of Real Happiness*, and articles in popular magazines of all kinds. But above all Peale was known through a 1952 book, *The Power of Positive Thinking*,[60] which in sales dwarfed even his own monumentally successful *Guide to Confident Living*. Peale claimed that his book's purpose was simple and limited: "This is simply a practical direct-action, personal-improvement manual." And so it was, but in style and content *The Power of Positive Thinking* came very close to the core of his teaching as a minister. Week after week those who came to Manhattan's Marble Collegiate Church were treated to sermons on many of the same themes covered in his books—how to obtain happiness, health, wealth, and success and avoid their opposites. The purpose of faith could be summed up in a single phrase: successful living.

In a culture given to the praise of successful living in all of its respectable forms, Peale was the perfect representative of the culture-religion of the hour. His examples drew upon the experiences of the best citizens. "One of the greatest executives in the country," "a prominent manufacturer," "a former member of a championship university crew," "a man of great influence in the community," and "a prominent citizen of New York" were just a few of the models of personal transformation through the "techniques of Christianity" that Peale brought to the attention of his readers. All of these demonstrated that religion and positive thinking were not just for losers, for those who were not making it. Society's losers, when they appeared at all, were merely people who had failed to meet the challenges of life in positive terms. More often than not, the losers became winners through the adoption of a few simple practices—

Bible reading, prayer before bedtime, thinking upon life's blessings, never using negative words in conversation—and became not only content with their lives, but gained wealth, new jobs, prestige, friends, and husbands. Yes, husbands. Husbands were the identified problem of most of the women who appeared in the book. Be they desired, drunk, or divorcing, husbands were the only window into the experience of contemporary women in *The Power of Positive Thinking*. The jobs and social stations of men were nearly always noted as they were discussed by Peale. With the exception of two black women Peale had encountered as domestic servants, women's occupations did not really figure into his demonstration of the this-worldly wisdom of positive thinking.

Also conspicuous were the doctors—"a famous psychologist," "a locally renowned surgeon," "an eminent psychiatrist"—who backed Peale's claims that his techniques were medically and scientifically sound as a means to health. His prescriptions for self-improvement often sounded like doctors' prescriptions: "A primary method for gaining a mind full of peace is to practice emptying the mind. . . . I mention it now to underscore the importance of a frequent mental catharsis. I recommend a mind-emptying at least twice a day, more often if necessary" (22). At other times these suggestions for improvement took on the tone of scientific laws: "The formula is: (1) PRAYERIZE, (2) PICTURIZE, (3) ACTUALIZE" (55).

Wealth, health, and happiness are the principal life concerns of human beings in any age. Those who turned to religion in the 1950s brought these preoccupations to religion and in Peale found someone who took these problems seriously. Though not unique, Peale was perhaps unparalleled in the extent to which he was prepared to assure people of optimistic outcomes for their worldly woes.

The link between success in being faithful and success in daily affairs was guaranteed. For those who found the lessons of the anecdotes too subtle, Peale offered another, a tale of a negative couple named Maurice and Alice Flint. The Flints were unhappy and indebted. Maurice had bounced from job to job and was lacking in future prospects. The couple hated everyone—either mildly or with a burning passion—and blamed their failures on "dirty deals" done them by others. Living in Philadelphia, Maurice Flint read a condensation of Peale's *Guide to Confident Living* in *Liberty* magazine that emphasized the idea of "mustard seed faith." (Based on Matthew 17:20, "If ye have faith as a grain of mustard seed . . . nothing shall be impossible unto you.")

The next Sunday Flint drove his family to Peale's church in New York, and kept coming to learn how he could get some of this powerful "mustard seed faith." He told Peale of his troubles and expressed feelings of hopelessness. Peale later reported that he had "assured him that if he would get himself personally straightened out and get his mental attitudes attuned to God's pattern of thought, and if he would learn and utilize the technique of faith, all of his problems could be solved" (165). As Flint began to grasp the "faith idea," he began to feel better. But outside the Sunday church service its power often waned. What he needed, he determined, was a physical reminder. He began to carry mustard seed in his suit pocket. Small as they were, the seeds quickly became lost and were hard to find in the moments of crisis when they were needed most. So Flint hit upon the idea of putting the seed in a plastic ball and, after some technical problems, succeeded in encasing a mustard seed in plastic without introducing air bubbles. His triumph in this effort encouraged him to produce other mustard seed items: a necklace, a bow pin, a bracelet, a key chain. Flint made a card for each of these with the title "Mustard Seed Remembrancer" and instructions on its use, and sent these plastic talismans to Peale asking about their commercial marketability. Though Peale himself expressed some doubts, the fashionable department store Bonwit Teller was soon selling "Symbol of Faith" bracelets like hot cakes, and before long Maurice and Alice Flint owned a midwestern factory producing Mustard Seed Remembrancers by the thousands. For Peale the moral was clear: "Curious, isn't it—a failure goes to church and hears a text out of the Bible and creates a great business. Perhaps you had better listen more intently to the reading of the Bible and the sermon the next time you go to church. Perhaps you, too, will get an idea that will rebuild not only your life but your business as well" (168).

What Peale did for wealth he proceeded to do also for health and happiness, morally legitimizing these goals and presenting religion as the means to obtain them. As seemingly without peer as Peale was, he was not alone in effectively appealing to the psychological needs of the American public. In this talent he had the company of the immensely popular radio and television figure, Bishop Fulton J. Sheen.

Fulton J. Sheen had been the radio host of "The Catholic Hour" since 1930 when he decided in 1950 to embrace a new medium. The radio program was carried on 118 NBC affiliates and enjoyed a U.S. audience of four million listeners each week, but television offered the chance to reach an even wider public. And so, in the fall of 1951, the newly consecrated Bishop Sheen began a TV series, "Life Is Worth Living," which was carried on 123 ABC television stations and 300 radio stations reaching thirty million persons each week. The half-hour show ran Sunday nights during prime time, opposite the Milton Berle show, and most of those nights beat Berle in the all-important ratings. "Life Is Worth Living" continued to run until 1957, when it was succeeded by a syndicated program on the life of Christ.[61]

In the new medium Sheen proved popular with Protestants as well as with Catholics. He received fifteen to twenty thousand letters a day every year his show was on television. Without actually soliciting, he regularly received money for missions, cookies for himself, and hundreds of pictures drawn by children. He also received not a few unusual compliments. A blind couple in Minneapolis were so grateful to Admiral for sponsoring Sheen's program that they bought an Admiral TV set. A New Jersey woman reported that her cat always sat in front of the TV and looked at Sheen during the show. An elderly woman in Iowa put on her best dress to listen in "just as if she were going to church." A young actor asked if he could use Sheen's last name for life and became known as Martin Sheen.[62] Sheen was so popular that his audience extended beyond the bounds of Christians and the unconverted to include persons of other religions. A Jewish boy in Pittsburgh, having been told he was too young to wear a yarmulke, secretly wrote Sheen and asked for his Zucchetto. Later the Pittsburgh newspapers carried the story, complete with photos of the boy in his "episcopal yarmulke."[63]

In appearance and style, Sheen was a study in contrasts with Peale. Compared to the somewhat homespun Peale, Sheen was strikingly handsome, possessed a mellifluous voice, and was always immaculately groomed in his clerical garb. His shows were filled not with personal stories of people counseled, but with references to Marx, Freud, Jung, George Bernard Shaw, Milton, and Shakespeare, to Communism, fascism, and the Renaissance. And yet his teachings, too, began with the problems of the average 1950s American: with peace of mind, peace of soul, filling a void in the heart, death, anxiety, loneliness, love, and suffering. His show on the subject of "Mental Fatigue" began as follows: "There are two general reasons why people are fatigued mentally. First because they have no target; second, because they have too many targets."[64] As Sheen saw it, those without targets became bored with life and lost interest "in shooting arrows," embraced deterministic philosophies such as Freudian and Marxian theories, and abdicated freedom of the will. Those with too many targets, on the other hand, were those who, unable to find any fixed philosophy of life, flirt with one after another:

"One year they are reactionaries, with their feet firmly planted in cement. The next year they are liberals with their feet firmly planted in midair." So much changing of one's aims led only to distraction and frustration with life. It was possible to constantly change one's instincts and habits, but as Sheen noted, "One university drove pigs crazy that way." And yet this was the contemporary situation, a situation in which "minds are bored, worried, exhausted, and burdened with ennui because life is purposeless."[65]

Happily, there was an answer to this dilemma in the form of "three ways to achieve power and to overcome fatigue." These three were: (1) having a master idea, (2) strengthening the will, and (3) having recourse to outside power. Each of these three ways led to God. The recommended master idea was that human beings were made for happiness, but to be happy the human being had to strive for "Perfect Truth, and Perfect Love, which is God."[66] God only provided additional resources to those who had strengthened their wills and exhausted their own resources. Finally, while the individual's will had to be exercised, the human will was necessarily dependent on an outside power. "The basic trouble with atheism," Sheen argued, "is that it breathes in the same air that it breathes out." God was thus the source of fresh breath and an undepletable outside power.[67]

Sheen used the psychological complaints of Americans of the fifties to turn their hearts and minds to God. By contrast Peale sought to put the power of religion at the disposal of humankind. The difference between the two men was as subtle as the difference between insisting that for humans to be happy they needed to rely on the will of God and insisting that to be happy all they needed to do was to express their will to God. The difference was subtle enough to be lost on the majority of Americans caught up in the religion revival. From the popular perspective of the 1950s, Peale and Sheen were saying the same thing. And what they were saying was in full agreement with what Henry Link had argued in the 1930s—religion was good; good for the individual and good for society.

The New Academic
Respect for Religion

The varieties of the return to religion could not be exhausted even by Bishop Sheen and Norman Vincent Peale, for the 1950s also knew another kind of revival of religion. Affecting fewer lives, perhaps, than the flocking to the churches or the proliferation of Dial-A-Prayer services, religion also enjoyed an enhanced status in academic and intellectual circles. The days when Henry Link found university professors unrelentingly hostile toward all forms of religion and only the dullest students retaining any faith had come to an end. The days when most intellectuals wholeheartedly breathed a sigh of amen to H. L. Mencken's stinging remarks about Protestantism had given way to a time in which the best minds of the age acknowledged the force of the ideas presented by a new generation of religious thinkers.

The clearest sign of the rehabilitation of academic religion's reputation was the cover of the twenty-fifth anniversary issue of *Time* magazine, published on March 8, 1948. On it was an illustration of the theologian Reinhold Niebuhr supporting his unsmiling head with his hand. Below the illustration appeared the caption, "Man's story is not a success story." Both Niebuhr's appearance and the caption were symbolic for religion's restoration to a place of honor, for the last academic to be so singled out for an anniversary cover of *Time* had been the philosopher John Dewey. The contrast between Dewey and Niebuhr was tremendous. Where Dewey stood for the natural good in every human being ready to be progressively developed, Niebuhr took the position that humanity was by nature both good and evil, both free and yet finite and thus limited. To Dewey's colleagues in the philosophy department at Columbia University, *Time's* selection of Niebuhr was a repudiation of more than a half-century of progress against superstition. But no matter what Sidney Hook, James T. Farrell, or John Dewey himself thought of Niebuhr, Niebuhr's presentation of Christian ideas was gaining wide acceptance in the postwar world of American arts and letters.

Intellectuals had been disappointed by one ideology after another in the 1930s and 1940s. In Niebuhr's own terms, neither the "Children of Light"—champions of liberal culture and bourgeois individualism—nor the "Children of Darkness"—moral cynics given to absolutist schemes of political organization—were able to deliver upon the promises of humane democracy. The liberals who had created modern society had underestimated the power of individual and national self-interest. Yet those who recognized the powers of the will and of property had unleashed upon the earth regimes of terror and utter disrespect for human beings. On the liberal side, neither the social gospel nor John Dewey's ideas could account for continuing tragedy. Meanwhile, the theoretically attractive ideas of Marxism resulted in Stalinist purges and forced labor camps. The result was a crisis for the intellectual: a realistic description of the world was needed that did not merely abandon its people to its forces. It was to this joint need for an explanation of tragedy and the vindication of democracy in a time of death camps and atomic warfare that Reinhold Niebuhr's appropriation of the Christian doctrine of original sin spoke so strongly. And so it was that Niebuhr became the theologian of the postwar American intellectual.[68]

Niebuhr was not alone in commanding attention from serious minds, however. He was joined by his brother H. Richard Niebuhr and by the German-born theologian Paul Tillich as leading figures in a renaissance of Protestant thought. Richard Niebuhr's work had focused on the relations between social forces, religion, and culture, freely admitting that other goals besides love and service of God often motivated religious people. Tillich probed deeply into the connections between theology and the major philosophical problems of the day, particularly existentialism, being, and mortality. Tillich also acted as an analyst of Western culture and its foundations, providing historical explanations of theology and theological explanations of history. Both the Niebuhr brothers and Tillich were at the zeniths of their careers in the 1950s.

Protestants like the Niebuhrs and Tillich were joined by major proponents of religious ideas from other traditions. Judaism was well represented by the Jewish existentialist philosophers Martin Buber and Franz Rosenzweig and by theologian and ethicist Abraham Joshua Heschel. Buber and Rosenzweig were proponents of "dialogue" who saw communication between the self and another not as a dimension of the self, but as the location in which the self came authentically into being. Heschel posed the big questions—the meaning of life, how to live, human nature, and God's nature—and led his readers to a greater appreciation of the profundity of the Bible's answers to these problems.

Catholic thought was receiving plenty of attention thanks to the Trappist monk Thomas Merton, the American theologians Gustave Weigel and John Courtney Murray, and the historian John Tracy Ellis. Merton's *Seven Story Mountain* paved the way for thinking men and women to accept the disciplined life of Roman Catholicism. Weigel and Murray were responsible for working out an American Catholic understanding and tolerance of religious pluralism. For his part, John Tracy Ellis posed the question, "Why has the Catholic Church produced so few intellectuals?" in such a compelling manner as to demonstrate that it had produced at least one in his person. Also much discussed were the French Neo-Thomists, Jacques Maritain and Etienne Gilson, whose representations of the ideas of Thomas Aquinas were appropriated by notable secular thinkers such as President Robert M. Hutchins of the University of Chicago and the philosopher Mortimer Adler.

What had happened to religious thought was that it had made its peace with the philosophic and scientific discussions of the contemporary academy while simultaneously seeking to reclaim traditional concepts like sin, salvation, and gospel—and indeed the Bible—from the dustbins of the liberal theologians and the proprietorship of literalist conservatives. Thus, at the decade's end, Sydney Ahlstrom could say of the transition that had taken place in Protestant theology: "The Gospels were untangled from the synoptic and Johannine problems to allow a concern for the gospel, and St. Paul was restored to the canon as something more than the villain who twisted the pure religion of Jesus into an Hellenistic mystery cult. Yet . . . there was no inclination in either case to repudiate historical methods of findings. Indeed, it must be emphasized at this point that one major feature of neo-orthodox thinking was its complete willingness to join contemporary philosophical discussion, to share the liberal respect for scientific endeavor, and to accept and extend the nineteenth century's massive tradition of religious scholarship."[69] Moreover, the transition from religious hostility to science to the incorporation of science into a religious worldview had proceeded apace no less in the Jewish and Catholic camps.

Another angle of interpretation on the intellectuals' renewed respect for religion was offered by David Riesman, who provided a five-part analysis of this aspect of the return to religion in a 1951 article in the *American Scholar*. The intellectuals of the 1940s and 1950s, Riesman noted, embraced Freud's version of original sin for their own uses, principally to explain the persistence of evil. This took them very close to the traditional subject matter of religion and heightened in some an interest in religion that turned the tide in favor of those who had a more than simply curious stance toward religion. In Riesman's words: "The revival of interest in religion (if not in church-going) among intellectuals means that many in the upper social strata who are affiliated with organized religion need no longer flinch in pressing the claims of religion and in attacking its few remaining foes."[70] Meanwhile, popular culture and sentiment had turned against criticizing religion and toward an allowed criticism of society, its economic system (as long as one did not advocate Communism) and the "rat race." It was as though a new sacred cow had been brought in to replace the old one. The third factor promoting the intellectual acceptability of religion was the recent rise of Catholics in social and economic terms: "As Catholics have increasingly moved into the managerial and professional classes they have been able greatly to influence the definition of 'good American,' and have taken the lead since they were among the 'earliest arrivals' in the crusade against communism in defining the 'bad un-American' as well."[71] At the same time, psychoanalysts and religionists were converging on similar territory. The psychoanalyst's typical patient in the 1950s was now not a young man or woman needing to release sexual repressions, but a middle-aged businessman who was asking, "What is the purpose of my life?" Religion, in part because of its intellectual renaissance, was, in Riesman's words, beginning to serve "much more than in the preceding several generations, as a center for discussion of fundamental problems of value."[72] Thus people were asking essential questions of meaning and ethics of both therapist and priest, minister and psychiatrist. Finally, Riesman presented psychoanalyst Erich Fromm as representing the new wave of understanding of the relation between religion and psychology. In two of his books written up until that time, *Man for Himself* and *Psychoanalysis and Religion*, Fromm had demonstrated a willingness to take religion very seriously as a source of illumination in the moral problems presented in analysis. Riesman joined Fromm in carefully drawing the distinction between moral problems and problems of morale, one that not every practitioner of religious psychology in the revival would appreciate.

Seen synthetically then, intellectuals of the postwar period were motivated on several fronts toward revising their estimation of religion. Political disappointments in the Old Left, the creation of a more intellectually satisfactory relationship between theology and other branches of knowledge, and psychology's openness to questions of meaning and value all predisposed intellectuals to reconsidering their former opinions of religion. The sheer quality of the minds working in the religious academy and the ability of those minds to propose answers to the problems of the age also helped restore some of the luster religion had lost in earlier years.

The effects of the renewed intellectual interest in religion could be found in books, in increased enrollments at seminaries, and in new programs as the collegiate level. Signals that intelligent readers found religious questions and institutions worthy of study and consideration could be seen in the new-found success of serious works addressing religious themes. The publication of Paul Blanshard's *American Freedom and Catholic Power* increased Beacon Press's sales 145 percent above those for the previous year. The book was one of the top ten nonfiction books in sales for 1949, equalling the sales of the fourth best-selling fiction book that year. Its popularity, together with the appearance the next year of *Church and State in the United States* by Anson Phelps Stokes, testified to both public interest and to the enduring problematic character of church-state relations in American public life.

The serious religious paperback was also an invention of the 1950s. Although theology was put between paper covers as early as 1941, in a softcover edition of James Cardinal Gibbons's *The Faith of Our Fathers*, the breakthrough in the field came in 1954 when Doubleday began its Image Books series directed at the "intellectual Catholic public." By 1956, Image had sold over 1.5 million books, had forty-three titles in print, and its leading title—*A Popular History of the Catholic Church*—had sold 105,000 copies. This placed it second in quality paperback sales only to David Riesman's *The Lonely Crowd* (which had sold 160,000 copies for Doubleday's own Anchor Books division). Two Protestant paperback publishers soon got into the act, with Meridian and Harper Brothers introducing Living Age and Torchlight books, respectively, followed soon after in early 1957 by Reflection Books, a popular line introduced by the YMCA's Association Press. These paperbacks brought a number of authors to the public, and particularly to college students who otherwise might never have read Reinhold Niebuhr, Søren Kierkegaard, Thomas Aquinas, Hilaire Belloc, Edgar A. Goodspeed, Etienne Gilson, and Paul Tillich.

Another aspect of the postwar revival was an increased interest among young people in the ministry. One Ivy League college had a preministerial club with 150 members—more than ten times the usual prewar number. The profession which in the twentieth century had always found difficulty filling its ranks was now given a great infusion of fresh blood. Not only were there new ministers, but they came to the seminaries and divinity schools better qualified academically than their counterparts of any other modern decade.[73]

Religious Emphasis Weeks, having begun at Bowdoin College in Maine, spread throughout the nation's colleges, both private and public. These weeks usually featured religious leaders of varying backgrounds and degrees of distinction speaking on topics such as "What Does Religion Have to Say to Our Generation?" American colleges and universities also began in large numbers at this time to add the study of religion to their course offerings. The movement was spread by such books as Howard Lowry's *The Mind's Adventure*, a plea for the recognition of religion as a basic part of any truly liberal education.[74] Previously, religious study at the collegiate level had often been done on an ad hoc basis, reflecting the fact that—particularly at denominational schools—so many of the professors were ordained ministers, priests, or ex-missionaries that instruction in anything religious besides perhaps the Bible was unnecessary. Vital piety was assumed to suffuse the teaching of all subjects: philosophy, physics, even mathematics. In the postwar years, however, increased student interest and the American theological renaissance combined to create departments where religion and religious ideas were taken seriously as the focus of objective study. This was a development that would bear various kinds of fruit as time went on, as college students of the 1950s were challenged to see religion as a human phenomenon only partially captured and certainly not exhausted by their own Sunday school, church, or synagogue experiences.

During these years, Will Herberg often made great hay out of survey results which revealed the fact that so many who professed a faith couldn't name a single gospel. More recently, however, Robert Wuthnow has made the point that further exploration showed that knowledge of the Bible was almost wholly dependent upon levels of education. Thanks to the increased academic respectability of religion, knowledge of the Bible, knowledge of other religions, and acquaintance with formal philosophical and theological categories were on the rise as the postwar generation went to college. And, in addition to learning the names of famous books, these students also learned how to answer public opinion surveys.

One figure who wanted the 1950s college student to go beyond just learning about religion was Harvard president Nathan Pusey. Pusey's first article as president appeared in *Harper's* under the title, "A Religion for Now." In the article, Pusey attacked the argument of his predecessor Charles Elliot, who had contended in 1909 that the time had come to put away the old superstitious religion and serve instead the new religion of scientific truth and the pursuit of knowledge. Pusey maintained that there was still vitality left in the old religion, that indeed there was no substitute for personal faith. Still, the beginning of "the present low estate of religion at Harvard" was ignorance. It was his experience that "when one inquires today about religious questions—at least outside professional circles—one is apt normally to be met with disinterest, ignorance, and apathy on the one hand, and too often where interest does exist, with ignorance and fanaticism on the other. We have not been well taught about religion, and there is as a consequence a very widespread religious illiteracy and correspondingly little religious practice."[75] But the problem was not simply ignorance of religious matters, a deficit that could be remedied with the addition of religious studies courses. That, Pusey argued, would be to "slip into President Elliot's error here by seeming to imply that all that is lacking is knowledge." Instead, for Pusey, what was lacking was "faith."[76] Pusey subsequently went on to make substantial improvements in the Divinity School faculty, adding distinguished scholars who were also known for their involvement in the life of the church. These appointments included Paul Tillich, Amos Wilder, and George Buttrick.[77] He also attempted to augment the religious life of the College by introducing programs directed at guaranteeing that students would come to have the personal faith that they—in his view—so desperately required. In this latter project he found his efforts frustrated by an uncooperative faculty, and his religious influence on undergraduates was largely reduced to advising students at baccalaureate that Harvard graduates should have "the ability to speak the word God without reserve or embarrassment."[78]

The resistance Pusey received from faculty members for his efforts to instill piety into each and every Harvard graduate demonstrated that an academic respect for religion, though part of the revival of religious interest, was not synonymous with a desire "to get religion." It was one thing to agree that Reinhold Niebuhr was a genius, but quite another to require his faith of every freshman. Indeed, even the most faithful of those academics engaged in religious discourse often had very little positive to say about the more popular aspects of the return to religion.

Reading the Signs of a Revival— Contemporary Observations of the Return to Religion

Trying to read the signs and evidences of public conduct and attitudes to see if a religious revival was genuine had been a characteristic activity of American religious thinkers since at least 1741, when Jonathan Edwards wrote his tract on "The Distinguishing Marks of a Work of the Spirit of God," followed the next year by "Some Thoughts Concerning the Present Revival of Religion in New England." The religious revival of the 1950s had its skeptical questioners as well—people who asked if the increase in religious interest represented a turning to God or something else. In the 1950s the question of the nature of the revival engaged both secular and religious thinkers, but perhaps no conclusion was as succinct or as sharply worded as that of historian Eric Goldman: "Some of the new attention to religion was undoubtedly a sincere turning to the rigors and consolations of faith," he granted. "But a good deal of it was certainly a false religiosity, compounded of social aspirations and a fervid desire to avoid thinking."[79] Goldman's conclusion was, moreover, fully in line with the weight of religious observers of the return to religion. The response to the popularly heralded religious revival proved ambiguous at best.

As the decade and revival wore on, it became clear that the dissatisfaction of religious thinkers with the popular revival was an important corollary aspect of the return to religion. It also became the necessary starting point for the suburban jeremiads on which the greater part of this book concentrates. The critique that reached its fullest expression in the better-known full-length works was mirrored in articles and speeches by many other religious intellectuals. Their work appeared in places like the Jesuit journal *America*, the Jewish *Commentary*, the Protestant *Christian Century*, the liberal Catholic *Commonweal*, and a host of smaller religious periodicals. They also found expression in the respectable cultural news and comment magazines of the day, in the *Nation*, the *New Republic*, and the *Saturday Review*. A few of the most prominent critics, like Reinhold Niebuhr, even had access to wide audiences such as *Time* and *Life* readers.

One of the most influential of these critics was *Commonweal*'s talented editor, John Cogley. Analyzing the new-found popularity of religion among Eisenhower's entourage, Cogley noted that "religiosity—or the God-bit as it is called in the more cynical capital circles—has long been a part of our political tradition." Cogley found nothing wrong with a public expression of piety on the part of politicians, arguing indeed that "whatever his motives, Caesar should bow from time to time, if merely to remind us that he is only Caesar." But he found a far more troubling development in the political rhetoric of the republic: "There has been a tendency in the last few years—bolstered, I am sorry to say, by the President himself—to identify greatness and godliness. America is great, Mr. Eisenhower said on one occasion, because America is good; when America ceases to be good it will no longer be great."[80] Cogley saw in Eisenhower's statement an interpretation of current American greatness, measured in material wealth and political stature among the nations of the world, as being a reward for its godliness. Cogley went on to argue that the war hero's memoir, *God Is My Co-Pilot*, captured in the arrogance of its title the character of the contemporary national delusion. It was as if God had enlisted on the American side for the duration of the Cold War, and as if the church was not the custodian of God's truth so much as a kind of "anti-communist protective society." Using Catholic moral theology's classic proposition that good ends do not justify evil means, Cogley sought to divorce success and morality, "for it is a fact that evil ends have successfully served good means, if success is to be measured in worldly terms." Nor did use of pure means insure a victory. "If religion has any message for society," he wrote, "this is it. God's justice cannot be measured by its practical successes in this life." Lest anyone miss the point of his attack, Cogley ended his essay with these words: "The cheerful religiosity of Positive Thinking may be successful. I wonder how much of it has to do with Christianity."[81]

Occasionally, the problem Cogley pointed to—the relation between success and faithfulness—was also probed at more popular levels. In June of 1955, *McCall's* magazine stopped to remark that "since 1940, thirty million Americans have joined churches—Protestant, Catholic and Jewish. This is considerably more than the population growth during the same period of time. In 1850, only 16 percent of the country's citizens were church members. Today, 60 percent are." With all this good news to report, the magazine asked, "Why, then, are so many of our religious leaders asking . . . is our religious revival real?" The range of religious leaders it found with concerns about the genuineness of revival was indeed great and traversed the theological spectrum from Billy Graham, who had to remind his head-counting followers that "God is interested in the quality of converts, not quantity," to Reinhold Niebuhr, who phrased his concern in a way more delicate, but no less damning: "The question is whether this generation is not expressing its desire to believe in something, to be committed somehow, even though it is not willing to be committed to a God who can be known only through repentance." Washington's Roman Catholic Archbishop Patrick O'Boyle agreed, seeing too much of religion's popularity coming from a desire to escape the anxieties of an age poised on the brink of atomic calamity. "Many people are turning to religion as they would to a benign sedative to soothe their nerves and to settle their minds," he said, adding, "I do not want to be cynical about any man's struggle for religious faith, but for me and for many like me, religion is not a thing of mere sentiment or personal escape from fears and dissatisfactions." The most telling judgment was probably that relayed by Riverside Church's minister, Robert McCracken, who said, "*The New York Times*, in a review of books published in 1954, points out that from a glance at the sales charts it would seem that the average American wants most of all to (1) get religion, (2) reduce, (3) refinish and antique a Chippendale highboy."[82]

The recurrent complaint of religious intellectuals about the revival was that it seemed to harness religion as a means to other ends. Sometimes the ends were located within the individual; sometimes they were the ends of communal cohesion. Judaism's most prominent sociologist, Nathan Glazer, wrote despairingly of the Jewish side of the revival: "American Jews, if they believe in anything, believe in the instrumental efficacy of religion. Judaism is good for the Jew, they feel; it keeps him mentally healthy and adjusted, and keeps the Jewish people together. Any thought that it is good in itself, that it embodies valuable truths, and that—God forbid—these truths should be propagated among non-Jews is foreign to the majority of Jews in this country."[83]

One of the most common arguments made on behalf of religion in educated circles was that it undergirded democracy. Religious instruction in the public schools might even be justified, some held, since religious citizens made better citizens. There were even proposals for inculcating children in a "Religion of Democracy." Under the auspices of the Fund for the Republic, John Cogley hosted a symposium on the topic "Religion in a Free Society" where such questions were discussed. The responses of three of the participants in that symposium—Gustave Weigel, Paul Tillich, and Abraham Heschel—merit close attention, for they indicate just how much hostility the major religious minds of the day had for the claims made for the social utility of religion.

"Religion can contribute to the welfare of the general community; it can help society. My only worry is whether it should," wrote Gustave Weigel in his contribution ro the symposium.[84] Weigel went on to make the point from a Roman Catholic perspective that it "certainly cannot be the prime purpose of religion to make secular society more beneficent and the secular enterprise more satisfactory. That can indeed be the consequent of religion. But consequents are not the goals of deliberation; they are casual accretions to the proper goals of a planned effort" (224). Weigel also saw the widespread cultural acceptance of religion as a potential trap. The political society, he wrote, felt "quite magnanimous because it generously gives every citizen the rights to be as religious or irreligious as he wishes. What then does the collectivity ask of its religious members? A favor in return for the favor of toleration granted. It is recognized that religion refuses to be intimidated by power. The civic community is now asking that the men and women of religion harness this resistance to the chariot of the natural commonwealth. Religion, which before was tolerantly given the right to exist, is now invited to become an active dynamism in the common enterprise." Religion could then be regarded by the polis as something not merely to be tolerated, but as something to be used, and worse yet, regarded as "valuable because it can be used" (229). For religion, being valued by larger society was very seductive, but potentially also disastrous: "It is intoxicating to feel one's self esteemed after a long period of contempt. Good will and a spirit to please can stir the recipient of this new esteem. But the desire to please may be a subtle trend toward suicide" (230). Weigel believed that the contemporary religions of America were faced with the choice of divinizing secular society or being true to the goal of the kingdom of God. In the long term, success and popular glory for religion were not worth seeking, for it was not the purpose of the church "to save the republic" nor was it the church's role to be "a ministry of defense for government." "It makes little difference if the church be numerous or meager," he added. "In either case it will be a light on the mountain and a leaven in the mass" (235).

In his presentation,[85] Paul Tillich played the role of iconoclast and displayed his displeasure at the prevailing assumption that postwar American life represented the final achievement of civilization. "I feel a certain uneasiness in talking about Religion and the Free Society," Tillich confessed to his audience at the symposium. What, first of all, was meant by the term "free society"? But beyond definitional problems that made him uneasy, he cited a more profound worry: "Can religion be used as a tool for something else?" Tillich's answer was no, for by definition, "if religion is the state of being ultimately concerned, then it cannot be the tool for something else. The ultimate cannot be the tool for something non-ultimate" (272–273).

Tillich's final response to the question, as he saw it, was that religion could help the free society by offering principles of judgment to society derived from religion's own social-critical and self-critical aspects. Yet he was not as sanguine as many of the other participants in the symposium about the extent to which religion might, by being itself, support the ideal of a free society. Disagreeing with the kind of analysis offered by Weigel, Tillich pointed to forces that—though authentic to religious life—worked to resist the development of a free society: religious conservatism, religious authoritarianism, religious intolerance, and religious transcendentalism (274). The hopes of many Americans for the cultural effects of the religious revival were, according to Tillich, bound to be disappointed.

Abraham Joshua Heschel[86] was even more pointed in his assessment of the limitations of contemporary religion: "Little does religion ask of contemporary man. It is ready to offer comfort; it has no courage to challenge. It is ready to offer edification; it has no courage to break the idols, to shatter the callousness. The trouble is that religion has become 'religion'—institution, dogma, securities" (244). Worse was the fact that, in the return to religion, so many had signed up for a religion that was not religion at all, committing what Heschel termed "the fallacy of misplacement." Misplacement occurred, he said, when people "define self-reliance and call it faith, shrewdness and call it wisdom, anthropology and call it ethics, literature and call it Bible, inner security and call it religion, conscience and call it God." Fortunately, he reflected, nothing counterfeit could last forever (245).

For Heschel, the engine that drove modern religion was the same force as that which drove modern society—human need. "Needs are our gods," he wrote, "and we toil and spare no effort to gratify them. Suppression of a desire is considered a sacrilege that must inevitably avenge itself in the form of some mental disorder" (247). Such an orientation made it impossible for contemporary men and women to get anything out of the Bible, or the faith it represented: "Now the most serious obstacle which modern men encounter in entering a discussion about the ideas of the Bible, is the absence of the problem to which the Bible refers. The Bible is an answer to the question, What does God require of Man? But to modern man, this question is suppressed by another one, namely, what does man demand of God? Modern man continues to ponder: 'What will I get out of life?'" (246). But this inability of biblical religion to satisfy the demands of modern people did not prevent religion from flourishing, for religion proved able to adjust itself to the modern temper by "proclaiming that it too is the satisfaction of a need" (251).

Heschel heaped other criticisms upon the faith represented by the return to religion. Religion had become too defined by public acts—religious observation, church going, for example—instead of inward disposition, as if the chief virtue sought were social affiliation rather than conviction (257). He claimed the contemporary issue was not simply the lack of faith, but also its "vulgarization" (267). Finally, he returned to the theme played upon by other observers of the revival, that a fatal error was to equate religion with success or faith with expediency. "God's voice may sound feeble to our conscience," he added, "yet there is a divine cunning in history which seems to prove that the wages of absolute expediency is disaster" (270). For Heschel, the faith exemplified in the return to religion was a faith headed for disaster.

Reinhold Niebuhr was more ambivalent about the revival of religious interest than Heschel. In an article on the nature of the revival for the *New Republic* in June of 1955, he saw both good and bad in the renewed level of interest in religion. On the one hand, he was gratified that so many intellectuals had finally rejected the "secular religions" after they had been refuted by historical circumstances. He argued that "One cannot understand the spiritual climate of our time if one does not see how catastrophically modern man's experience of contemporary history has refuted all the secular securities which had been established irrefutably in the past two centuries. History was not so simply redemptive as the progressive interpretations of its course assumed. . . . The old symbol of the climax of history consisting of the engagement between Christ and anti-Christ seemed strangely more relevant to our experience than all the progressive interpretations of the nineteenth century."[87] Thus Niebuhr embraced the sophisticated kind of people who embraced his kind of religion. But of the other aspects of the return to religion Niebuhr had less positive things to say. He wondered with foreign observers why this most secular of cultures had combined "good plumbing with religious faith in the 'American Way of Life.'" He also suggested that the popular expressions of religion most commented upon—such as the prayers offered by representatives of all three major faiths at the 1952 political conventions—were evidence of just how easily religion could become a source of complacency, for such public displays of religiosity usually amounted to no more than thanking God that America was great.[88]

A situation in which religious thinkers are at best ambivalent toward the popular success of their enterprise is a circumstance ripe for conflict. Religion in the decade of the 1950s was at its peak of popularity, and the religious revival was celebrated far and wide for filling the houses of worship, for captivating the hearts of millions, for leading the masses back to a belief in prayer, for engaging the intellectuals, and for meeting the needs of the modern world. Yet to its experts, religion had never been at greater peril, or less faithfully observed. In this apparent paradox—this radical difference in perception about the truth of the religious revival between its participants and its critical observers—lay the basis for the fifties' most intense religious debates, and for jeremiads that would follow.

The Return to Religion Analyzed:
Three Kinds of Religion

The disagreement between the religious experts, demographers, journalists, and ordinary men and women in the 1950s about the relative merits of the postwar revival of religious interest highlights the essential problem of interpreting the decade's return to religion. For it is difficult to assign causes to a phenomenon whose character is still in doubt. When faced with a situation in which the dominant question at stake was, as *McCall's* magazine put it, "Is our religious revival real?", the place to begin is not with what caused the churches and synagogues to grow, but rather with the definition of "religion" that each party to the disagreement brought to the debate. Once the nature of the debate is fully understood, we may move on to comprehend the causes of the revival.

As we have seen, the situation of the 1950s was indeed one in which the pollster, the theologian, and the woman on the street disagreed as to whether religion had made a successful comeback. Our first task is to ask, "Did they all mean the same thing when they said the word 'religion?'" Upon examination of the evidence it soon becomes clear that the definition that George Gallup used for religion differed greatly from that used by Abraham Heschel. For Gallup, religion was more successful if the average number of people attending a religious service in the last seven days went up. For Heschel, religion was not to be counted as more successful unless more people were led to an obedient relationship with the God of Abraham and Jacob. For the man or woman on the street, religion might well be defined as on the rise on the basis of the proportion of time people seemed to spend discussing religious topics over the barbecue or bridge table. Coming to terms with the differing meanings of religion and their respective measures of success is the next analytical task.

In her book, *America: Religion and Religions*, Catherine Albanese has proposed a distinction for understanding the phenomenon of religion between "ordinary religion" and "extraordinary religion." Ordinary religion is, she says, "the taken-for-granted reality we all assume . . . [putting] its premium on the things which are deeply present and unconsciously revered here within the borders of everyday culture." Extraordinary religion "involves an encounter with some form of 'otherness,' whether natural or supernatural. It is specific and particular, easily recognizable as religion, and possible to separate from the rest of culture."[89] Though there are problems with this sort of approach, it also offers some strengths.[90] Of particular note is the close identification she makes between everyday culture and ordinary religion. Her ordinary religion suggests a belief system in which one is so thoroughly immersed that one does not stop to question its doctrines, which of course have no need of being written down. On the other hand, extraordinary religion, with its emphasis on particular tenets and practices, necessarily is at least in part independent of culture.

An attempt to apply Albanese's distinction to the 1950s return to religion would soon prove frustrating, since it is quite difficult to tell when ordinary religion stops and extraordinary religion begins. However, a cue may be taken from the distinguishing features of culture-integrated and culture-separability of the respective kinds of religion. We could then propose a typology for religion in the 1950s that is a modified version of Albanese's distinction. The first kind of religion we will call "popular religion," the second type "ecclesiastical religion," and the third, "elite religion."

Working definitions for each of the three types are as follows:

Popular religion is the religion conveyed to a person as a result of growing up in a culture. It may partake of elements of other, more formalized belief systems and include ideas of God, immortality, reincarnation, and heaven and hell, but it requires no explicit instruction.

Ecclesiastical religion is the religion lived out within a formal institutional setting. The institution has rites, mores, and doctrines to which participants are in varying degrees required to assent to or observe.

Elite religion is the religious belief and tradition system maintained by a group of professional scholars and religious practitioners, and sometimes educated amateurs. Although individuals involved in elite religion may disagree with one another about the content of the religion, they place a high priority on proper understanding of and obedience to that content, and often appeal to traditions, texts, or other authorities in support of their positions.

The relationship between the kinds of religion is important as well as the kinds themselves, for it is often the case that the practitioners of elite religion will also be the keepers of ecclesiastical religion's doctrines and rites, and it is always the case that the participants in ecclesiastical religion will have come out of a popular religion background even if the ecclesiastical religion requires that they renounce popular religious beliefs or practices. Ecclesiastical religion is thus a potential meeting place for the practitioners of the two other kinds of religion. What is important in the overall religious situation within a culture is the congruence between the three types. In a situation where there is perfect congruence between the types, there is no religious conflict. In a setting where the congruence between the ecclesiastical and elite types is high, the belief system of the religious institution tends to be highly intellectual and religious observance rigorous. An example of this type of relationship might be found in Puritanism. Finally, in a setting where the congruence is high between popular and ecclesiastical religion, the requirements of the institutional forms of religion tend to be less rigorous, requiring little more than what participants in the general culture already subscribe to in terms of behavior and belief. It could be argued that Catholicism of the late middle ages represents this type of relationship, although it must be recognized that the church had already had a large hand in shaping the culture from which its adherents came.

Applying this typology to the 1950s and the return to religion, it appears that the congruence between the popular and ecclesiastical types of religion was greater than that between the ecclesiastical and elite types. It also becomes clear that the debate over whether the revival's religion was "real" was a debate between the elite and popular religionist, who each insisted that their definition of religion was the right one. For the popular religionist, God, country, church, Bible reading, the free market, human dignity, and the virtues of neighborliness and niceness formed a seamless web of belief and practice—and the churches and synagogues of the 1950s to a large degree reflected this definition of religion.

This state of affairs was disturbing to the elite religionists who saw too many Americans confusing God and country in the aftermath of World War II, but more perplexing was the possibility that some people were attaching themselves to synagogues and churches without a belief in so much as the existence of God. Thomas Hine has argued, "God may or may not have been the most important element in suburban religion, but it is clear that Tupperware was not the most important aspect of a Tupperware party."[91] To be sure, Earl Tupper's company reaped tremendous profits from the product. But critics who dismissed the parties as "commercial transactions masquerading as social events" misinterpreted the experience of the participants. For those who gave and attended a Tupperware party, the commercial transaction provided an opportunity at sociability with little risk. The worst that could happen to the hostess was that she wouldn't like the guests, but still end up with free Tupperware. If a guest turned out not to like the hostess, she might have to buy a translucent butter dish, but she was not obliged to invite the hostess and her husband over for a family barbecue. And yet if things worked out, people were introduced and friendships made that eased the lonely and insecure feelings that came with life as a suburban pioneer.[92]

But if Hine is right in his functional explanation of the Tupperware party, what then of religion? Cannot a similar case be made that God was not the most important element in suburban religion? It is conceivable that people wanted sociability and joined the church as a culturally acceptable way of obtaining it. That was the fear of the elite religionists, and their only way of countering this possibility was to insist that this thing called church was not necessarily true religion. More probable, however, and harder still to counter, was the possibility that the return to religion on both the popular and ecclesiastical levels, particularly in the suburbs, was fueled by the baby boom.

In 1952, the *Saturday Evening Post* ran a conversion story entitled, "God Saved My Baby," breathlessly introducing its subject: "Sam Binder had almost forgotten how to pray. He hadn't been to church in years when he came to the most frightful crisis a parent can know—and found proof that there is a God. This is his testimony." The account drew upon all the themes of a classical religious conversion story and added a few twists distinctly appropriate to the American fifties. Sam Binder had known success as the world counted it. He was happy, respected, had a beautiful wife and a beautiful home. And even after his conversion, he made it clear in his story that spending Sundays on the golf course instead of church had not damaged his character much. "I wasn't what you'd call a sinner. Neither was my wife. We had both been raised in Christian homes." Yet when Sam and his wife were told that their baby was going to die, that it was just a matter of time before the disease took its inevitable downward course, they began to try to pray. In the end, the baby made a recovery the attending physician described as miraculous, and his parents found faith in God and gave up the golf links for the church pew.[93]

The story is worth probing a bit further since it provides clues into the nature of the revival. Immediately apparent is the unwillingness to say, "I was a horrible sinner." The ideal mid-century conversion was the man or woman who was already a credit to his or her gender, community, and role in life. The fifties did not want to hear the story of the hopeless alcoholic, prostitute, or unsuccessful door-to-door salesman brought to faith. The standards for membership in the respectable ranks of ecclesiastical religion were the same as those for the popular religion. Indeed, Sam Binder made a point of noting that both he and his wife were raised in Christian families, as though a religious background was part of the basic requirements for membership in the general culture.

The second revelation is that the child in this story is essentially the cause of the religious questioning that brings Sam and his never-mentioned-by-name wife back to faith. In one respect this is not at all surprising, for there is a great deal of historical evidence to suggest that the timing of religious conversion is closely linked to life-stage changes. Thus an unexpected death of a teenager in a community is followed by a surge in religious experiences and conversions by other youths in the vicinity. Likewise, Mary Ryan has found a striking correlation between an approaching or recent childbirth and a woman's conversion in the mass revivals of New York's Genessee Valley from the 1820s through the 1840s.[94] The underlying engine of these conversions comes from facing the ultimate questions associated with human mortality for one's self or one's children.

Bearing these findings in mind, it appears that the great increase in religiosity and religious affiliation in the 1950s coming at the same time as the great baby boom is perfectly natural. Concern for one's children and concern for religion go hand in hand. There was, however, a dimension of this problem that would bother critics of the revival. Were the parents turning to the faith for reasons internal to religion or for effects collateral to their religion? Did parents of the 1950s sincerely believe and embrace the religious faiths they professed, or were they—in the words of the day—"doing it for the children"? These were the kinds of questions put to the revival by the elite religionists. Their suspicions that many new church and synagogue members had joined out of motives for which elite understandings of religion had no place found ready confirmation in stories like Mary Elizabeth Sergent's "Why Aren't They Like Us?"

A popular fictional account of one family's history in the postwar years, Sergent's story serves as a guide to popular American religious sentiment in the 1950s. In her story, Sergent describes what happens "when a normal, average young married couple becomes increasingly involved in our complex social and economic world, treats the church casually, and then wonders as the years go by why their children 'aren't like us.'" That, in a sentence, was the American dilemma—how to make something gold stay. The search for the cause of America's greatness and the search for the source of personal success kept leading back to the same source—religion. Imparting one's own values and religious heritage was a time-honored aspect of the popular religion, and with the cooperation of institutional religion the practice was encouraged as a step toward maintaining the culture which nourished that religion.

Ecclesiastical religion in the 1950s was not simply the willing victim of a kind of cultural religion, however, and to portray it as such would be a mistake. Protestantism in particular had institutionally experimented with more rigorous doctrines both on the right and the left of the theological spectrum, and the results proved disastrous. Now, in the postwar years, the theological positions of the 1920s and 1930s that had seemed to be the only possibilities were rejected as divisive. As Robert Wuthnow has written: "Prominent theological positions now seemed dated; the world had somehow matured beyond them. Fundamentalism was pictured as being overly narrow, negative, and separatist, capable of attracting few to its version of the gospel. Modernism was recalled as a preoccupation with obscure intellectual debates, too rationalistic, too concerned with vague social issues, lacking in drive, vision, and power to motivate a vigorous personal faith."[95] That is part of what happened. Another way to describe what happened to fundamentalism and liberal theology is that the American religious people, unable to cope with the assaults of the former on their reason and of the latter on their faith, settled for a warm, fuzzy, pragmatic faith that tried not to draw any distinctions too carefully. By the late 1940s the appeal of a broad modernism, such as that represented by Harry Emerson Fosdick, as opposed to either fundamentalism or an extreme modernism, was clear to the church and to its professional servants. This broad modernism was warm and sentimental and demanded little thought or defense of thought. Indeed, the commonsenseness of the Gospel was the theme repeated by all the leading popular religious figures of the day, and on this motif Fosdick, Peter Marshall, and Billy Graham sounded suspiciously alike. The center ground, relativistic and anti-intellectual though it was, possessed much charm for religious institutions burned by previous battles involving elite religionists of competing camps.

The elite religionists, for their parts, had very little influence on the early stages of the return to religion. No theological breakthroughs from the nation's ivory towers preceded the mass convergence on its religious institutions. Yet the very popularity of the churches and synagogues created a demand for new leaders, and these new leaders were schooled to think like the elite religionists who occupied the religious academy: an academy that itself was undergoing a restoration of reputation and popularity. For the time being, the elite religionists posed difficult questions to the religion of the culture in which they taught. In time their students would pose these challenges directly to the religious institutions they served.

The return to religion in the 1950s was in reality a simultaneous return of three distinct, yet interrelated, kinds of religion. While the popular aspects of the postwar revival of religious interest have gained the most attention from historians and scholars of American religion, it was the competing views of what constituted "real" religion provided by representatives of the three kinds—popular, ecclesiastical, and elite—that guaranteed that a vital debate would ensue concerning the relation of religion to American society and culture. The religious stage was set for the appearance of the suburban jeremiads.

3

Critics of the American Dream

■

The 1950s were a time of unparalleled achievement for American society and its religious bodies. The nation's economy, housing stock, birth rate, flow of consumer goods, international stature, and educational quality were all on the rise. The number of persons living in poverty was in decline; television offered the fruits of popular culture to people throughout the nation and helped create a truly national culture. If there were still imperfections in American society, some argued, they were temporary ones. For its part, organized religion was enjoying an all-time peak, with membership, giving, and popular identification with religious bodies at their greatest levels in American history. Yet such success had its limits.

Prosperity proposes dilemmas to societies that are fortunate enough to experience it. At the most basic level there is a fear of losing what has been achieved; the fear that luck will not hold and the fear of becoming complacent and losing one's gains by abandoning the struggle in which they were acquired. In the fifties, this led some within both the religious and more general cultures to attempt to explicate why America's postwar miracle was permanent, the result of unique factors in the American character and American democracy.

With economic success, the stakes also rise. So in the 1950s, critics who had focused on the failure of the system to clothe and feed America's people in the 1930s now took its material benefits as given and began raising the moral question: "Affluence for what?" And so for most social critics at work in the 1950s, the issues were personal and interpersonal, not systemic, political, or economic. That is, the social critics worried more about the distorting psychological effects of conformity, the meaninglessness of work, and the trivial uses to which leisure time was put than they did about the absence of political alternatives, the ownership of the means of production, and economic inequity. Still, the 1950s nourished a thriving company of writers who provided a continuous stream of critical comment that flowed in sharp counterpoint to contemporary celebrations of the American dream. The intellectual critics of the 1950s saw American society as a lonely crowd of white-collar workers and organization men, housed in lookalike suburban homes, and dominated by mass culture and the power elite. Their criticism is part of the story of the suburban jeremiads.

For the religious elites, the numerical growth of churches and synagogues and the popularity of prayer and piety represented a hollow success. In their eyes it was not real religion that was successful; it was something less than the religion of the God of Abraham, Isaac, and Jacob. In the language of the Bible, the critics believed the people had "gone off after idols and false gods." By the end of the decade they would call the nation's true faith "the American Way of Life," compare the suburbanization of the middle-class churches to the captivity in Babylon, and even suggest that God did not appreciate the sounds filtering up to him from America's solemn religious assemblies.

Both kinds of critics—the ostensibly secular social critics and the religious social critics—are important to the understanding of the phenomena of suburban jeremiads, that is, the prophetic religious criticisms of American life and religion. The secular critics are important on two levels. They are important insofar as they represent the thought world out of which the more religiously oriented Jeremiahs worked. They are also vital because in a real sense they too were religious critics. To attack culture in such a time as when culture and religion are identified is to attack religion. Thus, the social critics were critics in our terms of the popular religion as well as society. Indeed, the line between social and religious-social criticism proved an exceedingly fine line as the so-called secular critics decried social developments on moral grounds, used religious language to call America to account for its sins, and reserved some of their harshest criticisms for the churches and synagogues for failing to take a stand against the prevailing secular culture.

The first critics of postwar American society—both chronologically and in terms of the priority of their ideas—were the secular critics. Although there were other critics at work at the time, four deserve special attention in this work. First is David Riesman, principal author of *The Lonely Crowd*, followed by William H. Whyte, Jr., author of *The Organization Man*. Next is C. Wright Mills, whose central critique spanned two volumes, *White Collar* and *The Power Elite*. Finally, the thought of essayist Dwight Macdonald on the phenomenon of mass culture will be considered. These four thinkers and four books are important, for they are the social critics who received the widest reading and whose ideas, at least in simplified form, rapidly became commonplace opinion among educated Americans. The claim is not made here that they were the best or most original social critics working in the 1950s. But measured purely in terms of impact, these writers proved to be the outstanding critics of their day.

The Lonely Crowd

The Lonely Crowd began with the preparation for an interdisciplinary course on "Culture and Personality" at the University of Chicago where David Riesman, a law professor with strong interests in social psychology, was teaching in the social science program. Eventually the project attracted the support and collaboration of Reuel Denney, a literary critic, and Nathan Glazer, a prominent young sociologist. The project also moved, with Riesman, to Yale where it was part of the university's interdepartmental research program in national policy. It was thus written as a scholarly volume, and its nearly 400 pages and technical social-science vocabulary did not promise the average nonprofessional reader an easy time. Yet the title in its short form and with its subtitle, "A Study of the Changing American Character," suggested both sadness and recent change and attracted an enormous readership, much to the surprise of Riesman and his coauthors.[1]

The Lonely Crowd was first and foremost an argument that Americans were the most developed of a new kind of people living in a new kind of society. In order to make this historical claim the book began with a metatheory that related growth potential to society types. Where particular societies fell on the Malthusian S-curve of population growth, the authors argued, determined what kind of character their typical members had. Thus a society of high growth potential "developed in its members a social character whose conformity is insured by their tendency to follow tradition," or "traditional-directed" people. A transitional population-growth society was dependent on inner-directed members, and a society of incipient population decline was dependent on the tendency of its members to be sensitized to the expectations and preferences of others—and its people were termed "other-directed." Because the theory's characterological types were "ideal types" in the Weberian sense, no one person or society could be expected to represent a pure case of one of the types. Still the claim was made that in America the "other-directed" type was most perfectly realized.

Although Riesman expressed some misgivings about the theory even as it pertained to ideal types and, in the second edition of the book appearing in 1960, admitted that the correlation between population status and social character types was perhaps the weakest argument in the original book, it is important to note several things about the three social character types he discussed. First, all of the character types were conformist. Conformity was taken as a given need of every society. This was often lost in the popular discussion of the idea of other-directedness in the years following the original publication of *The Lonely Crowd*, as though *the* thing wrong with other-direction was that it resulted in conformity, as though there was another option besides conformity. Indeed, the inner direction that seemed to casual observers and critics to be the clearest alternative to postwar other-directed conformity was defined by Riesman to be the "social character whose conformity is insured by [people's] tendency to acquire early in life an internalized set of goals" (9). However much these goals were enforced from within the individual, they were not *produced* from within the individual. Instead these internalized goals—the honor of a Christian gentleman in the age of Victoria, to name but one—were acquired from outside, from the society interested in conforming its members to itself.

Further, the best discussion of the book was about the advanced Western society and why neither the folkways of the tradition-oriented society, nor the "psychological gyroscope" of the transitional society, were appropriate to a society such as the United States in the 1950s. The society of incipient decline in population was one characterized by abundance where the hard life of scarcity under former types of economies had ceased to exist. The inner-directed control of something like the Protestant work ethic was no longer necessary or particularly helpful. "Increasingly *other people* are the problem, not the material environment" (19). A new psychological mechanism was called for and that was an "abundance psychology" in which people must consume, enjoy, vacation, acquire for reasons beyond need alone, and so forth. The information to supply this new psychology came from peer groups on the playground or in the workplace, or from the media.

What Riesman and his coauthors were describing, of course, was not advanced Western societies in general so much as America. In terms of population decline, Great Britain showed it was possible without having dispensed entirely with either social role/class distinctions or inner direction. *The Lonely Crowd*'s authors did recognize that Americans were the other-directed types *par excellence*, however: "The American is said to be shallower, freer with his money, friendlier, more uncertain of himself and his values, more demanding of approval than the European" (19). Curiously, this was the same kind of observation that visitors to America had been making at least since de Crevocouer and Tocqueville. Still, Riesman defended his view of the American as the first in a new type of character type and not simply a singular historical development: "Tentatively, I am inclined to think that the other-directed type does find itself most at home in America, due to certain constant elements in American society, such as its recruitment from Europe and its lack of any seriously feudal past. As against this, I am also inclined to put more weight on capitalism, industrialism, and urbanization—these being international tendencies—than on any character-forming peculiarities of the American scene" (20).

Riesman described the transition overtaking American society as follows: "If we wanted to cast out social character types into social class molds, we could say that inner-direction is the typical character of the 'old' middle class—the banker, the tradesman, the small entrepreneur, the technically oriented engineer, etc.—while other direction is becoming the typical character of the 'new' middle class—the bureaucrat, the salaried employee in business, etc" (21). Other-directed's got their direction not from the past, not from a philosophical and/or religious ethic, but from contemporaries of two kinds—peers and the mass media.

Though the discussion of national character was the portion of the book that received the most attention, character was only the first third of *The Lonely Crowd*. Politics and autonomy were, respectively, the second and third parts. Both were extensions of, and responses to, the analysis developed in the first part of the book. In the political realm, each kind of character type had its own distinctive style of political involvement. The tradition-directed character was politically "indifferent" and understandably so, for who ruled and how was not the decision of that society's individual. The inner-directed society's political type was the "moralizer," who translated his self-interests into the "public interest" and crusades for them, feeling little ambivalence about them (191). The characteristic political style of the other-directed individual Riesman designated the "inside dopester." The inside dopester was aware that people were as important as things, and sought to be on the insider circle of political activity, not for the sake of what politics could accomplish, but with the goal of knowing what was going on or being close to the center of power. Moreover, Riesman argued, "No matter how politically active the inside-dopester may appear, he is essentially passive—a self-conscious puppet tolerantly watching and making sure that the strings that move him do not touch his heart" (201). As contrasted to the inner-directed type of character then, the other-directed and tradition-directed were strikingly alike in their essential attitude of helplessness in political life. In both cases, they sought not to change life politically, but only to minimize where possible political changes' effects on their lives and interests. This resulted in postwar American political life being characterized by veto groups: special interest blocks that set up an effective countervailing balance of interests such that politics accomplished nothing much.

The specter of a political sphere in which there was a great deal of activity and no action did not seem particularly bothersome to Riesman. Indeed, given the progress of American society under the New Deal, a system that provided the prospect of only minor change seemed a blessing. The possibility that America should undergo the kind of violent political upheaval that Spain, Italy, and Germany had experienced in the last two decades was thankfully foreclosed. This beneficial aspect of the other-directed society allowed Riesman to look to the personal sphere as the place where the most improvement was needed.

If the other-directed person did not seek power, Riesman asked in the third part of *The Lonely Crowd*, "then what does he seek?" At the very least, he answered, adjustment. It was possible to fail even in this and become anomic, but more was also possible, for occasionally the other-directed individual sought to be autonomous and succeeded in transcending the mere requirements of culture. Some social conformity was necessary to get along in life, but the obsessive ritualized other-direction characteristic of contemporary American life was not. Riesman's solution was premised on his belief that the *social* character was not all of character: "The individual is capable of more than his society usually asks of him, though it is not at all easy to determine this, since potentialities may be hidden not only from others but from the individual himself" (286).

Standing behind the views of Riesman were those of the psychological and sociological savants of the era. Erich Fromm's *Man for Himself* and C. Wright Mills's "The Competitive Personality" figure prominently in the finding of a new characterological type.[2] Fromm was Riesman's analyst and teacher, and it was from him that Riesman borrowed the terms "inner-directed" and "other-directed." Fromm, in turn, had absorbed them (as in *innige Mensch*) from the German philosopher Martin Heidegger.[3] Riesman's types, then, were second-hand intellectual goods, and his role was as a popularizer. But the question arises whether these terms went all the way down. Were they understood anyway after they had been disseminated? Only in part. As terms, "tradition-directed" and "other-directed" made sense, and Riesman could easily find examples of both types of people to which to point. But the "autonomous" person, like Nietzsche's *Übermensch*, was in some respects still waiting to be born. Though his book was meant to be both practical in description and recommendation, Riesman unwittingly cast himself in the role of prophet. In the time of the "other-directed" person and the veto-group, behold the age of the person with the truly "internal gyroscope" had come. That was the message of "autonomy," but few of the millions who referred to American society as a lonely crowd followed Riesman this far. In the forward to the second edition of *The Lonely Crowd*, Riesman remarked that "in an age when many educated Americans are preoccupied with the nature of their own identities and values, many non-professional readers have come to *The Lonely Crowd* for clues as to what they were like and how they might live. Indeed, many have read it as a test of their character, in the old-fashioned and non-technical sense of the word 'character'" (xxviii). What most of these nonacademic readers took from the book was a conviction that the other-directed way of life was wrong because it was so conformist, and that the essential choice that Riesman posed was between the sycophantic Organization Man and the lone cowboy on the range, secure in his saddle and held upright by his "internal gyroscope." This was not the choice that Riesman had in mind between adjustment and autonomy, but it was what the popular mind did with his book. Critics would complain that the autonomous individual was vaguely presented in *The Lonely Crowd*, but the general public did not care. On the whole, they preferred the cowboy. And they were prepared by *The Lonely Crowd* for another prophet of individualism, William H. Whyte, author of *The Organization Man*.

The Organization Man

The idea that grew into the book *The Organization Man* originated in a story William H. Whyte did as an editor at *Fortune* magazine looking at the college graduates of 1949. "I went around to colleges and bought the seniors steak dinners, and we had bull sessions," he recalled in a 1987 interview. "They were all talking about a possible depression and wanted to go to work for big companies." This came as something of a shock to Whyte, who himself had been a college senior only ten years earlier, when "all of us in the Class of 1939 wanted to be individualists."[4] The article created a lot of comment, and the men of the Class of 1949, and others like them who worked for large corporations and lived in the new postwar suburbs, became the focus of study for his book.[5]

At one level, *The Organization Man* was simply a good journalistic description of the changing shape of the American middle classes. It encapsulated their work, their rootlessness, their propensity to buy on a budget plan rather than save for purchases, their emphasis on being "well-rounded," their education, their living patterns, the interchangeability of their suburbs, their child-centered lifestyle, their mores. But Whyte's book was also a moral brief against the social ethic that undergirded this expanding new class of persons.

Whyte's theme was the decline of individualism, and the ascent of its successor, the organization. Whyte's book chronicled the rise of what he called the "social ethic." The principal features of this ethic were a belief in the safety found in numbers, a commitment to togetherness and communal cohesion at all costs, and love for and trust in an organization. The ideological foundation of the "social ethic" was scientism, "the promise that with the same techniques that have worked in the physical sciences we can eventually create an exact science of man" (26). Scientism evidenced itself in the prevalence of talk in the 1950s about social engineering" and in the rising status of the personnel director, the time and motion statistician. It found a corollary in the belief that, because of what had been learned about human behavior and how to control it since the Great Depression, a recession-proof economy had been created. One of the principal conclusions of scientism was that by aggregating individuals into groups, the risks of competitive individualism could be avoided while giving up none of the benefits bequeathed by older modes of social organization.

But Whyte also believed that beyond merely seeking groups for the goods that could be achieved nowhere else, people in the contemporary age saw groups as ends unto themselves. What most formulas for improving American life shared, it seemed to Whyte, was a belief that the thing most needful to modern persons and their societies was a sense of belongingness. There were different candidates for the source of this belongingness—the corporation, the community, the union, even the church—but wherever one turned spokespersons could be heard bewailing "the lack of an encompassing, integrated life," and, not surprisingly, generously volunteering their own group "to take over the whole messy job" (50). This belief in belongingness, Whyte emphasized, when combined with one of the precepts of scientism—that groups were proven to be more effective than individuals—led to the third characteristic of the social ethic, togetherness. In Whyte's words, not only did people want to belong, but they wanted to "belong together." Not only was no man an island, but an individual without a group was nothing at all. Group work was the rage at school and corporation alike.

The effects of these aspects of the social ethic were much the same as those of Riesman's other-directed style of character formation. The individual learned to distrust his or her own judgments and to subordinate personal tastes and preferences to those of the group. Whyte portrayed this subordination as tragic on two levels. On the first level, it was tragic in the dilemma faced by the middle-level manager who could obey the dictates of his conscience and save the lives of plant workers by throwing the off power switch in an overload situation, or follow his boss's orders and remain a good organization man—and gives primary consideration to the latter choice (269–275). And though not so obviously life-threatening, it was also tragic in the case of the suburban housewife who allowed the cultural tastes of her *Reader's Digest*-reading neighbors to tyrannize her out of joining a theatrical group, even though she felt culturally lacking.

The social ethic's greatest sin for Whyte was that it presented a false view of the world. The belief in salvation through the organization masked the reality that life as experienced by individuals in all times, places, and societies is difficult. The truth, as Whyte saw it, was that the tension between the needs of the individual and the needs of the society was an eternal conflict. Those who felt this conflict were made to believe that their doubts in the system made them abnormal. Far from being abnormal, however, those who saw the conflict were in possession of the truth that was necessary to put together an individually satisfying life. Like the little boy who said, "The emperor has no clothes on," the person who had doubts about the organization way was in the healthy majority, even if no others spoke up publicly to agree. The awareness of the truth, however, did not by itself lead to joy. "This duality is a very unpleasant fact," Whyte wrote. "Once you acknowledge how close the relationship is between conformity and belongingness—between 'good' participation and 'bad' participation—you cannot believe in utopia, now or ever. But progress is not served by ignoring it. Many current prescriptions for a better society ignore it, and thus are delusory. However shrewd their diagnosis of what is wrong, their precepts could intensify the very problems they are intended to solve" (400).

Whyte's book also reserved harsh words for suburbia, though not because a ranch house or a picture window was any worse in itself than the features of urban neighborhood living. Whyte's complaint was that suburban life was part and parcel of the organizational myth. The residents of suburbia were fond of seeing themselves living in a dream come true, a classless society, free of social conflict. If pressed, they would admit that perhaps it was not an unclassed society, but then at least they were living in a one-class society, a middle-class society where everyone had enough to live comfortably and no one had enough to lord it over others. "We are all in the same boat," they liked to say, but as Whyte pointed out, they were not. Far from the final resting place of a settled middle class, the suburbs were a study of a middle class in formation. For many, a move to the new suburbs was also a move to the middle class. Though college-educated organization men and their wives set the tone for suburbs, they were joined by many who had earned their wages in a factory, barely finished high school, and grown up in an urban ethnic neighborhood. When they came to the suburbs, these newer members of the middle class accommodated themselves to the lifestyles of those they perceived to be their betters (331). Indeed the suburbs served as a new melting pot where immigrants were schooled in what being a modern American was all about. Here too, as in the turn of the century's urban crucible, individuals learned to give up their distinctiveness in the interest of group consensus.

Yet even as they were the models for class formation, the Organization Man and his suburbs were also threats to the stability of the new middle class. For while people entered the suburbs with incomes very close to one another, those employed in the middle management of large corporations soon outdistanced their salesmen and white-collar clerical neighbors in earning power. The small improvements to homes and acquisition of more and slightly more tasteful furniture belied the myth of classlessness that had made the early years of pioneering in the suburb so satisfying to so many (338–342). Meanwhile, just beneath the surface of the enjoyment of prosperity was the fear of "going back," of suffering a loss in income that would not only rob a family of some luxuries, but its very style of life. For psychologically, Whyte argued, to a family on the "edge of the middle class," what others might classify as amenities were necessities. Despite this acknowledgment of the dark side of the Organization Man's residential trend-setting, Whyte remained hopeful about the future: "The phase in which people stand poised on the brink of the middle class is not a pretty one, but it is a phase. In somewhat the same way that Americanization affected succeeding waves of immigrants, acclimatization to the middle class will lessen the feeling of social vulnerability that can turn these newcomers ugly" (342). In discussing the purported classlessness of suburbia, Whyte also noticed another discordant note that lay just beneath the surface of life in Park Forest. "The classlessness also stops very sharply at the color line," he wrote. In the early 1950s, there had been an acrid controversy over the admission of blacks to Park Forest. For one minority of residents, integration would have meant the fulfillment of personal social goals. For another group, those who had moved out of Chicago wards that had been "taken over," the possibility of blacks as neighbors presented the return of the threat they thought they had left behind. Most residents, though probably also opposed to integrating the suburb, were primarily upset that their domestic tranquillity had been disturbed. As of 1956, no blacks had moved in, but Whyte said, "The issue had been brought up, and the sheer fact that one had to talk about it made it impossible to maintain unblemished the ideal of egalitarianism so cherished" (344).

The church of suburbia was also beholden to the "social ethic" of the organizational way. Wherever young organization people gathered in a community, Whyte noticed, "the urge for a more socially useful church manifests itself" (417). Whyte allowed that there was a strong social component in the current religious revival, but argued that separating the organization's people from people in general revealed that the trend among the former was even greater. This was only logical, he thought, since they needed to emphasize what others had historically taken for granted: "For those who stay put in one place, the church has always been socially useful, and the by-products of church affiliation they take as a matter of course. But the transients cannot. Stability, kinship with others—they want these demonstrated, and in the here and now" (417). The result of this need was that the churches and synagogues were faced with an "irresistible temptation" to make the provision of friendship their chief appeal. To illustrate his claim, Whyte cited a church advertisement from New York–area Episcopal churches that made the connection between the church and friendship explicit. The ad read, in part, "Lots of acquaintances—not many friends. Is this increasingly true for you? Look at your life. You may find that it lacks those spiritual experiences which bring people together in understanding and friendship" (418). The quest for friendship was the moral quest of the organization's suburban transient population. This quest placed an expectation on religious fellowships, an expectation that the churches were only too happy to adopt as their own. In the hands of the religious social critics, Whyte's analysis of the socially useful church would become a major point against the return to religion.

Whyte's answer to the dilemma posed by the organization was a two-part solution. First was the recognition that the dilemma existed, for "unless the individual understands that this conflict of allegiances [to self and group] is inevitable he is intellectually without defenses." Without this recognition, individuals would find themselves misled by the "facades of those about them" and feel isolated in their differentness and self-apparent abnormality. The fault was not the organization, Whyte maintained, but rather his contemporaries' "worship" of it. Indeed, this religious language was employed in other places where Whyte was at his most critical. He spoke of the current attitude toward organization work as coming close to "deifying it" (14). The real problem was that the idolization of the organization was symptomatic of a denial that there was a conflict between the individual and organization (443). But simply recognizing the conflict would not end it.

After the individual recognized his or her plight, Whyte offered the second part of his solution to the problem of the organization. In the end, Whyte's recommendation was that the individual fight the organization, to subvert it from within: "He must *fight* The Organization. Not stupidly, or selfishly, for the defect of individual self-regard are no more to be venerated than the defects of co-operation. But fight he must, for the demands for his surrender are constant and powerful, and the more he has come to like the life of organization the more difficult does he find it to resist these demands, or even to recognize them. It is wretched, dispiriting advice to hold before him the dream that ideally there need be no conflict between him and society" (448).

The reaction to *The Organization Man* was overwhelmingly favorable. The *New York Times* called Whyte "a brilliantly gifted student of the customs of his country," and Max Lerner accurately predicted that it would be read "for years to come." And, more telling still, another term passed into the vocabulary of the average literate American, "organization man." The term did not mean exactly what Whyte intended it would, for as it passed into popular usage it came to be virtually synonymous with the "man in the gray flannel suit." Both designations were applied to men working in large impersonal organizations to which they were bound in a kind of life commitment. Still, the absorption of the term into popular parlance indicated at least the willingness of American society to have its condition diagnosed, even if it was not ready to have its disease cured.

White Collar and *The Power Elite*

Of all the major social critics of the 1950s, C. Wright Mills offered the most politically radical, and perhaps also the bleakest, view of contemporary American society. Mills was a professor of sociology at Columbia University who had written several well received but little known books on sociology, politics, Max Weber, and higher education, when in 1951 his latest work, *White Collar: The American Middle Classes*, catapulted him into the national spotlight.[6] His fame was only further increased by the appearance of *The Power Elite* in 1956. Together the two books represent the only significant analysis of class dimensions of postwar American society to appear during the 1950s. Most contemporary social critics saw the broadened middle class as a benign, even beneficial, achievement upon which a more just and satisfying society could be built. Hence most critics left aside the formerly vexing economic and political problems and concentrated on the psychological and social problems of the emergent middle class. For Mills, however, the emergence of a large middle class was itself a symptom of deep troubles.

To C. Wright Mills, the one hundred years of American history leading up to 1950 could be best seen as the story of the slow but inexorable expropriation of the wealth and property holdings of the middle classes by big business, which in turn represented the interests of a power elite. The old middle classes of the nineteenth century had been shopkeepers, farmers, and small manufacturers. They typically owned the means by which their livings were made. The functions they performed were indispensible to the society and were conducted on such a localized scale that competition from large-scale enterprise was ruled out. By contrast, the white-collar workers of the mid-twentieth century were wage workers in suits. Not only did they no longer own their own businesses, but, as the great depression proved, they were subject to massive unemployment no less than the common laborer. The nation had been turned from a country of farmers and burghers into a nation of people captive to large-scale business. Even those who still technically owned a business were in reality merely agents of large corporations; agents who assumed risks, but whose prices and profits were limited for them from above by means of fair trade laws and exclusive retailing agreements.

By examining white-collar people Mills argued it was possible to learn something about what America was becoming: "What must be grasped is the picture of society as a great salesroom, an enormous file, an incorporated brain, a new universe of management and manipulation" (xv). Mills agreed with Riesman and Whyte that modern life was characterized by rootlessness and by psychological hardship, but the causes for these maladies he located not in the organization or other-directedness, but in the "workings of capitalist progress." The economic organization of modern society had moved on and left the great middle class with no understanding of their place in the new order, only old views that failed to explain: "In our politics and economy, in family life and religion—in practically every sphere of our existence—the certainties of the eighteenth and nineteenth centuries had disintegrated or been destroyed and, at the same time, no new sanctions or justifications for the new routines we live, and must live, have taken hold." The condition of the white-collar people was thus one lacking in any applicable order of belief, a condition that left them "morally defenseless as individuals and politically impotent as a group" (xv–xvi).

For Mills, the troubles of the white-collar people were the troubles of all men and women living in the twentieth century. To be sure, for a time the middle strata had been seemingly well-off and immune to the problems faced by the lower classes. Prior to the First World War, the "little men" had been few in number and held for a brief time a monopoly on high school education. Their skill and scarcity protected them from many "of the sharper edges of the workings of capitalist progress" (xv). But in the long run this was damaging, for it allowed the middle classes to entertain the illusion that the system was working for them, that America was in fact, as well as in principle, a nation of and for the middle class. Mills hoped in his work to make men and women aware of their conditions, but warned that the state of public consciousness was itself problematic: "What men are interested in is not always what is to their interest; the troubles they are aware of are not always the ones that beset them. It would be a fetish of 'democracy' to assume that men immediately know their interests and are clearly aware of the conditions within themselves and their society that frustrate them and make their efforts misfire" (xix). Indeed the problem was not being conscious, but being falsely conscious.

Throughout *White Collar* and *The Power Elite*, Mills offered a functional explanation of American society based on the paradoxical nature of false consciousness. White collar people believing themselves better served by the political economy than laboring men and women opposed the interests of organized labor and endorsed business values that undermined their own position in society by strengthening the hold of large-scale enterprise and bureaucracy over them. When they became frustrated by their wages, housing, entertainments, opportunities, and quality of life, they were apt—if politically conscious at all—to cede more power to the sphere of business that would in time only compound their frustration and add to their own powerlessness (320–323). More common among white-collar people were those who were politically indifferent, only minimally sacrificing their time and selves to meaningless work in exchange for the "private pursuit of activities that find their meaning in the immediate gratification of animal thrill, sensation and fun" (327). The middle classes, despite the huge numbers they represented, were therefore the most politically impotent group in American society.

In the meantime, the elites of the nation also were engaged in false consciousness. For while they expressed beliefs in democracy, the free market, the paramount importance of individuals, and the need for consensus, they continued to exercise power in a way utterly inconsistent with these avowals. The way power actually worked in the United States was that a handful of corporate, military, and political leaders composed an elite whose decisions affected not only their respective domains, but also one another's areas of activity. "If there is government intervention in the corporate economy, so is there corporate intervention in the governmental process," Mills wrote in *The Power Elite*.[7] "In the structural sense, this triangle of power is the source of the interlocking directorate that is most important for the historical structure of the present" (8). The elite themselves might deny their power. Indeed, the elite typically were less aware of their power than of others' resistance to its use. But the actor need not be accurately conscious of his place to act. People who listened to the reports of those involved in the great events of the day might be led to believe that there were no opportunities for decision and that the events "made the man," as generals and presidents often argued in their memoirs. But, as Mills pointed out, people in the contemporary world were aware that they lived in a world of great decisions, knew that they did not make any, and could properly infer that someone was in fact making those decisions (5).

The men who decided (and it was men who belonged to this exclusive club) were those located in the upper echelons of the hierarchies of state, military, and the economy, the major institutions of the modern society. They were bound together as an elite, Mills argued, by similar class, educational, religious, and ethnic backgrounds, by the structural similarities of leadership in one of the major institutions of the "permanent war establishment," and by explicit coordination between such groups in a great "interlocking directorate" (19–20). Such a view led to the rejection of Riesman's picture of American politics being composed not of powerful interest blocks, but rather veto groups who exercised power only by putting brakes on the occasional offense to their interests. Mills, by contrast, portrayed a politics in which every sphere of life was being brought into subordination of the three major hierarchies:

Families and churches and schools adapt to modern life; governments and armies and corporations shape it; and, as they do so, they turn these lesser institutions into means for their ends. Religious institutions provide chaplains to the armed forces where they are used as a means of increasing the effectiveness of its morale to kill. Schools select and train men for their jobs in corporations and their specialized tasks in the armed forces. The extended family has, of course, long been broken up by the industrial revolution, and now the son and the father are removed from the family, by compulsion if need be, whenever the army of the state sends out the call (6).

Thus the central locations of life activity for most persons were corrupted by the influence of modern society's three large-scale institutions. When education, religion, and family life became contingent upon the needs and sufferance of army, government, and corporation, they became disordered elements in a badly disordered society.

For all appearances to the contrary, Mills did not simply embrace a Marxian view of society. He lumped the Marxist and liberal together as being in error when it came to the matter of rationality, for both made the same false assumption—that people could see or be led to see their interest, and that when they saw their interest they would act upon it. Mills flatly denied this, for his overriding concern was to show how often in reality people acted irrationally in the face of their interests. Any political theory then was going to have to come to terms with these problems. Yet he was also uncomfortable with the political fatalism of much contemporary thought that portrayed all collective human activity as counterrational, or the work of fortune or an unseen hand. In *The Power Elite*, the twin villains he skewered were views of history that imbibed too deeply of either rationalized conspiracy or unreasonable drift. To accept either view, Mills maintained, "of all history as conspiracy or of all history as drift—[was] to relax the effort to understand the facts of power and the ways of the powerful" (27). Moments of decision came and went, and elites made, or failed to make, those decisions. These were decisions for which the public was well within its rights to hold them accountable, for not every person was equal in ability to make history. When America dropped the bomb on Hiroshima, it was after all not America who decided to use the weapon, but rather a man named Truman.

Beyond all else, Mills aimed his efforts at laying bare the truth about American society so that Americans could use their economic rights to organize themselves for the sake of their interests and exercise their latent political power to order society to promote full and satisfying lives. Like that of Riesman and Whyte, Mills's work was an exercise in political sociology. Unlike the purely descriptive sociologists or even the intellectual defenders of American democracy, all three were interested in criticizing American society with the aim of making it better. For all his doubts about whether the middle classes would ever rise up against the power elite, Mills continued to believe that certain areas of society should provide pockets of resistance to the overreaching corporate/political/military sphere of life that sought to harness all aspects of culture to its objectives. One place he believed this opposition should be located was in the nation's religious leadership. Mills ventured beyond even his usual passionate description of American society to offer what he called "A Pagan Sermon to the Christian Clergy" in the *Nation*.[8] There his complaint was that the churches and their clergy were failing to do what by their own profession and tradition they were committed to do. In particular, Mills found it offensive that the churches had so accommodated themselves to the prejudices of the day that they offered no resistance to, or even moral questioning of, public-policy reliance on the threat of nuclear war to accomplish national objectives in the world. The religious application of Mills's power analysis therefore had already been anticipated by

Mills himself. But his conviction that ministers, priests, and rabbis were called to be more than chaplains to the military-industrial complex would find ready acceptance and expression in the work of more religiously oriented critics.

Mass Culture

The final major critical approach to the American life in the 1950s was the criticism of mass culture. Unlike the preceding approaches, it is not represented by one central, overwhelmingly popular book by a single author. Instead of being a book, it was a debate involving many intellectuals, some favoring the development of mass culture in the popular arts, some condemning it, and some suggesting that mass culture be left to the masses while "real" (read high) culture be recognized as such and hermetically sealed off from those unable to appreciate it. The debate went on for most of the 1950s and was played out in the pages of such journals as *Dissent*, *Commentary*, the *New Yorker*, the *Nation*, the *Saturday Review of Literature*, and the *New Republic*. The debate also resulted in the publication of a college-level reader on the subject, entitled *Mass Culture: The Popular Arts in America*, edited by Bernard Rosenberg and David Manning White.[9] In Rosenberg and White's collection of essays and excerpts, the reader could find analysts, detractors, and even celebrators of mass culture. Predictably, the first selection was an excerpt from Alexis de Tocqueville's *Democracy in America*, in which the thesis that democracy leads to a cheap, uninspired, but widely available body of art and literature aimed at the masses was introduced. Also represented was the thought of S. I. Hayakawa, Irving Howe, Marshall McLuhan, T. W. Adorno, Paul Lazarsfeld and Robert K. Merton, and Jose Ortega y Gasset. Clement Greenberg's famous distinction between two kinds of culture, "kitsch" and "avantgarde," provided the basis for an essay that probed how one and the same civilization could simultaneously produce a poem by T. S. Eliot and a Tin Pan Alley song. Also featured was Gilbert Seldes's celebration of the possibilities he saw in the mass media, providing intellectuals and the "lords of kitsch" would stop underestimating the intelligence of the general public. For the purposes of this work, however, the arguments that most merit attention are those of social critic Dwight Macdonald.

In his excellent survey of 1940s and 1950s intellectuals, Richard Pells has described three common ways that intellectuals approached society in the 1950s. Some, like Sidney Hook, devoted their efforts to defending democratic ideals in the Cold War. Others embarked on "a sympathetic reexamination of the nation's political and economic institutions."[10] Most notable among this type were Arthur Schlesinger, Daniel Boorstin, Daniel Bell, and Seymour Lipset. A further option was to be highly critical of liberalism while remaining a liberal oneself. This last option was exercised by Richard Hofstadter, Louis Hartz, and John Kenneth Galbraith. Dwight Macdonald, however, approached his contemporaries' society in none of these common ways, for, as Pells observes, he "was temperamentally incapable of pursuing a strategy or following anyone's example."[11] And yet, Macdonald proved to be one of the more genuinely radical of all the 1950s writers concerned with contemporary affairs. Rather than representing a party of thought, Macdonald took on all comers. Beholden to no positive plan or ideology, he was perfectly situated to be critical of the grand designs and millenarian plans of others, whether they represented the movies, the Republican party, or intellectual or Soviet Marxism. His style was consistent with his background, as a 1920s film critic—satiric and sharp-tongued, he would provide a plot summary and then move straight to the problem spots, refusing to let the slightest detail or discontinuity go unremarked. "Whatever the forum," Pells writes, "Macdonald normally treated someone else's argument or a government policy as if he were responding to a particularly pretentious Hollywood epic. He derided the ideas of an author, a political leader, or a cultural spokesman by performing a vivisection on their language and imagery; how they wrote and talked was for Macdonald the essential indication of what they truly thought."[12] Macdonald's own use of language proved his point and revealed his thought on the powerlessness of the individual, as when he wrote that the individual citizen had "almost the same chance of determining his own fate as a hog dangling by one foot from the conveyor belt of a Chicago packing plant."[13]

Macdonald's 1953 article, "A Theory of Mass Culture" (included in Rosenberg and White's anthology), contains the greater part of his critique of mass culture.[14] In the article, Macdonald's analysis began with the positing of two kinds of culture, a "High Culture," the kind chronicled in textbooks and taught in universities, and a "Mass Culture," a culture "manufactured wholesale for the market."[15] Macdonald made clear his preference for the term Mass Culture over "Popular Culture" because it was at least theoretically possible for High Culture to be popular, as in the case of Charles Dickens's literature in the nineteenth century. High Culture originated in the patronage of an aristocratic class for individual artists in music, literature, painting, sculpture, and architecture. The people outside of the aristocracy might have their own folk art or culture, but this was not truly analogous to Mass Culture. Whereas folk art was "the people's own institution, their private little garden walled off from the great formal park of their master's High Culture," Mass Culture was imposed from above and integrated "the masses into a debased form of High Culture," and was thus an instrument of political domination (60). For Macdonald, the historical reasons for the development of Mass Culture were obvious: "Popular democracy and popular education broke down the old upper-class monopoly of culture. Business enterprise found a profitable market in the cultural demands of the newly awakened masses, and the advance of technology made possible the cheap production of books, periodicals, pictures, music, and furniture, in sufficient quantities to satisfy this market" (59). Thus, Macdonald's thoughts on Mass Culture owed debts to both Clement Greenberg and Alexis de Tocqueville. To the former, he owed credit for the notion of two cultures; to the latter, he was obliged for his view of the cultural effects of a leveling democracy. But Macdonald`s reputation as the postwar intellectuals' critic *par excellence* derived not from his originality, but from his ability to synthesize historical experience, class analysis, political commentary, and aesthetic judgment and to follow a thesis to its logical conclusion, however radical that conclusion might sound.

One of Macdonald's radical conclusions was that because the appearance of the masses on the political stage had had the effect of erasing the line between commoner and aristocrat, it also had the effect of breaking down the barrier between their respective cultures. Thus, whereas High Culture could formerly ignore the mob and simply live for the approval of the cognoscenti, it now was forced to "compete with Mass Culture or be merged into it" (61). Even in the modern age, however, this might be remedied if there were a clearly defined cultural elite. Then the elite could have their culture and the masses their kitsch, leaving "everybody happy." But such was not the case, the United States had no such cultural elite to speak of, and though people in metropolitan areas might have the real choice of going to a horror film or a classical music concert on any given night, or the choice of reading Tolstoy or the latest Mike Hammer detective story, they lacked a principle of discrimination. Mass Culture was a revolutionary force breaking down all former barriers, artistic values, and distinctions, and producing in its place a "homogenized culture" that made all forms of entertainment and expression equal, much as homogenized milk evenly redistributed the sweet cream throughout its liquid instead of allowing it to float to the top. In the competition of serious ideas with commercial formulae, the advantages were all on the side of the latter. Macdonald suggested that a kind of Gresham's Law must be at work in the cultural as well as in the economic realm: "Bad stuff drives out the good, since it is more easily understood and enjoyed" (61–62).

High Culture had, Macdonald maintained, tried to defend itself against the onslaught of Mass Culture through the 1920s in two opposite ways, which he called Academicism and Avantgardism. Academicism was the attempt to compete by imitation, to package Mass Culture music, paintings, novels, and so forth as High Culture. Macdonald cited the music of Elgar, the Beaux Arts school of architecture, and the novels of Somerset Maugham as cases in point of this kind of ersatz High Culture: highly praised when they first appeared, seen for what they were only by true artists, with time regarded with embarrassment, and slipping into oblivion with the other, cheaper products of Mass Culture.

Avantgardism, by contrast, was marked by a withdrawal from competition with Mass Culture. Novelists such as Joyce, painters such as Picasso, and composers such as Stravinsky were examples of the Avantgarde movement. The movement had represented a last, despairing attempt to define an area in which the serious artist could still work, responsible only to his or her own standards and not those of the marketplace. As such, argued Macdonald, Avantgardism "created a new compartmentation of culture, on the basis of an intellectual rather than a social elite" (63). But alas, since the coming of war to Europe in the 1930s, even Avantgardism had failed to press forward and had blended with the Academicism it had once disdained, and both older versions of High Culture now only provided a tinting to the color base of Mass Culture.

The emerging Mass Culture that partook of these two previous streams of High Culture, far from representing the raising of standards in Mass Culture—as others, such as Gilbert Seldes, argued—was resulting instead in "a tepid, flaccid Middlebrow Culture that threatens to engulf everything in its spreading ooze" (63). Thus, Macdonald's crusade against Middlebrow Culture was on, motivated out of the twin beliefs that it was actually a corruption of High Culture and that "there is nothing more vulgar than sophisticated kitsch."

Dwight Macdonald was not the only intellectual critical of the mass culture of the period, as he himself acknowledged. Conservative critics, such as Ortega y Gasset and T. S. Eliot, argued that because the "revolt of the masses" had led to the twin evils of totalitarianism and "California roadside architecture," the only solution was to reinstitute the old class systems and bring culture and society both back under control of an aristocracy. By contrast, liberals and Marxists believed the problem lay not in the masses, but in the diet of trash they were fed by the "lords of kitsch." Macdonald neatly summarized their solution: "If only the masses were offered good stuff instead of kitsch, how they would eat it up!" He held that both these positions were fallacious, arguing that they erred in assuming that "Mass Culture is (in the conservative view) or could be (in the liberal view) an expression of *people*, like Folk Art, whereas actually it is an expression of *masses*, a very different thing" (69).

The only answer to the dilemma posed by High and Mass Cultures for Macdonald, developed only slightly in his "Theory of Mass Culture" article, lay in a recognition that people lost their capacity for producing High Culture when their identities were submerged into a "mass." High Culture was properly the product of either a single mind, or a collective effort of like minds steeped in a common, deep, and stable tradition of high culture (as in the case of gothic cathedrals). Given these realities, Macdonald argued, there was no hope that mass culture would ever produce anything of quality. Meanwhile, the only hope for the survival of high culture was the revival of the cultural elite of the type that had supported avantgardism. What Macdonald saw in the contemporary intellectual life of America, however, did not sustain his hopes very much. "One of the odd things about the American cultural scene," he wrote, "is how many brainworkers there are and how few intellectuals, defining the former as specialists whose thinking is pretty much confined to their limited 'fields' and the latter as persons who take all culture for their province." Not only was there a dearth of intellectuals, Macdonald complained, but the ones that did exist did not "hang together" and had very little "esprit de corps" (71).

The import of Macdonald's line of thinking for social criticism was profound indeed, because it raised the possibility that—public opinion polls notwithstanding—120 million Americans really could be wrong. Moreover, this horrifying possibility undermined not only television, detective fiction, and pseudo-classical music, but—in the right hands—the very assumptions of much of the return to religion.

The Legacy
of the Secular Jeremiads

The studies of the four critics we have considered so far had made its way into public attention by 1956. Their work was foundational to the book-length criticisms of American religion's social position that were beginning to appear. Their legacy for the religious social criticism that would follow came in the form of style and substance. By their success, they crystallized a book genre that could then be employed by other critics to reach a mass audience of the newly college-educated generation of men and women who were concerned with great ideas and what was happening to their society.[16] The writings of these critics were marked by a journalistic style, cleverly coined titles, and terms for significant ideas. Even Dwight Macdonald, for all that he complained about pandering to "Middlebrow" tastes, eschewed footnotes and succumbed to the practice of letting slogans—Mass Culture, Folk Art, Avantgardism—carry the rhetorical weight of his argument. The secular jeremiads, directed toward the educated middle class and disseminated through the recent invention of the "quality paperback book," set a new style, and provided a new venue, for the discussion of societal morality and public life.

The secular Jeremiahs also bequeathed a set of ideas to their religious counterparts. Whyte and Riesman lent an intellectual legitimacy to the fear of conformism and presented autonomous individualism as a desirable goal. Whyte rejected organized activity and the suburbs as not being the panaceas they were made out to be. Mills, Whyte, and Riesman agreed that religion could be erroneously used as a means to an end at odds with its own goals. Mills introduced a notion of a power elite and power system that militated against the interest of average citizens. Finally, from Macdonald came the disturbing, undemocratic idea about the hugely flourishing mass culture, that what was "popular" was not what was real. As is clear by now, the close identification of religion with culture in the 1950s meant that these attacks on culture were by their nature simultaneously challenges to its religion. Yet as powerful and popular as these criticisms were, the American people did not apply these analyses to their religious institutions themselves. That task remained for other principal critics: Jeremiahs who were inspired by social critics of the 1950s, on one hand, and the Bible's social critics, on the other.

4

Critics of the
American Way of Religion

■

Building on the work of the secular critics of the American dream were a group of sociologically informed religious critics. Borrowing both style and data about American life from the secular critics, these writers took the jeremiad genre a step further by bringing it back to its original religious context and by arguing that much was wrong, but that all was not lost if only the people would again open their hearts to God and repent of their evil ways. Three works in this refined genre stand out with special significance: Will Herberg's *Protestant, Catholic, Jew*, Gibson Winter's *The Suburban Captivity of the Churches*, and Peter Berger's *The Noise of Solemn Assemblies*. First with his book off the press, and perhaps most responsible for the successful adaptation of the new jeremiad to religious discourse, was the contentious, self-educated, and enigmatic Will Herberg.

Herberg called his book "an essay in American religious sociology," but he was not a professionally trained sociologist. He thought of himself as the Jewish Reinhold Niebuhr, but his book was not celebrated, nor is it remembered, for its theology. Instead it was, like *The Lonely Crowd, The Organization Man*, and *The Power Elite*, a distillation of historical fact, sociological theory, and community studies into a coherent, popularly accessible essay. In *Protestant, Catholic, Jew*, however, more than with the secular jeremiads, there was an iron hand inside the kid glove, for ultimately the religion of the American Way of Life was wrong because it was against the will of God. Autonomy, individualism, and class consciousness—even Macdonald's strategy of elite withdrawal—were one kind of prescription for American society's ills; but a genuine return to the God of Abraham, Isaac, and Jacob, as Herberg called for, was a recommendation on a different order altogether. In order to understand the origin and force of Herberg's solution to the religious crisis, we must first comprehend his diagnosis of American culture and its religion.

Prostestant, Catholic, Jew

When he came to write *Protestant, Catholic, Jew*, Herberg was not a newcomer to polemical writing, nor even to religiously partisan discourse disguised as analysis. His background as a labor union education director accustomed to doing history and analysis in the Marxist sense of those terms prepared him well for doing "committed analysis" in the religious sphere. As with many other American Communists of the twenties and thirties, the Moscow show trials under Stalin, the fratricidal war within the American Communist party, and the initial complicity of Stalin with Hitler in World War II combined to sour Herberg on the possibilities of true progress within the ideology of organized Marxism. Even while his faith in Communism was being shaken, however, Herberg clung to the humanitarian ideals of socialism and began to see those values more perfectly represented in the thought of the current generation of religious thinkers, most specifically in the writings of Reinhold Niebuhr.

In the early and mid-1930s Herberg had lectured his students at the New Workers School that religion, and Christianity in particular, provided only the illusion of emancipation at times when this-worldly freedom was impossible.[1] By 1939, he had moved to a middle position, writing, "Unless socialism is humanitarian, unless it makes the cause of suffering humanity its own, it is not likely to develop much beyond the level of ordinary power politics without real hope for the future." He added, "If socialism prevents us from acting and feeling as human beings should, there is something spurious about it."[2] How, Herberg pondered, could socialism in the U.S.S.R. have degenerated from a people's revolution into a totalitarian dictatorship? By way of response to this question, Herberg discovered the concept of original sin through Reinhold Niebuhr's *Moral Man and Immoral Society*. Having already embarked on an ethical critique of Marxism, Herberg found the theologian's understandings of the moral ambiguities of human existence and human societies more adequate than those of the Marxist dialectician. He and Niebuhr met to discuss the book over coffee and began a relationship that would endure until Niebuhr's death in 1971.

Contact with Niebuhr would lead Herberg to find his own faith and to see socialism and Christianity as having, at root, the same belief system.[3] Yet Marxism was always in danger of forgetting its roots and falling into the errors of positivism and humanistic naturalism. Its only hope for preservation, Herberg believed, was to permanently ground itself in the Judeo-Christian tradition out of which it had sprung and to which it owed its humanity-valuing ethical impulses. To the end of becoming a better, truer socialist in his new and refined understanding of socialism, Herberg considered becoming a Roman Catholic, but Niebuhr convinced him "to establish his religious perspective in Jewish terms." Therefore, Herberg set out to do for Judaism what Jacques Maritain had done for Catholicism and Karl Barth and Emil Brunner had done for Protestantism; he attempted "a great theological reconstruction in the spirit of neo-orthodoxy equally distant from sterile fundamentalism and secularized modernism."[4]

For his view of Judaism and its relation to Christianity, Herberg looked to Franz Rosenzweig, whom he interpreted as arguing that Judaism and Christianity were essentially a single religious reality. Judaism was for the Jews alone, a constant living testament to the one God. Christianity, meanwhile, was the attempt to extend word of that one God to the gentile world.[5] Moreover, the two religions shared a biblical theology that told of the nature of God and the nature of the human being, and was full of enough paradox to adequately reveal the tragic dimensions of human existence and societies. As such, history was not the solution, as in Marxism, but was instead the "very crux of the human condition."[6] From this time in the early 1940s forward, biblical faith would become Herberg's designated antidote for "power mad cynicism, secular utopianism, and other worldly quietism," all ills that distorted the society which failed to acknowledge the source of all life and goodness.

Herberg's determination to be "the Jewish Reinhold Niebuhr" led to his writing *Judaism and Modern Man* between September 1947 and July 1950.[7] Herberg considered the book to be a restatement of Jewish tradition seen in light of recent existentialist philosophy, particularly as represented by Martin Buber and Franz Rosenzweig. More importantly, he admitted it

was his own "confession of faith" and a "declaration of total commitment" as an individual committed to the "biblical-rabbinical tradition."[8]

After having paid his theologian's dues in *Judaism and Modern Man*,
Herberg turned to the project that became *Protestant, Catholic, Jew*, and
to the application of his theology to the nature and problems of contemporary society.[9] It was the magnum opus to which all his earlier work had
been leading, the intersection where his religious and social concerns
joined. Though the new project was most keenly his own, Herberg's book
began with two observations from others. From Barbara Ward's essay,
"Report to Europe on America," he took the observation that America
was in the midst of a "notable 'turn to religion.'" From Oscar Handlin, he
borrowed the insight that in the mid-twentieth century, "the trend toward
secularism in ideas was not reversed."[10] *Protestant, Catholic, Jew* thus
opened with a paradox: America was at the same time becoming more
religious and more secular. In exemplary Niebuhrian fashion Herberg
had found the paradox that would serve—in its explication—as his central theme. Herberg illustrated the existence of this paradox with a deluge
of statistics. No piece of evidence was perhaps as telling, however, as his
report that a recent survey had found that four-fifths of adult Americans
believed the Bible to be the "revealed word of God," but that when these
same survey participants were asked to name the "first four books of the
New Testament of the Bible, that is, the first four Gospels," 53 percent
failed to name even one (2).

Many other critics of the return to religion had dismissed the revival as
simply so much empty emotionalism and shallow escapism, but Herberg
parted company with these critics by asserting that those returning to
religion took it quite seriously indeed.[11] The real question for Herberg,
therefore, was not "Are they really religious?" but rather "What is their
religion?" A primary goal of the book was to answer the latter question
and thereby explore the religious/secular paradox.

In pursuing this exploration, Herberg confronted the major cultural
trends and realities of his day. While allowing that God might finally have
other plans for the world, Herberg argued that for now, social forces
accounted for the shape of both religion and society. Furthermore, Herberg
was convinced that much of what drove the culture's growing secularism
was identical to what impelled changes in its religious character. The
early chapters of *Protestant, Catholic, Jew* are given over to enumerating
these social forces.

In essence, Herberg's enterprise in *Protestant, Catholic, Jew* was a thoroughly Niebuhrian one in the sense that he borrowed heavily on the characteristic approaches of both the Niebuhr brothers. From Reinhold he took a sense of irony and paradox. From Richard, he borrowed the technique of explaining religious difference and change in terms of human, nontheological categories. To this task, Herberg also brought all his years of Marxist analysis; he was intellectually predisposed toward seeing the difficult situation in terms of a central paradox that was driven by great social forces.

In chapters 2 and 3 of *Protestant, Catholic, Jew*, Herberg outlined his immigration/assimilation-driven model of religious choice and change. American history was, Herberg believed, as Oscar Handlin had argued in *The Uprooted*,[12] the history of immigration and immigrants (6). The cause of the immigration to America was the economic and social upheaval of nineteenth-century Europe. New machines and products, along with new methods of production and farming techniques, displaced millions of agrarian peasants from their homes—from Ireland to Russia and from Norway to Italy. If from the beginning immigration was caused by economic forces, then too the immigrants' chief concerns were economic. They did not come to America for religious freedom but for a better life conceived largely in terms of material comforts and progress.

Most immigrants to America probably hoped to take advantage of the vast amount of land open on the continent to reestablish their agrarian way of life. Some succeeded, notably the Germans and Scandinavians in the mid- and upper-midwestern states. But for the great majority the move to America meant exchanging a rural farmer's life for that of an urban laborer or factory worker. Moreover, the economic "carrot" of mobility through assimilation virtually guaranteed that carryovers from European culture would be greatly diminished during the lifetimes of the second generation of immigrants (9).

Yet even in the first generation, factors were at work to deconstruct the immigrants' old-country identity. The immigrant thought of himself or herself in terms of a local village, a particular village church or synagogue, even a particular patron saint. But in America the village and its institutions could no longer serve as a bond, and thus language became the basis of ethnic unity. Religiously, this meant that the immigrants "inevitably transformed the church they thought they were transplanting" (11). Those who had thought of themselves as Poznaniskers or Mazhevoers in the old country now were forced to conceive of themselves as Poles. The religious institutions they created in America also followed these linguistic-national lines.

It was the second-generation American who most experienced the conflict between the ethnic culture of his or her parents and the dominant culture. Taught in school and on the streets to speak English and think in ways American, the person of the second generation lived in a home where the language and customs were very different. Thus the second generation were men and women living on the margins of two societies and not fully at home in either.

For the third generation, however, the issue of identity posed a different problem. The question of identity for second-generation Americans was what identity they desired, and their answer was, "Americans stripped of all ethnic peculiarities and imperfections." The third generation's quest for identity asked "What am I?" This generation was much more willing to hear and bear the answer, "an Italian-American," than the second had been, for they bore out what Marcus Lee Hansen called "the principle of third generation interest."[13] At its most basic level, the principle, also called Hansen's Law, stated, "What the son wishes to forget, the grandson wishes to remember" (30). The third-generation American no longer faced the problem of seeming un-American—they knew they were American—but they wanted to know, "What *kind* of American?"

Still, even curiosity and ethnic pride could not bring the third generation back to the culture of their grandparents. For one, they did not speak the language of their forebears. They were not sustained by the newspapers, periodicals, and songs that had nurtured immigrant life in the urban Polonias, little Italys, and little Bohemias. The melting pot had done its job well. The third generation spoke English, listened to American popular music, paid attention to American politics, and viewed world events from an American perspective. What was left to remember? Herberg's answer was religion. The one thing America did not ask of its immigrants was that they give up their religion. When young men and women of the third generation sought to return to their inheritance they found religion still there, though with most of its ethnic features removed or muted. Thus, third-generation Polish, Italian, and southern German Americans could return to the same Roman Catholic parish church, and German and Russian Jews could be found in attendance at the same synagogue.

The melting pot had really proved to be a triple melting pot. People could be melted down into Protestants, Catholics, and Jews, but no further, it seemed. Americans' twentieth-century marriage patterns bore out this conclusion, as researchers discovered it no longer made sense to speak of endogamous marriages in terms of ethnicity but only in terms of religion, where intrareligious marriages continued to be the rule (32). An individual's religion became the critical piece of recoverable culture once the search for identity began in the third generation. The impact of this fact on religion was great, Herberg maintained, for given the social necessity of belonging—in a society in which belonging was defined in terms of one of three religious groups—the pressure to identify with one of the three was tremendous (41).

Having established a narrative of American immigrant experience that would support the third generation's revival of interest in religion, Herberg turned to the contemporary upswing in religious interest. It was characterized, in his view, by increases in publicly expressed religious preference and self-identification, as well as heightened church membership, attendance, religious education enrollment, status of religious leaders, and religious building construction.

Next, Herberg related the revival of religious interest to the theory of the "triple melting pot."[14] If indeed the way to be an American was to be a Protestant, Catholic, or Jew, then a person naturally began to think of himself or herself in these terms. To socially locate or identify oneself along religious lines, Herberg argued, is not itself intrinsically religious, but such a process does make one favorably disposed toward that religion. It came as no surprise to Herberg, then, that more people would identify themselves as members of a religious body than were claimed by the religious bodies themselves. Even so, social identification could also lead to actual affiliation, and increasingly men and women of the fifties joined churches and sent their children to church school out of conviction that "the church supplies a place where children come to learn what they are" (57). Religion was therefore in fact, as well as in theory, a means of achieving what Herberg called "belongingness."

To belongingness, Herberg added another factor to explain the revival—the transition from inner to other-directedness. Applying David Riesman's terms and analysis of culture to religion, Herberg argued that, though inner-direction was still dominant in America at large, in the new suburban middle-class society composed of professionals and junior executives and their families, other-direction was already prevalent and would soon spread upward and downward within the social hierarchy. The turn toward religious institutions was, therefore, "a reflection of the growing other-directedness" of the culture (59). Herberg went on to suggest that the current vogues of hanging Van Gogh and Renoir prints in the suburban home and joining a suburban church might not be totally unrelated. Having the right taste in all things brought manifold satisfactions to the other-directed conformist.

Herberg cited other factors promoting the return to religion. There was the hydrogen bomb, the crisis of Western civilization, the constant threat of Communist totalitarianism. To these dilemmas, religion seemed to offer the prospect of peace; indeed for many, religion was "synonymous with peace." For others, those inclined to fight fire with fire, religion was heralded as a "secret weapon" ready to combat these same problems. Herberg also recognized that the increased emphasis on finding meaning within the private world of the family might have the tendency to drive individuals back toward religion's stress on the things that are permanent (61). Finally, and least concretely, Herberg cited the "depersonalizing pressures of contemporary life" as forcing modern human beings to return to religion to provide themselves with an "inexpungable citadel for the self" (63).

Herberg turned from assessing the reasons why the revival of religious interest was taking place to the content of Americans' religion. Here again Herberg used the statistics that were by that time familiar to the public. Polls showed that 97 percent of Americans expressed a belief in God, while 90 percent prayed; they believed in an afterlife, and by an overwhelming majority they held religion to be of very great importance. Then Herberg sought to find the true significance of these apparently encouraging statistics. When he probed beneath the survey findings, he found that though 73 percent of respondents believed in an afterlife with God as judge, only 5 percent had any fear of going to hell. Indeed, 80 percent indicated that their priority was living well in the here and now, not in some life after death. Moreover, in their own opinion, "they were not doing so badly even from the point of view of divine judgment," with 91 percent replying that they could honestly say they were trying to lead a good life and more than half maintaining that they followed the Golden Rule "all the way" (63).

Though Americans' claims to their own virtue were strikingly high, Herberg found one statistic even more significant: when Americans who had confessed to believing that religion was "very important" were asked, "Would you say your religious beliefs have any effect on your ideas of politics and business?," 54 percent answered "No." Religion, they felt, did not have an effect on these key areas of human life. The survey's administrators argued that this discrepancy pointed to an acute division between public and private realms of religious life among Americans. Herberg saw it differently. Some ideas, he insisted, must have a guiding influence over people's political and economic actions. If these ideas were not those readily identified as religious by the survey respondents, then it "would seem to indicate very strongly that, over and above conventional religion, there is to be found among Americans some sort of faith or belief or set of convictions, not generally designated as religion but definitely operative as such in their lives in the sense of providing them with some fundamental context of normativity and meaning" (74). Thus began Herberg's search for a super-religion, a religion that stood above, and even under, the three large historic communities of faith that operated in the United States.

Herberg based his belief in such a super-religion on the assertion of sociologist Robin M. Williams, Jr., that "every functioning society has to an important degree a *common* religion." From the fact that America was a functioning society it apparently followed that there must be a set of rituals, ideas, and symbols that were shared to bind Americans together. Herberg called his candidate for this common religion the "American Way of Life." It was only the American Way of Life that could be said to provide American society with, in Williams's terms, "an overarching sense of unity." Moreover, while Americans were tolerant of members of other religious faiths, when it came to challengers to the American Way of Life, such as Communists, they were "admittedly and unashamedly intolerant." By both positive and negative criteria, therefore, Herberg was able to make the claim that "by every realistic criterion the American Way of Life is the operative faith of the American people" (75).

Lest someone argue that he had simply put a new label on materialism, Herberg hastened to indicate that the contents of the American Way of Life were at root spiritual, conceptual, and ethical convictions about the right way to live: "It embraces such seemingly incongruous elements as sanitary plumbing and freedom of opportunity, Coca-Cola and an intense faith in education—all felt as moral questions relating to the proper way of life. The very expression 'way of life' points to its religious essence, for one's ultimate, over-all way of life is one's religion" (75).

By now it was obvious that the American Way of Life was not simply the lowest common denominator of America's three great faiths. Instead, it was a belief structure that was superimposed on religious communities which allowed for and encouraged their formal existence but was not contained by them. The central tenets of the American Way of Life could be summed up in the word "democracy," Herberg believed, if democracy was used in a "peculiarly American sense" to mean a belief in the Constitution, economic free enterprise, and social equalitarianism. This kind of democracy also necessarily featured a pragmatic individualism that judged people by "deeds, not creeds" and a humanitarian idealism that tended to become moralistic and see even self-interested acts as justified by "higher" principles.

According to Herberg, the American Way of Life had been greatly shaped by the ethos of American Protestantism. Indeed, he argued, the American Way of Life might best be comprehended as "a kind of secular-ized Puritanism, a Puritanism without transcendence, without sense of sin, or judgment" (81). Thus, the distinctive features of the American Way of Life—its action orientation and commitment to service, its ideal-ism, and its distrust of powerful central government—were derived from the Puritans' senses of vocation, asceticism, and responsibility before God, and from the Calvinist's awareness of the ambiguity of human nature and motivation. Other strands of early American religious life also left their marks on the American Way of Life, Herberg contended. He pointed to the examples of pietism and frontier revivalism as being jointly responsible for promoting the American Way of Life's pragmatic, anti-intellectual insistence on "deeds, not creeds" as the principle for public life.

Even as the American Way of Life had religious roots, it also had worked its way into the branches of religious life and practice. These influences could be seen in the things that the historic faiths shared, as practiced in the United States. It went almost without saying that when the various religions of Europe were transplanted to America, they began to take on features that to European observers made them look more like each other than they were like their European antecedents, but Herberg went to the trouble of saying that this observed phenomenon was noth-ing less than the result of the shaping influence of the American Way of Life. Under this influence, the historic expressions of Judaism and Chris-tianity became integrated into a single entity—religion—which was val-ued for its culture stabilizing effects by the American Way of Life. Likewise, belief in God by an overwhelming majority of Americans was prized principally because it undergirded and sanctioned the shared faith in democracy. That is, the fact of a common belief in a supreme being provided a seemingly unassailable epistemological foundation to the val-ues and beliefs that Americans really shared and cared about. Indeed, Herberg charged, the object of faith was not significant to contemporary Americans. Having faith was what mattered, faith qua faith; in fact, faith with no particular object was enough to give peace of mind and make the nation secure against the enemies of democracy. Faith, as a disposition, guaranteed that a positive, "can do" attitude was being maintained (90). Herberg was coming very close to suggesting a solution to the paradox with which he began, since, having noticed the reversal of the traditional ends-and-means relationship between religion and other goods, he commented that "secularization of religion could hardly go further" (83).

Though religion had both influenced and been influenced by the American Way of Life, Herberg noticed that there remained pockets of resistance within the overall religious community. Withstanding the onslaught of the American Way of Life in Herberg's view were the ethnic churches, which included portions of the Lutheran, Reformed, and Catholic churches with close ties to Europe; those individuals and groups with a specific theological perspective—be it "orthodox," "neo-orthodox," or "liberal"— that was at odds with the "implied 'theology' of the American Way of Life"; and finally the "religions of the disinherited," those holiness, pentecostal, and millenarian sects that had not yet been domesticated by the common American faith. Herberg thus tipped his hand that there were alternatives to the American Way of Life, but further exploration of this theme would wait until the end of the book.

The next three chapters of *Protestant, Catholic, Jew* consisted of Herberg's largely derivative sociohistorical descriptions of the three religious communities. For his chapter on Protestants, Herberg was most dependent on William Warren Sweet and H. Richard Niebuhr. For his analysis of Catholicism, he employed the older work of John Gilmary Shea and Peter Guilday along with the more contemporary writings of John Tracy Ellis, but his most often cited source on Catholicism was Willard Sperry's 1946 book, *Religion in America*. Besides his own writings, Herberg looked to Oscar Handlin and Marshall Sklare for the data and interpretation for his chapter on Jews in America. In each case, however, Herberg took the historiography of the day and spun it to support his interpretation of the historical development of American religion.

Herberg's description of Protestantism declared the story of Protestantism in America to be the epic of a vital religious movement encountering and subduing the ever-expanding western frontier. Yet it was also a story of decline. Through domesticating the frontier, the churches became victims of their own success and were themselves so domesticated that they no longer were a vital movement but rather an ossified, denominationally divided set of quasi-established churches.

Herberg admired the Puritans for their zeal and their dedication to a religious ideal. He recounted with relish each revival movement that accompanied the westward expansion of the nation. With the end of the frontier period, however, Protestantism's motivating religious dynamic also came to an end. The churches that had begun as "religions of the disinherited" became ever more bourgeois. This clearly offended the old socialist in Herberg: "Frontier religion, essentially the religion of the 'religious proletariat,' imperceptibly became transformed into more or less conventional denominationalism, still bearing the old names but harboring a very different social and spiritual content" (108).

By the end of the nineteenth century, the pattern of American Protestantism had been very largely set, with two exceptions—the ethnic churches from Europe and the black churches. European ethnic Protestantism had eventually succumbed to the acids of Americanization. Meanwhile, though Herberg conceded that the African American church constituted "an anomaly of considerable importance in the general sociological scheme of the 'triple melting pot' along the lines of religious community," he declined to deal further with this problem (114).

Pressing ahead with his account of Protestantism, Herberg declared that the practical result of Protestantism's origins and its American development was that it was bound to stress individualistic piety and to expect that through the righteous living of individuals social justice would naturally result. There was, Herberg admitted, the turn of the century attempt of the leaders of the social gospel to challenge the easy accommodation of their religion to secular culture. There was also the more recent attempt of the neo-orthodox theologians to hold Protestantism to its historical biblical and theological foundations. Both of these he dismissed as largely peripheral movements, led by intellectuals and reaching only slightly into the life of the churches, despite the attention these movements had received in the religious press those same intellectuals controlled.

Turning to the second of the "religions of democracy," Herberg outlined a history of Catholicism in America in which the English Catholicism of the colonial era was supplanted by an Irish-dominated American Catholicism forged in the crucible of the trusteeism crisis of the early nineteenth century. The next moment of significance was the "know nothing phase," in which Protestants turned upon their Catholic neighbors in the context of economic pressure, brought forth by swelling Irish immigration in the period 1820–50. Nativist bigots helped to force Catholics to become more cohesive. Here again the Irish occupied a pivotal position. They formed a bridge between the Catholic immigrants and the English-speaking Protestants; they were foreigners themselves, but they spoke the language of the majority. Later, at the turn of the century, the crisis of Cahenslyism and the church's response of a limited accommodation to ethnic Catholicism led to a controlled process of Americanization. Again the Irish, because they were already deeply nationalistic and identified their patriotism with religious devotion, were able to lead the way in easily transferring this religious patriotism from the old country to America: "[The Irish Catholic's] Americanism took on the same religious fervor and soon came to be identified with his Catholicism. It was almost as though to be a Catholic meant somehow to be an American, even though it was obvious that the converse was not as true as it had been in Ireland" (146). To a greater or lesser extent, Herberg argued, all American Catholicism had taken on this patriotic coloration. The next step in Catholicism's progressive accommodation to the American Way of Life came in the twentieth century, as large segments of the Catholic community moved into the middle class and—insofar as America was preeminently a middle-class nation—thus became even more American than before.

In two particular features, American Roman Catholicism was more like other American religions than European Catholicism. First in its activism, which bordered "on what Pius XII in 1950 described as the 'heresy of action,'" and second in its position on the proper relation between church and state, Catholicism as actually practiced in America resembled nothing so much as another denomination. Though the average Catholic might not explicitly reject the idea that his church was the one true and universal church and custodian of the truth—indeed such a rejection was unthinkable—still, he "could not help but regard American society as intrinsically pluralistic, and his own church as one among several" (151).

Catholicism had come of age in America, and the Catholic Church was "recognized as a genuinely American religious community, speaking to the American people not in terms of a unique treasure of revelation entrusted to it alone but in terms of those 'ideals and values' which the American feels is at the bottom of all religion" (161). Like Protestantism, Catholicism had succeeded in becoming fully American by becoming less than its distinctive self.

The Americanization of Jews took a different path from those followed by Protestants and Catholics. According to Herberg, the small size of initial Jewish migration and the differing language groups from which Jews came to the United States tended to guarantee that, until the late nineteenth century, Jews would find themselves far away from large numbers of people with the same ethnic and religious backgrounds. This diffusion, combined with the pressure to be like those around them in America, caused many in the second generation to discard everything associated with the immigrant heritage of their fathers and mothers, including Judaism. The solution to this problem for leaders of the German

Jewish community was to quicken the pace of institutional adaptation to American culture and modern belief. The American Reform movement sought to purge Judaism of its ethnic, superstitious, and antiquated features. This movement culminated in the Pittsburgh Platform of 1885, which tried to define Reform Judaism, but in Herberg's view it reflected an attempt to reconcile Judaism with German Idealism and American Protestant Liberalism. It replaced Saturday with Sunday for sabbath worship, relegated the Talmud to the margins of Jewish life, rejected Zionism, and converted messianic expectation into a nineteenth-century doctrine of progress.

This accommodation went too far for some leaders, and out of reaction to the theological excesses of the Reform movement Conservative Judaism was born. More importantly for the future of American Judaism, a great wave of immigration of Russian and Polish Jews was underway at this same time, which would ultimately bring 2.5 million Jews to the United States in the fifty-five years after 1870. This time the Jewish immigrants were not dispersed, nor were they part of a larger group of immigrants sharing the same language. Instead, they tended to find themselves concentrated in America's large eastern cities. Even so, these new immigrants divided themselves into two groups. There were the religious Jews who tried to transplant the heder and yeshiva as they had functioned in the Eastern European ghetto, and the "labor-radical secularist" Jews who channeled their energies into radical reform for the urban proletariat (181).

The American Jewish population of the United States at the turn of the century was thus deeply divided into German and Russian with further subdivision into religious and secular Jews. However, these divisions were already being overcome by the growth of voluntary societies drawing members across these lines for the purpose of supporting such causes as charity, education, and Zionism for all Jews.

If Jewish institutional development was one force promoting homogenization and Americanization, then the desire of the second generation of East European Jews to be unequivocally American was another. Here Herberg returned to the three-generation hypothesis left untouched since his third chapter. While Protestantism accommodated itself to the American Way of Life as a religious movement that had lost its way, and Catholicism became Americanized as a way of proving its loyalty through a unification of nationalism and faith, Judaism's contemporary character was determined by the application of Hansen's Law. The second generation's uncomfortable feeling of living in two worlds—one Jewish, one American—was relieved by ceasing to be Jewish. But even in choosing secularism, their choice often still had, Herberg felt, a Jewish tinge to it. Some became radicals and "internationalists" (Herberg was always careful in the mid-1950s not to use words like anarchist, revolutionary, and Communist); others became ardent Zionists, but Herberg pointed out that "both were somehow strangely 'Jewish,' for was not internationalist socialism a secularized version of the 'universalist' aspect of Jewish messianism and Zionist nationalism a secularized version of the 'particularist' aspect?" (185).

Finally, in the forties, the third generation of Jews tracing their American origins to the great Eastern European migration of the late nineteenth and early twentieth centuries came of age. As they did so, Herberg maintained, they followed Hansen's Law: they wished to remember what the second generation had wished to forget.

In returning to the religion of their forebears, the third generation accomplished many of the same effects that had taken place in the other religious communities. Where a marriage of a Lithuanian Jew and a German Jew would likely have been opposed by the couple's families and communities in the 1880s, few in the 1950s would bother to differentiate one Jew from another on the basis of their ancestors' national origins. At the same time, the Jewish proletariat of the turn of the century had disappeared completely, and Jews were now almost completely occupied in the professions and in business—more thoroughly middle class than Protestants and Catholics—and thus, in this one way, more American than those of other faiths.

Herberg's viewed the religion of American Jews at mid-twentieth century as "characterized by far-reaching accommodation to the American pattern of religious life which affected all 'denominations' in the American synagogue" (191). He pointed out that the typical synagogue had the same corporate structure and organizations as the typical Protestant church. Jewish worship, with slight modifications, also closely resembled Protestant church service, as evidenced by the centrality of the sermon, congregational singing, the use of organs, abbreviated services, and the practice of concluding a service with a benediction. The transformation of Hanukkah to be an equivalent holiday to Christmas was just one more instance of the isomorphic tendencies of American Judaism in practice.

Herberg saw mixed meanings in the new return to religion in his own faith group. The old style of turn-of-the-century secular Judaism was obsolete. The old Jewish organizations had nearly ceased to exist. Being Jewish had come to mean being religiously affiliated. In the fifties, Herberg noted, virtually every child became a bar mitzvah, unlike the case in the preceding thirty or forty years. But if the bar mitzvah was nothing but a "lavish and expensive party," Herberg asked, what was the significance of near total affiliation with religious institutions for Jews? Contemporary Jewish life posed a paradox of its own, Herberg believed, for "much of the institutional life of the synagogue has become thus secularized and drained of religious content precisely at the time when religion is becoming more and more acknowledged as the meaning of Jewishness" (196–197).

The extent to which religion had become secularized even as it became more popular was, for Herberg, seen in its most acute manifestation in American Judaism. Yet Judaism was not alone in trading religious integrity for popularity. For each of the three faith communities, Herberg sought to demonstrate how their faith had helped make them American. He also aimed to show how they had adapted their faiths to America. But for Herberg the ethical question—what does this religiosity of Americans count for?—kept arising. The underlying tone of his inquiry often amounted to a plaintive cry: "Is this all there is to religion?" His own answer was expounded in the last quarter of the book, as he began to synthesize his findings and theories into a jeremiad against the low state of contemporary faith.

As Herberg compared and contrasted the three communities of faith, he recognized that important differences remained between them and provided for tension within the overall culture of America. Protestants, Catholics, and Jews formed three groups who thought like minorities. In the case of Catholics and Jews, they truly were members of minority faiths. But for Protestants the experience of feeling as though the culture was no longer wholly under their control was enough to confer the mindset of minority status. The place where these groups brought their anxieties to the fore, Herberg argued, was in the vexing area of church-state relations. Catholics tended to see society in pluralistic terms and to favor the maintenance of a set of parallel institutions of schools, charities, and voluntary associations related to the Church. Protestants, concerned with their loss of status and defined at base by a negative stance toward Rome, tended to ask questions such as: what is wrong with the public schools? why do the Catholics need a separate bar association? Finally, marked by a long history of living within an overwhelmingly Christian nation, Jews adopted the position of even more extreme separation to serve as a protective strategy against Christian encroachments (239).

Given these defensive postures toward one another, it was remarkable that Protestantism, Catholicism, and Judaism could be said to have functioned together in America to produce anything like Herberg's construct of the American Way of Life. Yet the religions of America, though suspicious of one another on at least an official level, still saw enough common features and commitments to recognize one another with a tacit understanding. At this level, a kind of unification occurred through what Herberg termed "the interfaith movement." This movement featured an attitude that was also characteristic of the American Way of Life: a willingness to do anything for the sake of "brotherhood" or the "future of democracy" except discuss the actual theological beliefs that divided the three groups. One's own religion was important, and deserved to be cherished, but should not be "flaunted" before others. Herberg found this attitude disturbing (242–246).

In view of his dissatisfaction with interfaith approaches, it was perhaps surprising that Herberg's critique of American religion was offered not, as one might expect, from the perspective of a particular community of faith, but from the position of what he called "Jewish-Christian Faith." This he defined as the underlying unity of Christianity and Judaism that was found in the Bible, a God-centered faith in which "all being finds its beginning and its end in God, and its unity, reality, and order in its ordination to Him" (254). His project therefore was to hold religion as practiced accountable to its theological roots. Religion in American life was not accountable to Catholicism, Judaism, or even American Protestantism. It was to be judged as were these historic faiths, by the neo-orthodox concept of biblical faith.

Herberg's point in moving from sociology to theology was to move from description to prescription. The Jewish and Christian religions might *do* many things, sanction and forbid many things, but what they *should do* was indicated by the Bible. Above all, the lesson of Jewish-Christian faith was that actual human life is corrupted by idolatrous self-love which perverts all relationships, and that this worship of self instead of God is repaid with judgment. For evidence of this retribution, Herberg quoted Ezekiel (28:6–7): "Thus saith the Lord God: Because you count yourself wise as a god, behold I bring strangers against you. . . . Your heart was proud because of your beauty; you corrupted your wisdom by reason of your splendor. [Therefore] I cast you to the ground" (254).

The word of judgment on human pride and self-sufficiency was also, to Herberg, "a word of judgment upon human religion, or the human element in religion" (255). Herberg drew upon A. Roy Eckardt and Reinhold Niebuhr to support him on this point: "Scripture has no ax to grind for religion," wrote Eckardt; "on the contrary it is highly suspicious of much that passes for religion" (255). Religion as practiced in America also suffered in comparison to biblical religion because of its individualism. In the Bible, Herberg maintained, a Jew approached God on the basis of membership in the people of God. Later this was extended as the covenant was expanded, such that, for Jews and Christians alike, biblical faith was "the faith of man-in-community." Religiosity was not a good thing if practiced apart from a community of faith. But even in community, religion was not an unqualified good, for the Church and the People Israel, insofar as they were human entities, were "subject to all of the temptations and corruptions of human institutions" (256).

The religious situation in America, where nearly everyone identified himself or herself as a Protestant, Catholic, or Jew, Herberg believed, was a situation that was good for religion but not necessarily good for faith or for Protestantism, Catholicism, or Judaism. America's return to religion was evidence that America had an underlying "culture religion" in which the three conventional religions were deemed to be "equi-legitimate expressions." Herberg did not dispute that there were areas of commonality between the three faiths. He believed, after all, that one could speak of a "Jewish-Christian faith." But he argued strongly that "the very existence of this common ground makes the unique and distinctive witness of each communion, even the advocacy of universal claims where such are felt to be justified, all the more necessary for the life of faith." Indeed, in a culture where no one would make a universal claim for his or her own religion for fear of offending the American spirit, Herberg believed, the "authentic character of Jewish-Christian faith is falsified." The faith that went under the names of Protestantism, Catholicism, and Judaism in America was thus reduced to the mere "status of an American culture-religion" (262).

Culture-religion or, as Herberg interchangeably termed it, "civic religion," played the role of sanctifying the American society and its political and economic values. This sanctification, without any possibility of judgment or self-critique, made the civic religion of Americans idolatrous on its face to Jewish-Christian faith, just as it rendered all forms of civic religion idolatrous. At its worst, the contemporary religiosity of the American public thus came to serve as nothing less than the spiritual reinforcement of national "self-righteousness" and the "spiritual authentication of national self-will" (263).

This inability to achieve any critical distance from self-interest was also the product of the kind of people Americans had become. How was the other-directed person interested in adjustment and conformity supposed to relate to the God who demanded nonconformity? How was that person to understand the alienated zealots of the Lord, Elijah, Amos, Isaiah, or Jesus? The prophetic faith of the Bible had been rendered nearly incomprehensible by the contemporary outlook and by the institutions that were charged to be its bearers (261).

After demonstrating the dubiousness of an American religion that was both culturally self-serving and personally undemanding, Herberg went on to argue that much of what was called "faith" in American religion was faith per se, and faith per se, faith without an object or purpose, was not the faith of the Bible, or Judaism, or Christianity.

Herberg had begun *Protestant, Catholic, Jew* with the observations of a European visitor to America. Now, at the end of the book, he returned to the view that European visitors had of American religion. He quoted the Norwegian Lutheran Bishop Eivind Berggrav, who said that his impression of religious life in America was that American Christianity was "real, true, and personal," and that its congregations were "true organisms of fellowship." Herberg went on to note that other recent visitors from the continent had found in American religious life a vitality, a popularity, and a widely shared sense of the importance of religion that they found most impressive. Yet, Herberg also noted, this was the same American religion that he had argued was so empty, "so conformist, so utilitarian, so sentimental, so individualistic, and so self-righteous" (269). "Americans," wrote Herberg, "fill the houses of worship, but their conceptions, standards, and values, their institutions and loyalties, bear a strangely ambiguous relation to the teachings the churches presumably stand for." The answer to the paradox lay in the fact that, far from disparaging religion, Americans cherished it, but defined its role in their lives in such a way that it posed no serious challenge to their politics, their business affairs, or the conduct of their personal and family lives. This was the way of secularism, for Herberg asked, "What is secularism but the practice of the absence of God in the affairs of life?" In this way it was true that America was "at one and the same time, one of the most religious and most secular of nations" (270).

And yet after all his invective against the contemporary low state of religion, Herberg still ended his book on an optimistic note. He argued that within the overall framework of a secularized religion there were "signs of deeper and more authentic stirrings of faith" (271–272). His exposure to college students in the course of lecture tours had made him hopeful. "Certainly among the younger people," he wrote, "particularly among the more sensitive young men and women on the campuses of this country, and in the suburban communities that are in so many ways really continuous with the campus, there are unmistakable indications of an interest in and concern with religion that goes far beyond the demands of mere social 'belonging'" (272). Even the more conventional forms of American religion that Herberg had done so much to criticize he now maintained should not be completely written off. Nothing was too unpromising to serve the will of God. After all, he wrote, "the God Who is able to make the 'wrath of man' to praise Him (Ps. 76:10) is surely capable of turning even the intractabilities and follies of religion into an instrument of His redemptive purpose" (272). The format of the jeremiad would not permit Herberg's book to end any other way. Herberg's overall purpose was fulfilled neither by pure sociological description, nor by critique. His tract utilized both these elements to plead for reform and to suggest that there was a way for those who were drawn to religion to authentically claim the name Protestant, Catholic, or Jew.

Herberg's masterwork, therefore, like its secular forerunners, was an exercise in more than social description. It was a tract for its times that presented normative judgments in a well-disguised form. It presented a description of American life that sought to appall the reader into reaching precisely the same sense of moral outrage the author had, and this just in time to convert the reader into adopting the author's positive approach as the only way to reverse the manifest evils that had been chronicled. As for Whyte, the answer had been to fight the organization and for Macdonald it lay in sealing off high culture from the taint of middlebrow culture, so for Herberg the answer was the adoption of the prophetic faith.

Herberg's choice of the prophetic literature as the portion of tradition upon which he would make his religious stand is not surprising when seen in the context of his life. There was a decided elective affinity between Herberg's neo-orthodoxy and his earlier devotion to Communism. Although his biographer, Harry Ausmus, has interpreted this as the result of Herberg's need to always believe in absolutes, this interpretation hits wide of the target. Herberg's quest for answers was driven by his passion for righteousness. In his earliest phase, Herberg identified righteousness with the side of the proletariat oppressed by the rich and powerful. As Communism ceased to share this zeal for the rights of the downtrodden, Herberg slowly became soured to that ideology even as he was schooled in the ambiguity of human solutions and motivations. Neo-orthodoxy's biblical faith—as interpreted for Herberg by Niebuhr and Rosenzweig—gave Herberg an ideology that incorporated human ambiguity into its worldview and still reflected, in its emphasis on the prophetic tradition, the zeal for righteousness that led him to seek out Communism in the first place. In his review of Ausmus's biography, Richard Fox is correct when he asserts that Herberg's move from "right to right" is not, as Ausmus argues, from the right-wing of American Communism to right-wing conservatism, but rather a continuous association with those things that were most concerned with what was "right" in the moral sense of the word.[15]

Critically it could be argued that Herberg's work was unoriginal. He was dependent on Marcus Lee Hansen for his three-generations hypothesis, on Ruby Jo Kennedy for the notion of a triple melting pot, and on David Riesman for the idea of other-directedness. He owed intellectual credit to H. Richard Niebuhr (and through him to Ernst Troeltsch) for the critical insight that social factors were powerfully determinative of religious groups' histories and behaviors. Even his theology was second-hand, owing to Reinhold Niebuhr, Franz Rosenzweig, Martin Buber, and Paul Tillich. But the tremendously positive reaction to *Protestant, Catholic, Jew* on the part of the public and even intellectuals in the late fifties and early sixties argues for another position, that the work was original in the breadth of material it attempted to synthesize. For the average reader it talked about religion in ways that were wonderfully new and yet made perfect sense. Popular discourse about religion to this point in the twentieth century had almost always focused on whether religion was true or not, and sometimes on whether it was useful. Here was someone who left aside those tired questions and argued that people thought of themselves as Catholics because their grandfathers were Neapolitans, that people attended church because it seemed to be expected by their new suburban neighbors, and that a great deal of religion did not seem to count for very much. Here was a man who spoke the truth.

For intellectuals, Herberg's appeal was found in his application of theory to fact in a cross-disciplinary way, so that even though they might quibble with his understanding of their own particular fields of expertise, his word was accepted as gospel truth on other matters.[16] Like *The Organization Man*, *The Power Elite*, and *The Lonely Crowd*, *Protestant, Catholic, Jew* was a book that dared to paint in broad brush strokes across an immense canvas. And like its more secularly focused forerunners, the book soon became the statement of record on this particular aspect of the contemporary culture; what *The Organization Man* was to American business life, *Protestant, Catholic, Jew* was to American religious life.

More persuasive than the charge of unoriginality, however, is the criticism that Herberg was guilty of overgeneralizing on the basis of his own experience and his own religious and ethnic group's experience. Catholics did not fit the three-generations hypothesis quite as neatly as East European Jews did, and Protestants, even of late immigrating groups, hardly fit it at all. Herberg's central point of criticism of America's religious people was that they did not live up to the norms of their historic faiths. But even Herberg had to admit that Catholics came remarkably close to fulfilling this obligation (219). It was American Jews who had most accommodated their actual faith to the secular ways of modern America and were the most extreme of the three groups in their departure from their historic faith. And yet, even though Herberg had written of religion in America from the perspective of a second-generation Russian Jewish immigrant, and had taken the extreme case as indicative of the norm, public reaction to the book again argues that the jeremiad may have overstated the case but disclosed a vital truth nonetheless.

Despite all the criticism leveled at the book, Herberg's description of the state of religion in America proved generally satisfactory to a generation of readers. More importantly, it captured the flavor of the faiths' new interrelation in a way that could be discussed. Whether readers agreed with Herberg or not, *Protestant, Catholic, Jew* set the tone for the debates that would follow. Religion's social function, its political role, civil religion—all these were topics that were opened up for discussion by Herberg's probing synthesis. Herberg made another contribution to American religious history as well. By arguing that Jewish and Christian faith and practice should be regulated in response to the prophetic core of the biblical witness, he established one potent line of attack on the popular religion of his day. The prophetic demands for justice, true worship of God, and love of neighbor would be increasingly taken up as cudgels against the contemporary religious establishment as the fifties gave way to the sixties.

The Suburban Captivity
of the Churches

If ever there was a piece of criticism that deserved the title "Suburban Jeremiad," it was Gibson Winter's attack on suburban Christianity. When it came to the suburban church, Winter knew of what he spoke. He was raised in suburbia and did parish work as an Episcopal priest in suburbia. After service as a naval chaplain in World War II and graduate study in social relations at Harvard, he spent the next several years in suburban Detroit helping to establish the Parishfield Community, a training center for lay people designed to help them relate Christianity to contemporary industrial and cultural life. Gibson Winter knew suburbia well; as a Christian and a person trained to think sociologically he did not like what he saw. Suburbia was, for Winter, the ultimate extension of 200 years of industrialization. It was also a very real peril to the soul of the Christian church. Winter first published his charges about the churches' suburban captivity in the *Christian Century* on 28 September 1955, just weeks after Herberg's *Protestant, Catholic, Jew* appeared in bookstores. In an article titled, "The Church in Suburban Captivity," Winter began by recognizing that suburbia had become a major social phenomenon in American life.

In calling suburbia "a dominant social group," Winter meant to indicate what he perceived as the swing of power of all types from the cities to suburbia within the generation just past. Recognizing that suburban locations varied considerably from one to another, he still argued that they formed a single group, "by reason of their state of mind rather than by their geographical similarity." The overall balance of Winter's article was dedicated to probing the meaning of this state of mind for the churches. To do this, he first had to define the suburban state of mind, given his allowance that, spatially and economically, suburbia ranged from lower income to top salary residential areas and from ranch houses to colonials. The elements of the suburban mind were threefold. The first and most important was the principle of advancement in life. For the suburbanite, success was not defined in terms of skill or service; rather, success equaled "advancement with a pay raise," this being "the real meaning of work." The second element in this mindset was the permeation of the management point of view. Even the members of lower suburbia saw work "in terms of production needs, cost problems, and profit drives." It did not matter that most suburbanites lacked the prestige and checkbooks of top management; one of the first steps on their way to advancement was to think like top management. The final principal characteristic of the suburban mind was the attitude that came with a high degree of mobility. Suburbanites never saw themselves as "rooted, anchored, placed," and though they might live in the same place for a dozen years, their attitudes would still suggest "temporary friends and provisional organizational commitment." All of this added up to a pattern that promoted the overextension of activities. The suburbanite, out of a desire for advancement and the insecurity of mobility, found himself "unable to refuse organizational obligations . . . one of these being the church."[17]

When it came to church life, suburbia had introduced its conception of success into every aspect of the church's being. In spite of infusing the church and its programs with energy and enthusiasm, and filling the offering plates, pews, and educational facilities to overflow, suburbia, Winter believed, could, be said to have brought the churches into captivity—with all the negative connotations the term implied. Suburbia had imposed its mindset on the church. The "criteria by which suburbia measures all things"—advancement in financial terms and numerical growth—had crowded out more traditional measures of Christian success, such as salvation, redemption, care of the poor, and witness to the power of the cross. Indeed, the very success of the churches in suburbia posed a danger for the identity of the Christian churches overall: "Despite a nominal church background, this is an unconverted, untrained mass of people, who make the problem of church membership comparable to what it was in the time of Constantine, when Christianity became a recognized institution of society."[18] With church members being added more quickly than clergy and dedicated lay people could assimilate and train them, there was a virtual guarantee that more of the world would be brought into the church of Christ than Christ be taken by the church to the world.

Finally, suburban life undermined the life of the church insofar as it had "nailed up an impenetrable layer of insulation between the churches and the world of work, community, housing, and daily bread."[19] Winter recognized that the isolation of the church from daily life was not created by suburbia, but maintained even so that in suburbia secularization had found its fullest and final expression. This, he believed, constituted a national tragedy, for it was happening at a time when America's world leadership necessitated "a prophetic church at home." The suburban church was anything but prophetic. "Suburban domination may well be God's word of judgement upon us as his church," Winter wrote. "For our trespasses and complacency we have been delivered to Babylon." Like the prophets he admired, Winter ended his essay, "May this word be heard in the churches!"[20] The reaction to Winter's article was immediate—so much so that *Time* magazine carried news of the essay to its readership, together with extracts from it as its lead religion article under the title, "Last Train to Babylon."[21]

Six years later the focus of Winter's work had shifted somewhat from the meaning of the impact of suburban life on the churches to a religious concern with the "creation of a human environment in the metropolis."[22] The urban-suburban divide that had received a paragraph's notice in the 1955 *Christian Century* article now was the focus of a great part of his 1961 book, *The Suburban Captivity of the Churches.* The ethics of the urban/suburban divide was the focus of Winter's religious concern, for in his view there was no greater test of the churches' faithfulness to God's vision for human community than whether they challenged or merely accepted the "vicious circle of demolition, redevelopment and spreading blight" that characterized life in the contemporary metropolis (9).

The first contention of Winter's book was that for the immediate future, the metropolis was the primary site of mission for the Christian churches. The metropolis had become the center of the United States. Politically, socially, culturally, and economically speaking, the United States was no longer a country that looked to its small towns and rural areas for leadership. Rural clothing, once offered in the Sears catalog as a perfectly normal option, was distinctly out of fashion; the print and broadcast media were centered in large cities. The idea of metropolis, as Winter understood it, was key to his point. It was not the much-talked about process of urbanization that Winter wished to bring to the attention of his readers, for a metropolis was not merely a large central city and, since 1920, he pointed out, the preponderance of growth in metropolitan areas had occurred on the periphery of central cities (17). The social effect of this trend would not be remarkable but for the fact that as one moved out from the central city to the "series of rings of decreasing population density," one found "progressively more expensive housing, more education, and higher incomes," while moving toward the core one discovered that "the residents are increasingly unskilled, their incomes lower, their dwellings poorer" (18).

Winter allowed that it was possible for industrial workers to live in a suburb and industrialists to live in high-rise splendor within the center city, but insisted that the pattern was sufficient to argue that "the spatial distances between people mirror the social and economic distance between them" (18). This economic division, Winter noted, had also taken on a racial character that further deepened the problem of the metropolis. The "job ceiling" had worked to keep most blacks in poor-paying jobs and thus unable to upgrade their standard of living as other groups had, and segregation had further limited black residential mobility. The net result was that "the central city, as administrative and political heart of the metropolis, is becoming a Negro community" (19). Issues of race, segregation, and exclusion remained in the forefront of Winter's thought throughout *Suburban Captivity*.

There was also more of a class consciousness in Winter's work than there had been in Herberg's *Protestant, Catholic, Jew*. Herberg had moved away from identifying the problems of contemporary religion with class, viewing them instead as coming from an alternate ideology that was in competition with real biblical faith. Winter's social criticism more closely corresponded to C. Wright Mills than did Herberg's, for he believed it had been class or race consciousness of an unthinking type that had brought Protestantism into the captivity of the petit bourgeoisie and only class consciousness of the deliberate, progressive type could set it free.

The story of Protestantism in modern America was one in which the churches had repeatedly sought out better and better demographic markets to exist in, a process Winter termed "upgrading." Such upgrading, however, necessarily entailed the collapse of central-city churches, "abandoning large numbers of the congregation to an inadequate ministry, while suburban gains mean increased recruitment from the upper social ranks." Such social upgrading through residential relocation was not new, Winter recognized. After all, he noted, "many congregations changed the location of their churches every decade or two after 1850" (42). The metropolitan Protestant churches had moved further and further out with each new wave of urban immigration. Roman Catholics, foreign-born Protestants and Jews, rural white Protestants, and Negro Protestants followed one upon another as the latest arrivals on the urban landscape. Each new group posed a threat to WASP hegemony, so the churches of the WASPs chose to move rather than assimilate.

The Protestant mainstream churches had staked their futures on a residential scheme of association by likeness. This made eleven o'clock in the morning not only the most segregated hour of the week in terms of race, but also in terms of class, income, and lifestyle (27). Winter's complaint, as always, was not that this made for unsuccessful churches. On the contrary, as an observer trained in sociological theory, he recognized that association by likeness was a superlative basis for the social success of any group enterprise, at least in the short term. His difficulty with association by likeness was that it made for unfaithful churches. How, Winter asked, "can an inclusive message be mediated through an exclusive group, when the principle of exclusiveness is social-class identity rather than a gift of faith which is open to all?" (29).

Despite the apparent success of the mainstream churches in suburbia, Winter recognized that the link between inclusion in a church fellowship and social class could spell trouble for the long-term survival of the Christian church. At present, the problem of residential discrimination most acutely impinged itself on the black community. But even a solution to racial discrimination, Winter argued, would leave the metropolis "with its basic difficulty unresolved." The metropolitan principle of impersonal interdependence was bound to undermine every attempt to create an autonomous local community, and hence every autonomous fellowship: "The metropolis is inclusive. Churches that identify with local areas become exclusive and antimetropolitan." The short-term danger to churches from being locally identified was obvious: they became "victims of the pathology that assails neighborhood life, whether it be small-town gossip or metropolitan discrimination" (29). The long-term danger was that of extinction. Winter compared the suburban American class-identified church with the early Christianity of North Africa. The churches of North Africa became centers of upper-class culture but had never formed a widespread base among the common people. When Islam expanded into North Africa, it was able to sweep away Christianity. Nestorian Christianity had likewise perished after a single century in China despite its appeal to elites. This led Winter to observe that "where Christianity has become identified with upper-class elites, it has lacked a substantial base in the working population and has been unable to weather social change" (50).

More than anything else, the problem with the alliance between neighborhood and church that 1950s Protestantism had endorsed was that a suburban neighborhood was a location, but not a true community. He wrote about the suburban congregation, "assembled from no real community and witnessing to none, it merely contemplated its own budget" (35). *Suburban Captivity* was full of these one- and two-line trenchant remarks in which Winter made clear that the contemporary church was all too mercenary in its motives. "Denominational leaders have watched the new residential areas surrounding the central cities with greedy eyes," he noted. "In fact, denominational leaders call these 'high potential areas,' and they do not mean potential for prayer" (31).

In an obvious reference to William Whyte, Winter argued that the "peculiar coalition" between these denominations and the emerging middle class gave birth to the "organization church" (37). The suburban congregations with building programs resembled nothing so much as "a cult of consumption" (79). For all his criticism of the white suburban, superficial organization church, Winter's challenge to it was remarkably simple: "Ultimately, the only important question about any congregation or religious group is this: in what ways is it an expression and ministry in faith and obedience? The tragedy of the organization church has seen its substitution of survival for ministry. Its promise lies in its resources for ministry in a mass society" (37).

Winter had thus laid the foundation of a classic jeremiad: the suburban church had developed in such a way that it was unable to measure up to the ethical standard of faithful obedience. The survival-oriented church, by definition, was well on its way to being no church at all. And yet even at this late hour, this church was not without its resources, and hence not without hope. The dilemma was clearly set before "Metropolitan Protestantism": it had to choose fellowship or mission, success or service (37).

To date, Winter believed, the Protestantism of suburbia had opted for fellowship and success. He wrote about this choice to be a fellowship driven by class considerations with the passion of an Old Testament prophet and the vocabulary of a mid-twentieth-century social analyst: "A new image of this church is emerging . . . created by the domination of contemporary life by economic activities. . . . For every rung on the ladder there is an appropriate congregation" (66–67).

Winter sought to strengthen this case by suggesting that the fact that 66 percent of church members owed their decision to join a church to "friendly contact," combined with the fact that the impact of educational activities, worship, preaching, and publicity on member recruitment was insignificant, added up to a pattern in which the "extension of economic integration through co-optation is the principal form of mission in the contemporary church." This contrasted sharply with the mission of faithful churches who extended themselves through "proclamation" of what they saw as essential truth (72–73).

Given the strong impact of the economic peer group, why was the church so popular? Winter had written, "The local Republican Club should serve as well as the local church." So then why did the American middle classes "turn to the church as a vehicle of social identity"? Winter himself believed, like Herberg, that the choice of a religious institution as the place to search for identity was not entirely accidental. "The search for identity in the churches seems to be a grasp for traditional symbols of stability by an uprooted and alienated social class; the religious interests of this group are an expression of an authentic search for values and stability in the rapidly changing milieu of an industrial and metropolitan world." The middle classes—C. Wright Mills's white-collar men and women—were newly placed, politically powerless, and insecure in their status; they were without tradition and virtually unaware of a sense of a "continuing place in the world." As such, they had religious concerns arising out of questions of identity, self-worth, and the ultimate meaning of life. And, by reason of these same questions, their churches were destined to be exclusive fellowships. Viewed from the perspective of the need for ministry to the metropolis, Protestantism was fighting a losing battle (75–77).

Denominational Protestantism was, in sum, defective, or in Winter's words, an "arrested development as a form of the church." The church could impart a true identity to its members only when its members represented "the interdependencies of human life." The identity of whites and blacks, rich and poor, were interrelated in the metropolis, Winter argued, and a man could no more discover who he was without men and women of other types than he could have discovered his identity as a child by cutting himself off from his parents (77). But this was precisely the pathology in which suburban Protestantism was immersed. Middle-class people, therefore, were denied the only genuinely religious thing they sought from the churches. Trapped by children, consumption, and conformity, they sought their true identities and the "ultimate meaning of life," and the church only further sanctioned their enslavement by blessing their culture. The quest for the ultimate led the middle class to the trivial: "The cultus of the Church has given way to the manipulations of the organization. In place of the sacraments, we have the committee meeting; in place of confession, the bazaar; in place of pilgrimage, the dull drive to hear the deadly speaker; in place of community, a collection of functions" (79).

The organization church was first and last a church of membership-oriented activities. As a form of the Christian church, the organization church raised two problems for Winter. First, what was the religious significance of the organizational network in such a congregation? Second, to what or whom was loyalty owed as a result of this organizational life? In determining religious meaning of membership activity, Winter, following W. Lloyd Warner, compared the kinds of exchanges that went on in connection with a church fellowship supper with a gift exchange of the Potlatch among the Indians of the Northwest. How else could one explain an activity where members contributed the food, prepared the meal, bought tickets, served the meal, cleaned the dishes, and when it was all over bought back the leftovers? Members of the church who were involved in such an activity often were disproportionately elated over the success of their ventures, given the amount of money they had raised. "From some perspectives," Winter wrote, "such an expense of energy seems wasted, but those who participate feel that it deepens their sense of belongingness to the church" (95). Viewed as an exchange of gifts, however, between people who do not already know one another and who need to develop a community feeling and a sense of trust with others, the fellowship supper could be seen to have produced far more in the realm of social utility than its mere economic proceeds.

Moreover, there was an additional puzzle. Why would members really want to do things that would "be considered intolerable drudgery at home: hours of telephoning, cooking, cleaning, serving, endless correspondence"? Some members, Winter allowed, might be trying to find an outlet for their energies or to achieve status through an organization. However, he believed another interpretation was far more likely, writing that activities might "provide some members with a means to work out feelings of guilt through sacrifices of time and energy in organizational drudgery. . . . The idea of atoning for guilt through organizational drudgery suggests that the activities of the churches provide a Protestant system of penance. Members do penance for their faults by sharing in the organizational work" (96). Winter believed that Protestantism, by rejecting sacramental penance, had "opened the way for the development of secularized penance." The performance of some unpleasant tasks for the organization church seemed far removed from repeating the Hail Mary, but for Winter, the organizational network had become "a secularized penitential system and the pastor who solicits their labors becomes the punishing father" (97). Religiously, the problem with this system of penance and absolution was that the church became party to a system of what Dietrich Bonhoeffer had called "cheap grace" (97).

There was also the problem of to what or whom loyalty attached, even in the organization church. Why is it that the organizational style made sense in middle-class culture, Winter asked, and what were the consequences for the church's mission? Here Winter relied on the findings of Yoshio Fukuyama. Fukuyama had found that, of all church members, two-thirds enjoyed a "cultic-style" of membership, either being only nominally involved or being organizationally addicted. The remaining members distributed evenly to those devoted to a devotional style (with an orientation to personal prayer), an intellectual style (with an orientation to religious ideas), and a creedal style (oriented to traditional beliefs). Winter's first conclusion, given Fukuyama's findings, was that perhaps as much as two-thirds of the official membership of the churches were religiously bound to an organization rather than to God, to beliefs, or to teachings. The Protestant church—which had rebelled against the institutional character of Roman Catholicism—had emerged in the twentieth century as itself an institution promoting works righteousness.

At this point Winter was, like Herberg before him, focusing the critiques of neo-orthodoxy on the religious culture of his day. Where Herberg's neo-orthodoxy had been the biblical kind derived from Franz Rosenzweig and Reinhold Niebur, Winter kept speaking of cheap grace and reconciliation, thus drawing upon the neo-orthodoxy of Dietrich Bonhoeffer and Emil Brunner. As Herberg's Russian Jewish roots had shown through in his analysis, so too did Winter's tradition influence his work. It was clear, for example, that Winter preferred a system of diocesan ownership rather than congregational ownership of local churches, for it allowed ministry to continue in a place even after its founding members had moved on to greener pastures and/or postage stamp lawns. With its higher sacramental theology, Anglicanism was also able to serve as a more balanced alternative to client-centered Roman Catholicism on the one hand, and to member-oriented free church Protestantism on the other.

In his final two chapters, Winter turned to setting a positive agenda for the churches and their missions in the metropolis. He began by quoting the Evanston Assembly of the World Council of Churches concerning the term "responsible society": "'Responsible society' is not an alternative social or political system, but a criterion by which we judge all existing social orders and at the same time a standard to guide us in the specific choices we have to make" (129). In picking up the term "responsible society," Winter was aiming at a similiar objective standard to which any and every church could be subjected, that is, the responsible church. In Winter's view, the first thing the churches needed to do to become responsible was to cease being complicit in the removal of religion to the private sphere of life. On Winter's account of the matter, the churches could never be responsible until they realized that the context of their responsibility was broader than the home and the local neighborhood. Good intentions on the part of the churches, even good results in their chosen context of mission, did not add up to responsibility if their conception of their field of responsibility was too small. As Winter saw it, at one time the neighborhood was an appropriate area by which to define

community concern. However, as a consequence of industrial development and the expansion of metropolitan areas, the neighborhood and
residential area became a private sphere and only a very restricted portion of the entire metropolitan community. Yet it was in this narrow
milieu that religious congregations continued to "center their memberships." The net effect, Winter wrote, "was to insulate the churches within
a privatized sphere—thus disengaging them from public responsibility"
(131).

Nor was the church alone. Residential space was still the basis of local
school systems, Winter allowed, but this only served to demonstrate the
folly of excessive privatization. As Winter pointed out, the major forces of
contemporary culture—literature, mass media, the movies—were not in
any way neighborhood-specific. Modern men and women, Winter believed, found themselves living in two distinct worlds. One was the world
in which they worked—the metropolitan community of economic and
political interests. The other was the private sphere—the world of family
and leisure interests. It was with this latter world that the church had
completely identified itself, ceasing in Winter's view to have anything to
say to the larger world in which people spent so much of their lives. The
recognition of this radical change in Protestantism led Winter to conclude
that "the attentiveness of the churches to this sphere is certainly legitimate, but exclusive identification of religion with the private sphere creates a special culture in congregational life; the inevitable consequence is
social irresponsibility, which means that the churches have abandoned
the context of public accountability in order to serve exclusively the
emotional needs of selected groups—those who are co-opted by the
membership" (134–135).

Lest anyone doubt the validity of Winter's assertion that there were
two worlds, and that the private world was socially irresponsible, he
called attention to the attitude toward racial integration evidenced in
suburban residential areas, noting that churches and residential associations almost without exception opposed racial integration while the government, the military, and educational, business, and medical groups all
made progress toward it. The morality of the metropolis was a dual
morality: "Public morality governs facilities, courts, and economic activity; private morality rules the spheres of housing, family nurture, religion,
the elementary school, and in many cases the high school" (136).

The solution as Winter saw it was two-fold: first, to construct congregational units that crossed "the racial and social class barriers that now
embody the economic ethos and undermine the religious community";

second, to stake out in the center of these "inclusive congregations a middle ground where economic, political, and metropolitan concerns can be discussed and faced in light of the Christian Message" (138). Without the accomplishment of these two goals, Winter believed the contemporary churches would fail to fulfill their missionary role of proclaiming Christ's Lordship.

When it came down to cases, the ministries Winter had most in mind were inner-city experimental ministries. He singled out for approval Kilmer Myers's work in Chicago with suburban ministries to urban areas, Judson Memorial Church's ministry to New York's Greenwich Village, the Cincinnati ministry to southern mountaineers led by Michael Hamilton, and the East Harlem Parish under the direction of George Todd. Such ministries, Winter noted, often involved risks both physical and social, for in working with persons in the inner city, such as gang members, persons transplanted from Appalachia, derelicts, and the poor, the church was brought into association with those whom society had declared failures. Winter, however, focused on ministry within the inner city in the interest of demonstrating a sensitivity of an even deeper and more fundamental sort. "To be the Church is to be involved in mission," wrote Winter, setting out mission as a condition for the church to be the church. Further, Winter went on to make mission to the inner city the essential test of the church's identity. This was not because it was the most important part of the metropolis, but because it was the test of an inclusive church. Without saying so explicitly, Winter was applying the test of Matthew 25—"Whatever you have done for the least of these, my brethren, you have done unto me"—not only to individual believers but to the church as a whole. The degree to which the church was good and responsible was dependent upon the extent of its mission.

Winter had criticized contemporary Protestantism for being too preoccupied with works and for fostering an attitude that said activity is the measure of Christian success. Now, however, it was clear that Winter's standard of Christian success was also one that depended upon activity of a certain kind. His positive standard—a kind of ethical neo-orthodoxy—he defended on biblical grounds: "There is strong warrant in Scriptures for the poor of the earth—as the decisive point for estimating the form appropriate to the task. God's deed for men conformed to the human plight; the Church must also conform to that deed, and its mission achieve the form of the Servant" (140).

Even if the inner city was the essential place for the contemporary church to be in ministry, Winter did not want to make the mistake of saying that urban ministries were the only real ministries. Instead, he asked, how was it possible for suburban churches to participate in a ministry to inner-city youth gangs, to different racial groups, and to different social classes? (144). Furthermore, how was it possible to attract and retain competent ministers for inner-city ministries if suburban ministries paid much better? Winter's answer was to stake out pie-shaped areas of Christian responsibility from the outer edge of the cities into the heart of the inner cities along major lines of access or freeways. This area would extend across the divisions of metropolitan societies—from blight to suburb, black to white, poverty to privilege, and blue to white collar. All the resources of the church, including finances, buildings, clergy, and lay ministries, would be allocated within these sectors by the decision of councils, composed of representatives from the entire area. In Winter's plan, such a sector would constitute "both the basic unit of ministry and the minimal unit of the Church" (145).

Winter's goal in all this scheming about a sector-based ministry was to unite Christians in different positions and conditions throughout the metropolitan area in a community of common interests. In this he was not unlike C. Wright Mills, who challenged the white-collar middle class to see themselves as needing to make common cause with wage laborers. Winter hoped that by making the church's basic unit cross the lines of race, class, and neighborhood, Christians would be forced by organizational realities to concentrate on finding common interests, much as the formation of a common market in Europe had forced European peoples to think less parochially (149). The sectoral ministry approach was also designed to stop the unchurching of the inner city by shifting the church's concern away from congregational survival and toward the issue of the adequacy of ministry within the total sector. Winter's plan, therefore, was nothing less than a radical attempt to restructure the economic and organizational incentives for the provision of ministry services, in order to break what he saw as the unchristian continuation of "ministry on basis of power to pay" (150).

As he closed his section of advice to the churches, Winter reflected on the writings of Martin Buber. He saw his earlier two-world split in terms of Buber's I-Thou, I-It dichotomy. The church had attempted to separate itself from all I-It relations in the dirty world of politics and work. But Winter felt that this religion-in-a-bunker approach had "imposed a cleavage in the Message which distorts its real meaning, and separates man even further from God" (158). Even so, Winter was not despairing, and he looked instead for signs of hope where he could find them. He cited the examples of suburban persons joining inner-city churches and articulated his belief that beneath all the organizational activity, the majority of church members had been drawn by a deep religious need to find the meaning of life. One indicator of this religious quality that provided hope was what had happened in churches that had practiced racial desegregation. "Despite the conflicts that have preceded integration," Winter maintained, "the average loss of members over this issue is infinitesimal." It was at just such crisis moments when the "chips are down" that the church was freed to be the church and its members realized the opportunity to share in its life, "a life which is essentially mission and ministry" (158). Once the church was reorganized to let form follow function (function understood as being in mission), then it could begin renewing the metropolis, the subject of Winter's last chapter.

From beginning to end, Gibson Winter's writing could not be said to lack narrative movement or purpose. The structure of *Suburban Captivity* moved from the dilemma of metropolitan Protestantism as it was rooted in the nature of the metropolis to the great exodus of Protestantism from the cities. It progressed from the identity of the churches as either fellowships or missions to the emergence of a new religious style he called the organization church and branded "introverted," and finally to the possibility of renewal. Now in the last chapter, he moved back to where he had begun—the metropolis and the question of what the church would do about its situation.

It was appropriate that Winter's final chapter would begin to sum up his jeremiad with a jeremiad. In a few brief sentences, Winter sought to put the dilemma clearly before his readers once again: "Citizens of the metropolis realize that their future and the lives of their children depend upon the creation of a safe, healthy environment in the metropolitan area. The exodus to suburbia has failed to check the spread of blight. There is no retreat from the disorder and deterioration which plague metropolitan society. Many of the new residential areas on the edge of the central city may be slums within a generation" (161). If some of his suburban Christian readers were still hoping after 160 pages that they could ignore Winter's call to mission and live out their lives of faith within the tranquil bounds of their residential enclave, Winter meant to forever shock them from their complacency. There was no place in the metropolis that was safe from the specter of spreading blight. But if this was the bad news, there was also hope. For in spite of all the mistakes the churches had made in the metropolitan strategy, they were still in the possession of a gift that could be used for metropolitan renewal. The church in its role of defender of values was in a position to "best represent the interests of the whole in the midst of conflicting economic interests, and can speak out most strongly for life and human values" (162). But time was running out and the Protestant churches, reliant on voluntary congregations and insistent on individual piety, were easy prey to social forces beyond their control.

After once again making clear the eleventh-hour position in which the churches found themselves, Winter pointed, like Herberg before him, to the signs of hope he saw that might yet avert disaster. Enumerating the "powerful forces" of renewal evident in contemporary Protestantism, Winter listed seven. Historical criticism had led to the production of a new and vital biblical theology, one that was renewing preaching and Christian education. The disciplines of developmental and group psychology were being applied to the teaching task of the church, while depth psychology enhanced its pastoral care. Liturgical renewal was also underway. But most striking for Winter was the contemporary reemergence of lay leadership in the churches. Winter saw in the renewal of the laity an opportunity for a deepening of the understanding of faith along with the rejection of some of the mindless activism of the organization church. The final signs were the growth in new ministries to nonresidential structures—hospital chaplaincies, ministries in higher education, industry, and even political organizations—and a heightened awareness of metropolitan needs in the form of church planning. When these forces of renewal already present began "to shape the ministry," Winter predicted, "Protestantism will become the central force for renewal in metropolitan life" (167–169). If only the church would take up anew its public responsibility, metropolitan community would be created, for they were, in Winter's words, "two sides of the same coin" (170).

In affirming a ministry to all of the metropolis, the church had everything to gain, including its soul. And if this were not enough, Winter also wrote of a different kind of reward, telling the story of a Lutheran parish on Chicago's south side that had desegregated in the beginning of black migration to the neighborhood. While other churches were put up for sale and attempts were made to bomb homes occupied by black persons, this church integrated its fellowship. Winter could happily report that "today, some six or seven years later, that church is probably the only church on the South Side that is half Negro and half White, and exerts an influence in the community far exceeding its numbers" (174). If this success story sounded a bit too glib, it only demonstrated the limitations of the jeremiad as a rhetorical form. Still, the "all this and heaven to" aspect of

Winter's hoped-for outcome was in full accord with the general conclusion of his book, that "the Church [was] deformed by the struggle to survive and reformed only as ministry in mission." In this task, Winter believed, the church could rely not only on its own resources but also on those from above, for the church was itself a gift of the Holy Spirit, and in reliance upon this fact was empowered for the renewal of the metropolis (176).

Winter's criticism of the suburban church was, in the final analysis, a call for its reform and not a revolutionary demand for the smashing of idols. In his temperament and in the scope of his overall objective, Winter would stand in conspicuous contrast to Peter Berger, the last of the principal critics of contemporary religion and the least optimistic about its future.

The Noise of Solemn Assemblies

Each of the religious critics produced a different intellectual legacy for religion in America. Will Herberg was the first to openly tell the truth about American religion and thus initiate an endless round of truth-telling about religion that would extend well into the 1970s. Gibson Winter promoted alternative visions of ministry that provided the intellectual foundation of the experimental, socially and ethically relevant ministries of the 1960s. Peter Berger must certainly be regarded as the proximate intellectual force behind the anti-establishmentarian and anti-institutional impulses in contemporary American religious culture. Even his title suggested this was going to be the work of an iconoclast: *The Noise of Solemn Assemblies*, as the fronticepiece indicated, was drawn from the book of Amos:[23]

I hate, I despise your feasts, and I take no delight in your solemn assemblies. Even though you offer me your burnt offerings and cereal offerings,
I will not accept them, and the peace offerings of your fatted beasts I will not look upon. Take away from me the noise of your songs; to the melody of your harps I will not listen.
But let justice roll down like waters, and righteousness like an everflowing stream.
(Amos 5:21–24 [RSV])

The Noise of Solemn Assemblies was subtitled, "Christian Commitment and the Religious Establishment in America," but it could have been just as accurately subtitled, "A Sociologist Christian Looks at American Religion." For Berger's book was really two distinct, though related, essays. The first looked at American religion sociologically, attempting to analyze and describe what was the case from the standpoint of Berger's discipline. The second part of the book examined the results of these findings from the perspective of Christian faith. But from the very beginning, Berger showed his hand. The "religion business" might be doing very well, but that did not mean that God was pleased. Berger addressed his essay to a state of mind he believed might be called "a sort of Christian malaise." This malaise often expressed itself in the "embarrassment" that could be observed in intelligent Christians when they spoke about their churches. The essential question to be posed in the essay was, "Could a contemporary person be both a Christian and intellectually honest?" Berger, writing his essay for the National Student Christian Federation, observed that this question of religious identity came to the fore for many young people when they hit the college campus, a place charged with intellectual energy and full of skepticism about taken-for-granted truths. For some, this intellectual encounter marked a definitive break from their religious backgrounds. For others, the result was a "permanently defensive posture, a reaction all too often encouraged and nurtured by the religious organizations of the campus." For what was, quite possibly, the majority, the reaction was a vacillation between affirmation of and embarrassment about their religious beliefs.

Berger saw this last reaction as a "capitulation to permanent half-honesty" and regretted that it should be regarded by contemporary culture as a sign of maturity, while those who rebelled were regarded as immature. To the contrary, Berger argued that "the moments of intellectual passion, far from being phases in a process of 'growing up,' are the crucial points of decision in life." The years in which an individual was a student could be regarded as the years in which a basis for intellectual honesty or dishonesty, authenticity or inauthenticity, was formed. Religion, like any other commitment in life, deserved to be more than half-believed. But Berger went further to argue that there was something in the Christian faith that internally resisted its being interpreted as "the religious rationalization of the process of 'maturation.'" "We would maintain," he wrote, "that Christian commitment demands a relentless intellectual honesty, because it concerns God, who is truth, and who is offended if He is worshipped as anything less than truth" (10).

Berger believed that for his time the greatest challenge to Christian commitment was posed not by history, biology, or psychology, but by his own discipline, sociology. Religion had survived the intellectual challenges of higher criticism, Darwinism, and Freudianism, and sophisticated Christians had managed to incorporate them into their religious worldviews. It was, however, Berger's experience that when attention was directed to the sociological function of religion, many of the same people expressed shock and dismay. This was to be expected in societies where religion had become "only a matter of social establishment, a part of the taken-for-granted order of society" (12). To illustrate this point, Berger referred to the passage in Matthew 10:16, where Jesus enjoins his disciples to be "wise as serpents and innocent as doves." Wise, he noted, meant sensible or prudent, or to be practically intelligent. His meaning of innocence, however, was not, as one might suppose, "unknowing," but rather "unmixed" or "pure." If Christians were to be "unmixed," they must resist the temptation to "mix" the message of God's love with the messages of this world. Thus began Berger's attacks on syncretism and on popular religion, for to hold such a popular notion, that the gospel brought with it mental health and was validated in its promotion of social progress, was to "mix" it and thus to lose innocence. What passed for innocence by contrast in the church was too often plain stupidity. Gently biting the hand that fed him, Berger noted that campus religious organizations were "all too often the gathering place for the most conformist, the most anti-intellectual, the most prejudiced segment of the campus population." Moreover, the view of society held by clergy he believed to be "often a collection plate for every delusion to be found in the market." Some of the most apparently committed Christians, lay and clergy alike, therefore, were those who were also committed to lifelong acts of self-deception (13–14).

To counter this bad faith and intellectual dishonesty, Berger proposed that idols be unmasked so that the true God could be seen. The tool he proposed for such debunking was, not surprisingly, sociology. In Berger's view, the sociologist was peculiarly able to help examine the truth of religious claims because of his or her nagging propensity to point out the truths of everyday existence. "Again and again," he wrote, "the sociologist will find himself addressing those who would seek the truth in the clouds, pointing out to them what is to be found at their very feet, and telling them that this is also the truth and that the truth of the sky must be reconciled with the truth as it exists on earth" (15). The insistence upon the unity of truth was the cornerstone for all intellectual integrity and for courage in the Christian faith. What Aquinas had done to reconcile Aristotelian philosophy with Christian revelation and what biblical criticism had done to square scripture and history, Berger now proposed to do with social reality and Christian belief. If God was truth, then the believer had nothing to fear from the truth uncovered by this kind of inquiry. Still, sociological analysis carried some kind of risks for the fainthearted and particularly for those engaged in popular religion: "It is only fair to add that the decision to see clearly at all cost may well be to insights which destroy the various elements with which all of us seek to 'mix' the Gospel—such as the delusion that the Christian faith is socially useful or acceptable" (16).

Berger began the first major division of his essay—the sociologist's part, which he called the nature of the religious establishment—with a look at the "American Situation." Here his basic point was that America represented the future more than any other contemporary society, for it was in America that the industrial revolution had most completely transformed a whole culture (19).

Against this social-historical context of change and innovation, Berger sought to depict the situation of religion in America. Bracketing his Christian faith for the time being, Berger wrote as a social scientist and observed the same paradox that had bothered Will Herberg, namely, the simultaneous growth of the popularity of religion and an increase in secularization. To account for the first part of the perplexing equation, Berger cited the then-familiar statistics. In a country whose regard of religion had been noticed even a century before by Tocqueville, the social prestige of religion had never been higher. The percentage of the American population belonging to a church had risen from 43 percent in 1920 to an estimated 66 percent in 1960. Berger also drew attention to the place of religious discourse in intellectual magazines, the growth of religious publishing, the growing number of religion departments in colleges and universities, and the heightened degree of religious rhetoric to be found in American politics. The place of religion in American society had become secure, even taken for granted, and in this sense it could be said that in America there existed a de facto establishment of religion (33).

As for the second part of the paradox, America's secularity, Berger needed to look no further for evidence than to the statements of organized religion's spokespersons. "On the one hand," he wrote, "[they] may praise America for its religious stance and hold the country up as an example to the rest of the world. On the other hand, they may complain about what they themselves call the increasing secularization of American life" (34). Religious leaders themselves were thus uncomfortably aware that religious motives appeared to be irrelevant to large areas of economic, political, and social life. Moreover, Berger argued that, without risk of much exaggeration, one could say that the religious institution was irrelevant to any of the revolutionary forces transforming American society. Denominational or ecumenical bodies might well make social pronouncements on current issues. Back in the local church, however, members represented the "economic outlook of the small business man" and, as C. Wright Mills had predicted, denied the reality of class while thoroughly immersing themselves in a radically new class system (36). The social pronouncements of solemn assemblies did not reach the church at the local level. Berger also dismissed as a delusion the belief of clergy, that what they said on Sunday morning had an effect on what their church members did the rest of the week. As important as this belief might be to maintaining the self-image of the minister, it was mistaken: "When our typical church member leaves suburbia in the morning, he leaves behind him the person who played with the children, mowed the lawn, chatted with the neighbors—and went to church. His actions now become dominated by a radically different logic—the logic of business, industry, politics, or whatever sector of public life the individual is related to" (37).

Far from being the most important aspect of people's lives, religion turned out to be a "leisure time activity." Berger, the sociologist, sensed a challenge. For if religion was so largely irrelevant to social life, and a weekend activity akin to bowling, why was it accorded so much prestige in American society? For anything to be assigned that much prominence in a society, it was axiomatic to the sociologist that that thing be functional to that society. For religion to be popular, it had to "fulfil a need, have social value, probably be conducive to the maintenance of the society in question." Berger explained American religion's functionality with the concept of cultural religion (38).

The term "cultural religion" was adapted from the earlier term of cultural Protestantism, which was first used by German theologians and philosophers to describe the great nineteenth-century general assumption that German religion and culture formed a "harmonious whole." As nineteenth-century German Protestant culture achieved a high degree of consensus, so too, Berger believed, had contemporary American culture reached a remarkable level of "cohesion and consistency in terms of its values" (40). In practice, religion functioned to promote cohesion and mold consensus in American society, and to prove the point Berger cited

Robert and Helen Lynd's second Middletown study. For those living in Middletown, the Lynds had written, "the role of religion is not to raise troublesome questions and to force attention between values and current practice."[24] Rather, religion served to undergird the value system of the community, what the Lynds had called in their case "the Middletown spirit." Going to church thus became a kind of "moral life insurance policy" (40). For Berger, the implications of this attitude were clear. Religious institutions no longer generated their own values; rather, they ratified and sanctified the values prevalent in the general community. In fact, the difference between the values endorsed by the religious institution and those promoted by educational and political institutions was negligible, and boiled down mainly to a difference in the amount of religious rhetoric employed. Even here, however, Berger believed that the difference between the churches and other institutions was not sharp. Putting it simply, he wrote, "the churches operate with secular values, while the secular institutions are permeated with religious terminology" (41). Such terminology, though derived from the so-called "Judaeo-Christian tradition," had been "radically voided" of its traditional religious content. It now supported a vague religiousness Herberg had termed "the common faith" and Martin Marty had described as "religion-in-general."[25] In terms of values held, it was nearly impossible to pick out the religious. Berger believed that "church membership in no way means adherence to a set of values at variance with those of the general society; rather, it meant a stronger and more explicitly religious explanation of the same values held by the community at large" (41).

Closely following Herberg's discussion of Americans' "common faith," Berger outlined the contents of this cultural religion. The common faith of contemporary culture was intensely this-worldly. Religion was a matter of morals and psychology, of relations between human beings and not between humanity and divinity. Even prayer, that most spiritual of activities, became an occasion for "moral preachment" or "psychological manipulation." This trend also undermined attempts to grapple with religion's intellectual dimensions. Even among the clergy, theology was "rather a bad word, something that one may leave to eccentric seminary professors but that has little relevance to the on-going business of both corporate and individual religious life." With this anti-intellectual bias to contemporary religion, no wonder the truth of religious claims appeared to matter so little (42).

Another characteristic of the common faith was success competitively achieved. A stranger to American culture who had read the sayings of Jesus relating to the lilies of the field might expect that the Christian churches would find themselves in tension with this value, but he would find them instead maintaining that the best argument "for morality itself is that it does not hinder success and might even help in achieving it" (43). An additional central value was activism. This carried with it a denigration of the contemplative life. Prayer, like theology, was the province of experts, and the person who took intellectual or spiritual matters seriously had no place in the world of business or even in the ministry (45). The most successful ministers were not those who saw their office as part of the great prophetic tradition, but those who in "the eyes of their flock are still those who manage to be 'regular guys.'" As an intellectual, Berger clearly found this appalling. It represented the church's capitulation to the conformist social world of other-direction that Riesman had described. This predisposed clergy and their churches to a conservative, status-quo affirming viewpoint. Therefore, wrote Berger, "one sees ethical problems in divorce but not in marriage, in crime but not in the law, in rebellion rather than in conformity." The culture was also rendered unable to deal with tragedy, passion, and evil, and sought to shield its members from all "visible signs of suffering and degradation" (47–48).

All of these characterizations, Berger allowed, applied most strongly to the central core of American Protestantism: Methodists, Presbyterians, Baptists, and Congregationalists. However, these churches had also exerted strong cultural influence on American Anglicanism and Lutheranism, and even, to a lesser extent, on American Catholicism and Judaism. Indeed, Catholicism found some favor in Berger's eyes for its ability to maintain a critical tension with the dominant culture. These reservations aside, Berger argued that the apparent fact of a common faith brought into sharp relief American religion's most important social function, that of "symbolic integration" (51). The words "function" and "symbolic" integration echoed the religious sociology of Emile Durkheim and the functionalist theories of religion and their application associated with Bronislaw Malinowski and J. Milton Yinger.[26] Berger, however, was not interested in their stronger claim that religion always functioned to support society, only in suggesting that at least in the case of contemporary American society it did. If a person saw religion in America from this functionalist perspective, Berger allowed, the next step would be the not-all-together flattering move to think of contemporary religion as an anthropologist would. "The figure of the modern religious functionary solemnly sanctifying the values of society," he wrote, "begins to have a disturbing similarity to the shaman twirling the sacred rattles as the tribe goes about its ceremonial dances" (52).

Indeed, some observers had already noticed the similarities and Berger cited W. Lloyd Warner's analysis of Memorial Day ceremonies as a case in point.[27] More disturbing than these displays of civic religion, however, was religion when its function was also ideological. By ideological religion, Berger specifically meant to indicate religion that was being used as "a set of ideas serving the vested interest of a particular social group" (53). Suburban religion in modern society was particularly vulnerable to ideological religion, for as life became more complex and stressful, institutional religion provided a context for pretending that suburbanites lived in an old-fashioned, warm, simple, neighborly small town, instead of an exurban community dependent upon the city and its "rat race." "As the mortgages pile up and the ulcers keep growing," Berger wrote, "one mows one's lawn, gossips with the neighbors—and goes to worship in the white-washed monuments of the idealized past." Berger went on to make the point that while religion could rather easily integrate societies having little stress, it had a much greater tendency to become ideological in times of rapid social change and economic pressure. In times like those in which he was writing, Berger believed interest-serving religion was a highly likely outcome of cultural religion (57).

One of the interests 1950s religion served was political cohesion. In the real world of politics, there were many manifestations of a de facto religious establishment. People might debate the election prospects of a Protestant, Catholic, or Jewish candidate, but everyone knew an agnostic or atheist stood no chance at all. Affirmations of national religiosity appeared on stamps, coins, and currency. America's religion separated her from godless Communism. Prayers opened the events of political parties. Legislatures and the military had their paid chaplaincies. Perhaps the most significant fact of all was religion's tax-exempt status, which Berger believed was no less a support of religion than the direct subsidies provided for state churches in Europe. When combined with what had already been said about cultural religion, the implication of the establishment of religion was clear: "Affiliation with a religious denomination thus becomes *ipso facto* an act of allegiance to the common political creed. Disaffiliation, in turn, renders an individual not only religiously but also politically suspect." Indeed, in many states it was impossible for parents who professed no religious faith to adopt a child. And in some places avowed atheism was a bar to public office (63).

Americans were trained in this politically established cultural religion in the public schools. More and more "sectarian" religion was being forced out of the daily curricular routine. In its place, a religion of democracy was taught where "American values and American democracy take on the nature of a religious cult" (65). The public schools were but one place where this cult was promoted. In the military the co-optation of denominational religion into the nation's political religion was even more pronounced. There, the chaplains were expected not only to perform the rights and functions their religions dictated, but also to engage in what were called "nonsectarian" operations. The military called these operations a "character guidance program" and compelled soldiers and sailors to attend chaplains' lectures. The military conceived of this function in turns of morale building, but Berger thought of it along much more anthropological lines: "The religious functionary here performs the shamanic role par excellence—the religious indoctrination of the tribes' warriors as they go out to face the enemy" (67).

In the late 1950s frequent comparisons were beginning to be made between the Roman and American empires, much as earlier comparisons had been made between Great Britain and Rome. Berger believed the analogy fit indeed. In America as in Rome, religion was endorsed by the government because it was useful. This was only possible because it was assumed that the "religion of democracy" formed the lowest common denominator of all American religions in their particular and sectarian forms. One of the central tenets of this religion of democracy was tolerance, but it was tolerance with a peculiar flavor. While it provided that everyone should have the right to his or her own views, it demanded that those views not include intolerance as to the truth of the views of others. Americans thus had a right to any belief as long as they kept it to themselves. Those who rejected this condition lost all rights of conscience whatsoever. Berger pointed out that it was instructive that the Romans had persecuted early Christians not because of the Roman intolerance but because of Christian intolerance for the demands of Roman toleration (69).

Political religion served the function of symbolic integration as had cultural religion, but it served another purpose as well, that of social control. Religion then became a coercive means available to a society for bringing its deviant individuals or groups into line, and in alliance with the state it became an agent of social cohesion both for its own and for the state's purposes. Berger put it bluntly: "The same government budget that builds the walls of penitentiaries provides the salary of the prison chaplain. And, as any convict will tell you, the clergy are normally on the side of the cops" (72).

Beyond symbolic integration and social control, there was a third social function religion in America performed, a function peculiarly, if not uniquely, American—the function of status symbolism. To this dimension of the religious establishment in America Berger gave the rubric "social religion." Though Herberg and Winter had talked about the class and status aspects of religiosity, Berger was much more direct and incisive in his observations. He wrote about a Baptist salesman who became an Episcopalian sales executive and a Swedish Lutheran couple who joined the Presbyterian church because they concluded that becoming Episcopalian would be "pushing it socially." What Berger had described with these anecdotes was the process of social climbing by denominational switching. To characterize the phenomenon in such unequivocal terms was at this time a novelty, although throughout the sixties and the seventies it would become a much-sung refrain by sociologists of religion.

H. Richard Neibuhr, the premier analyst of denominationalism in the previous generation, had been much less suspicious than Berger of the motivations of denomination switchers. The charge that people would actually choose a church on the basis of what it could do for them socially had not appeared in print before, perhaps because ministers, as Berger noted, were the one group who "habitually" denied the reality of such charges due to the adverse impact on their own professional and religious identity if they proved true (75). It was not coincidental that most of the writing about religion in the United States was still being done by ordained clergy and Roman Catholics with religious vocations. It was only with Berger's generation that this tendency was reversed and the secular scholar of religion became more and more the rule. Still, the social fact of the link between religious affiliation and social status, Berger argued, was obliquely recognized by those who routinely denied it. Taking a page from Max Weber, Berger concluded that church membership had begun to perform this status function during the "frontier phase of American society," when the need arose to have an easily discernible sign of a person's creditworthiness. As society developed, membership in a particular congregation came to serve the purpose of social identification in combination with individuals' other voluntary associations. Thus, Holy Trinity Episcopal and the country club went together, as did membership in the Second Methodist Church with being a benevolent Elk. In a complex society like the United States there was a great need for "such badges of belonging." But the fact that one could signal others that one had "arrived" by eating filet mignon or "consuming" Congregationalism opened the way for persons to acquire religious affiliations purely or primarily for the sake of the social status they thereby attained. Like Winter, Berger found that religion in America was highly segregated by class, but here his concern was not so much the moral problem of class stratification and the unchurching of lower class persons; rather it was the role religion played in socializing people to the dominant middle-class values of the culture. Thus, where Winter was concerned that the mainline churches had failed the poor, Berger was interested in how Holiness sects and evangelical organizations served as stepping stones into the middle class. Berger found that "the values inculcated by the lower-class churches are conducive to upward movement within the class system. . . . Affiliation with a working-class church thus becomes the first step in the 'right' direction for individuals whose sights are set on the middle-class heaven above them" (76–77). All up and down the social-status scale, religion accommodated itself, indeed, identified itself with the social mores of its class setting (85).

Where social religion became an ethical problem for Berger was the point where ministers no longer dared stand for any unpopular moral imperatives before their flocks. Because the success of a particular ministry was gauged to be so utterly dependent upon the popularity of the minister, religions operating under the voluntary principle had a strong built-in bias against hearing words of judgment against their positions on such "secular" matters as segregation. To Berger, therefore, the fact that black Baptist ministers served as NAACP secretaries and white Baptist ministers headed white citizens' councils came as no surprise. In both cases the result could be a reflection of social religion. The fact that one side might have the moral high ground was, for the moment, beside the point. "The possibility of specifically religious values," Berger wrote, "apart from group interests or even opposed from them, is very rarely in evidence in the entire situation." Put differently, the only way to tell that the phenomena of social religion was absent would be if, for instance, the Montgomery bus boycott leadership had come from "those *white* groups whose (real or imagined) interests demand the continuation of segregation." Social religion appeared as a very strong force indeed (88).

There was also a psychological side to the religious establishment. This aspect Berger termed "psychological religion." The idea of psychological religion encompassed a variety of popular beliefs about the relation of religion to individual well-being that Berger summarized as follows:

"Religion is highly beneficial, perhaps even essential, to the psychological integration of the individual. Religion provides meaning and purpose in life. It gives inner strength to cope with both minor and major crises. It alleviates anxiety and makes for a mature approach to one's problems. It helps the individual to relate to others, in the family and beyond. In general, religion is conducive to mental health" (90).

Organized religion itself participated in psychological religion through the contemporary emphasis on the use of the language and tools of psychotherapy in the parish and in the relatively new profession of pastoral care. This was to say nothing of the promises made on behalf of religion by the Bishop Sheens and Norman Vincent Peales of the world. Religion all too often amounted to a "cult of reassurance" and moreover tended to reinforce individuals' racial and ethnic prejudices. Those individuals affirming a conventional religious outlook tended to hold the prejudices of their society with greater tenacity than those without the religious commitment (100–102).[28]

At this point, Berger returned to the riddle of religion's apparent prestige (and thus functionality) coupled with its seeming irrelevance. By now, he believed, the point had been adequately made: "The social irrelevance of the religious establishment is its functionality" (103). If contemporary religion had not been passive, if it challenged society and its institutions, it would not be as popular. Analytically, the popularity of religion in America was anything but a positive index of its independent influence upon the culture.

Berger stopped at this point before continuing with the second part of his argument, the portion where the Christian responded to the sociologist's findings. In the interlude between the book's two major parts, he posed two questions—what was left out of the analysis and what difference did the analysis make. As to the first question, Berger tried to be conciliatory. He had, he recognized, left out any mention of Reinhold Niebuhr, neo-orthodoxy, or other intellectual movements within Protestantism aimed at coming to terms realistically with the nature of human beings and their society. Also neglected were the well-intentioned attempts of denominational and ecumenical bodies to speak relevantly to social issues and problems. Still, there was very little real evidence, he thought, that the religious establishment had been affected either by the work of its intellectuals or the pronouncements of its solemn assemblies. The failure of integrationist manifestos to desegregate local congregations was a prime case in point (106–107).

The second question, "So what if the sociological analysis were true?," posed an additional challenge to Berger. If American society, though not perfect, was not perfectly evil, then even Berger had to acknowledge that for it to remain intact it needed integrative symbols. On this account a case could be made that religion, by contributing to the functioning of a society, contributed to the good of that society's members and to the society's own coherence and decency. But this defense of the religious establishment left one thing out in Berger's eyes; it left out the Christian faith. For those who wished to retain the assumption that Christianity had anything to do with the New Testament, the Old Testament, and the God of Moses, Kadesh, and Golgotha, to view religion as a means to support society was to tempt God and commit blasphemy. For followers of Jesus Christ, Berger claimed, the attention now had to turn from the acknowledgment of the religious establishment to the faithful imperative of its very "disestablishment" (112–113).

As Berger's description of the religious establishment had broken down into its components of cultural, political, social, and psychological religion, so too did his proposal for the future—what he called the "task of disestablishment"—subdivided into several smaller "tasks." The first of these was the task of personal conversion. Conversion was the first task because it was the oldest and the most basic requirement of Christian life. From the time of the New Testament, Berger wrote, the Christian tradition had "spoken of conversion as the decisive turning point that occurs in a human life as a result of encountering the message of Jesus Christ" (114). A person could not be said to possess the Christian faith without consciously coming to terms with its claim to truth and the demands such truths put on his or her life. The Christian life, Berger believed, began with an encounter. The problem with the religious establishment was its effectiveness at preventing this encounter from happening.

In attacking the religious establishment as an obstacle to Christian conversion, Berger was aware that he was covering ground already trod by Søren Kierkegaard's attack on "Christendom" and Barth's critique of theological liberalism. Though the form of his criticism was thus not unique, Berger was convinced that it was all the more applicable to the American situation. The suburban middle-class church with its family- and child-centered religiosity and progressive philosophy of religious education was peculiarly complicit in the process of closing the door to the religious encounter: "There occurs a process of religious inoculation by which small doses of Christianoid concepts and terminology are injected into consciousness. By the time the process is completed, the individual is effectively immunized by any real encounter with the Christian message" (116). The church experience produced people who were "religiously mature, socially respectable, and psychologically adjusted." But it did not produce people who could deal with the "naked horror of Calvary or the blazing glory of Easter." Indeed, Berger suggested, the church member thus socialized came to terms with the grittier elements of the Christian faith only at the peril of his or her social respectability and mental health. For Berger, being a Christian entailed a measure of alienation. The person who wanted to "encounter truth" must pay the price of being alone" (118–120). Berger was returning to the theme raised in the work of Riesman and his associates, the problem of achieving autonomy. Under his own category of authenticity, Berger addressed the need for Americans to shrug off the ideology of togetherness. Conversion was the only way to become authentically Christian, and authenticity required a believer to become autonomously Christian, to be independent of institutions and other-directedness in one's faith.

Like Herberg, Berger did not want to make the error of asserting that God could not come to those in suburban churches. Still, Berger believed that some situations made salvation more difficult than others. The ancient Hebrews left the fleshpots of Egypt behind and entered the wilderness, he pointed out, and because of this, their encounter with God was aided and became more authentic (123).

Berger called on Christian students to do much the same thing as William Whyte advised young people to do. They must fight the system, resist, rebel, not out of stupidity but out of a higher commitment. For Whyte the higher commitment had been the sanctity of the individual. For Berger the commitment was religious truth. Yet they were not so far apart, for as Berger pointed out, given the principle of the unity of all truth, "Christian truth and human integrity [could not be] contradictory." Berger and Whyte recognized that their calls to rebellion would be disappointing to the organization's representatives. Both dismissed this institutional disappointment as a cost of individual integrity (123).

Berger was laying the foundation for an anti-institutional religiosity wherein it would be understood that some of the most authentically Christian people would be found outside the church. If not the most faithful people, then at least the most authentic could already be found outside the church. Americans protested against the hypocrisy of religion, not publicly like Europe's intellectuals, but quietly, mostly through withdrawal. Still dissent was to be found if one looked: "The protest may be found in the colorful obscenities whispered by soldiers herded into an auditorium to listen to a lecture on 'character guidance' given by a military chaplain. It is the core of inner integrity of a skid-row derelict who will bear the shame of taking the supper but not of singing for it. It lies in the anger of a suburban housewife, one of the millions of our unchurched population, finally breaking out against the one visitor too many trying to entice her into his religious fellowship" (121). The discomfort of these authentic protestors was, in Berger's scheme, the precondition to the development of an authentic faith.

The next task in Berger's program for the disestablishment of religion he called the task of theological construction. The milieu of the current establishment, Berger argued, was unconducive to theology. Theologians rarely rose to positions of significance in the churches, any more than intellectuals rose to positions of power within the general culture. Both of these facts could be attributed to America's strong streak of anti-intellectualism. In the case of the church, however, Berger complained that such a bias was disastrous, for theology as the "intellectual articulation of the Christian faith" provided the criterion under which both institutional and personal aspects of the Christian life could be evaluated. In the absence of theological standards, other "dangerous criteria" tended to be substituted. In institutional matters, the criteria was expediency; in personal matters, it was experience (124).

Expediency and experience were not the tools chosen by the organized religion out of conscious deviousness, but rather the standards left when the church and its members had abandoned all attempts to rationally justify the faith. As a Lutheran, Berger knew that he could be accused of special pleading for a narrow confessionalism. This, he made clear, was not his intent. Instead, he wished to reject all things offered as substitutes for hard thinking about the Christian faith and life, including facile subscriptions to creedal formulas, be they from Rome, Geneva, or Augsburg. A disturbing sign, for Berger, of this anti-theological mood in the church could be found in the contemporary seminary. Expediency was corrupting the current generation of seminary students who had lost interest in the question "What is the truth?" and asked instead, "How can I preach this?" Berger's great fear was that the clergy itself was abandoning theology except as a rationalization for the rites of its profession, and "as a bag of rhetorical tricks to play the professional role with effect" (125).

This rise in clerical theological dishonesty was paralleled by the growth of emotionalism among the laity. Berger called the results of this trend a "cult of experience" and located its cultural roots in general American pragmatism. Its specific religious antecedents were to be found in the pietism of eighteenth- and nineteenth-century revivalism and more recently in theological liberalism. In different ways, both movements had encouraged believers to seek religious answers not in the reason of the mind but in the heart. Substituting feeling for thought, the individual made a move from asking "what is the truth?" to asking "what do I feel?" From here, Berger wrote, it was but a "step to the next question: 'how does this make me feel?'" The religious seeker soon became the "religious consumer" and could shop the "denominational supermarkets" seeking out "just the right combination of spiritual kicks and thrills to meet his particular psychological needs." The question "what is the truth?" no longer had any significance (126).

To Berger, the truth of religious claims was the fundamental datum worth knowing. Because truth claims could not be sorted out apart from intellectual activity, theology was important to anyone who truly wished to be a Christian. Theology was therefore too important to be left to the experts; it was every Christian's duty (127).

The critical power of theology would also prove to be the undoing of cultural religion. The identification of the Christian faith with one particular culture's value system would always paralyze its prophetic mission. In addition, the association of the faith with certain American cultural values was particularly problematic. Berger named this-worldliness, moralism, success, activism, conformity to cultural norms, and suppression of metaphysical concerns to be values that "must be in tension with the Christian view of the human condition" (132). To demonstrate his point, Berger turned again to the life of Jesus—who together with the prophets was the source of most of neo-orthodoxy's liberal criticisms of culture—and painted a Jesus who failed to measure up to many of the cultural values of contemporary American society. Jesus had proclaimed that the Kingdom of God was not of this world; he was a sabbath breaker; he associated with undesirables; and "in human terms his life was a total failure." Theology opened the way for Christians to feel the tension between the eschatological character of their faith and the this-worldliness of their culture; the tension of the cross with success and happiness (133).

Berger went so far as to challenge his readers to think how an intellectual passion for the faith might interrupt the easy flow of church life. What if people began thinking of the cross in less than mystical terms— and instead thought of it for what it was—a Roman method of execution? What if worshippers arrived on a Sunday morning to find in place of the cross a gilded miniature electric chair? What if the figure in the electrical chair was that of a black man? Berger recognized that the church's minister might have a hard time pitching for contributions to the building fund, yet added, "but on that morning he would have an excellent opportunity to preach the Gospel" (134).

Berger's hope was for an American Christianity patterned after the development of the Confessing Church in Nazi Germany. He quoted with approval from the Barmen Declaration of 1934:

We repudiate the false teaching that there are areas of our life in which we do not belong to Jesus Christ but another lord, areas in which we do not need justification and sanctification through him. . . . We repudiate the false teaching that the church can turn over the form of her message and ordinances at will according to some dominant ideological and political convictions. . . . We repudiate the false teaching that the church, in human self-esteem, can put the word and work of the Lord in the service of some wishes, purposes and plans or other, chosen according to desire (134).

These repudiations, Berger maintained, were as applicable to postwar America as they had been to Germany in the 1930s. They also gave a clue to the kind of theology Berger deemed constructive, for after quoting Barmen he went on to Karl Barth, one of the Declaration's principal authors on the church and society under Communism, and then went on to acknowledge a particular debt of gratitude to "what is popularily called the 'neo-orthodox movement.'" Under the heading of neo-orthodoxy, Berger grouped Barthian theology, the work of the Niebuhr brothers, Paul Tillich, and Dietrich Bonhoeffer. However, Berger hastened to add that what was most needed among Christians was not that they become partisans for neo-orthodoxy, but that they embark on theological inquiries of their own (135).

The third and last of the tasks of disestablishment was that of social engagement. If the great fact about the religious establishment was its social irrelevance, then the overall obligation of a disestablished Christianity was to be socially relevant, even at the cost of its former popularity. In choosing the term "engagement," Berger indicated his conviction that Christianity would always find itself historically situated and thus never in a position absolutely to affirm or deny cultural values. The term also conveyed his sense that the church must claim its freedom to make at least a "relative choice of courses through the terrain of culture" (138). Berger outlined four models for this social engagement, labeling them Christian diaconate, Christian action, Christian presence, and Christian dialogue.

Berger defined the Christian diaconate as "the helping outreach of the Christian community to individuals in distress" (140). Though in a modern society, earlier Christian concern might well be institutionalized in the programs and policies of the welfare state, there were still areas of life where no secular institution was likely to meet human needs adequately. What was distinctively Christian in concern for human suffering, Berger believed, was most likely to come out in nonorganized ways. He used the problem of aging as an example, for even after governments and markets had done their best, basic human needs would remain. These included psychological difficulties of retirement in an action-oriented culture, "those coming from the social fact that there is no real place for the aged in our modern nuclear family—and last, but not least, the perennial human problems of boredom, loneliness and the fear of death." The Christian diaconate could address these problems by providing meaningful activities for the elderly, by rejecting the bias against old age and perhaps even by helping families with older persons "overcome the egotism that uses economic alibies for unthinking cruelty" (143).

Christian action was the next model for engagement; a model that dealt not only with individuals but also tried to "induce social change in some direction thought desirable from the viewpoint of Christian ethics" (145). Such action could take a variety of forms, but included democratic political activity in support of laws or policies, nonviolent resistance to certain societal practices such as racial discrimination, and even violent revolution, as in the case of the Christian conspiracy against Hitler in 1944. Much of what already went on in the Catholic Church and Protestant denominations under the name of social action fit into this category. Though reluctant to completely dismiss social action, Berger expressed pessimism about the efficacy of political action conducted in the name of religion, finding it "difficult to imagine that these efforts will induce any significant changes in our social situation" (147).

The next model of social engagement also received a lukewarm endorsement from Berger. This model, "Christian presence," was defined as the "erection of Christian signs in the world." As a form of social engagement, Christian presence was particularly susceptible to the charge of being a form of quietism that avoided "real social issues." However, Berger allowed that there were times, when Christians otherwise had their hands tied, that Christian presence was the only appropriate response (147–148).

Berger's preferred form of social engagement was the way of "Christian dialogue." This he defined as "the attempt to engage the Christian faith in conversation with the world" (149). Looking at the contemporary situation, Berger found it remarkable how few places the society provided for people to come together and talk freely about human problems and social issues. Generally, when these issues were discussed at all, the people speaking about them spoke as negotiators, scientific researchers, executives, union leaders, or others called upon to represent the interests of an organization or group. The "academy movement," patterned after the lay theological academies in Europe, promised to fill this social gap by providing a place where contemporary human and ethical problems could be discussed. In this form of Christian service, the religious institution would make an invitation to a number of concerned and affected parties, without reference to their religious affiliations or lack thereof (149–152).

Berger went on to indicate examples of where such dialogue was taking place. Notably, all his examples took place at the supra-parish level. This, like the work of Gibson Winter, raised questions about the viability and ethical responsibility of the local congregation. Berger would have more to say on this, but it was clear that these "proto-encounter groups" played a key role in his vision of what was the appropriate response to the American situation as he had defined it. Christian dialogue, he believed, served the function of "de-ideologizing" society. If all groups, professions, and institutions were capable of, and inclined toward, producing illusions that rationalized their existence and ratified their social status, then Christian dialogue could perform the useful function of breaking down the myths and illusions by providing a place for the truth to be told (157).

If, as Berger had made it seem, the most profound thing a Christian could do about the emptiness of the religious establishment in America was to promote Christian dialogue, then where did that leave the church? Berger was frankly pessimistic about the church's ability to transcend the religious establishment. It might make a positive contribution to the task of personal conversion and even help its members on their way to theological construction. But aside from a ministry of the diaconate, its prospects for social engagement were slim. It was on this account that Berger took on other critics of contemporary religious life who, like Gibson Winter, had come to many of the same conclusions about the relation of church and society, but had concluded that the churches had within themselves the resources to respond to social needs. Berger singled out his fellow Lutheran Martin Marty for special criticism because of his "essential conservatism concerning the institutional forms of religion" (158). Marty, in his book, *The New Shape of American Religion*, had argued vehemently against the anti-institutional solutions of other contemporary religious critics: "Too often the critics of contemporary religion join in massive assault on congregation, seminary or denomination. New iconoclasts, they would shatter the forms that centuries have developed and the good sense of Christian people has brought to maturity" (159). Berger argued that for all the apparent common sense of Marty's position, the radical questioning of contemporary religious institutions was at least an intellectual duty for seekers of truth. Moreover, he went on to maintain that his neo-orthodox friends were wrong in asserting that, since in every age the church had had a socially conditioned form, the critical problem in the contemporary world was for the church to find its socially relevant expression. To the contrary, Berger believed, the essential problem was what individuals should do. Here Berger rejected the communitarianism of Gibson Winter and went even beyond Will Herberg in championing the radical individuality of Christian belief and practice.

Berger also argued against placing too much hope in institutional religion on the basis of the organizational limitations the local church faced. Regardless of its form, polity, or ecclesiology, the typical American congregation had strong built-in resistance to engaging society. It was true that there were exceptions to this rule, usually urban experimental parishes, but as Berger pointed out, "the typical situation of American Protestantism is not in East Harlem but in Westchester County." The bottom line was that "the sharp edge of Christian engagement with the modern world is not likely to be in the parish" (167). The radicalism of this position on acceptable forms for Christian endeavor became apparent in Berger's last chapter, entitled, "Postscript on Commitment." For although Berger had followed the form of the jeremiad and was prepared to offer a positive way out of the dire situation he had depicted, he was not willing to conclude in bad faith by urging his readers to "go out and get busy in the religious organization of [their] choice" (173). The tasks of disestablishment—personal conversion, honest intellectual search, and social engagement—he contended were Christian imperatives, yet none of the imperatives required the Christian to be a church member. Instead, their importance suggested that Christian membership was beside the point. Or, as Berger formulated it: "Involvement with organized religion is a Christian vocation." In using the category of vocation he relegated religious organizational involvement to an option without denigrating those who chose it as an option. He compared this vocation to the vocation of nursing. Nursing was important, but not everyone was required to be a nurse (174).

The contemporary context presented other vocational options to Christians. These choices reflected the changing historical context, but also mirrored the biblical texts that were chosen as appropriate to the times—and Berger made it clear that his preference was for the major and minor prophets rather than courtly histories and priestly codes of liturgical observance. The times, he argued, called for a differential appropriation of the biblical witness. A proposition such as *Extra Ecclesia nulla salus,* he wrote, "has one significance when Christians are dying in the arena and quite another when Christians are spectators in the stalls." Indeed, participation in organized religion under such a time as the Spanish Inquisition might actually be a seal of damnation. Berger backed up his reading of the Bible with the teachings of Jesus, particularly a text from the Sermon on the Mount (Matt. 7:21): "Not everyone who says to me, 'Lord, Lord,' shall enter the Kingdom of Heaven, but he who does the will of my Father who is in Heaven" (175).

Berger recognized that there was something frightening about such thinking, for participation in the life of the church ceased to be a guarantee that one had faith. It even raised the possibility that the prayers rising up on Sunday mornings from "countless pseudo-Gothic edifices across the land" might receive the same cool reception as that reported by Hosea (1:9): "You are not my people and I am not your God" (176).

Berger's book would have violated the form of the jeremiad, however, if he had ended with this pessimistic view of the possibilities of organized religious activity. The ultimate note of hope he sounded was that individuals were free from the bondage of the religious establishment. The good news was that one could be a Christian without the "solemn assemblies," but rather was free to work outside them to "let justice roll down like waters," as Amos had said God preferred anyway. Christians were even called to rebel: "Christians may freely choose *not* to become members of local congregations, *not* to identify themselves with a denomination, *not* to join the weekly traffic jam of the religious rush hour on Sunday morning" (177). The present era had enough organization men, Berger believed; what it most urgently needed now were insurrectionists and rebels. "We have had enough soft-spoken manners in the Christian community," Berger wrote; "we now need loud-mouthed morality" (178). Berger looked to the recent student uprisings in the South as examples of just the kind of loud-mouth morality that was called for. It was a morality free of liberal delusions about the future and conservative myths about the present. It was a rebellion that ignored the principles in favor of persons. The uprising of southern Christians was exactly in this spirit, for it was not against the "principle of segregation" or in favor of the "principle of democracy"; it was rather "against oppressors and for those they oppressed" (179). The Christian rebel was called to be free of institutional bondage, free of ideological baggage, and committed to truth, justice, and passion. And here Berger ended. The choice of establishment or rebellion was finally an individual one. He had set the choice before the people.

Two Kinds of Jeremiads
and the Three Faces of Neo-Orthodoxy

As argued in chapter 3, at a time when religion and culture are close to synonymous, the work of cultural critics is a form of religious critique. It is because of this basic fact that it makes sense to speak about the social criticism of the more secular critics as contributing to the understanding of the relation of religion and culture in the postwar era. But here we wish to consider a further aspect of the close relation of the work of cultural critics to that of the religious critics in the particular context of the 1950s. Afterwards we will come to an appraisal of what made the three religious jeremiads distinctive and of what they contributed to the intellectual attack on the religious synthesis of the 1950s.

The connections between the religious critics and their more secular social critic counterparts were manifold. At the most basic level, it is clear from the religious critics' footnotes that they drew a major part of their social critique and intellectual inspiration from the work of the secular critics. David Riesman's *The Lonely Crowd* and William Whyte's *Organization Man* figure prominently in all three jeremiads, and C. Wright Mills is also cited in all three. Even stronger connections exist between the secular and religious social critics at the level of intellectual concern. Herberg and Riesman shared a deep fear of social control and unthinking capitulation to conformity. Herberg's promotion of biblical religion as an answer to the problem of conformity was in line with Riesman's prescription of autonomy. The prophetic tradition of the Bible provided norms and standards for behavior and belief that were neither of the character of the deontological, rule-based, simple morality of the nineteenth century's inner-directed conformity, nor of the completely relative morality of the contemporary other-directed style of conformity, wherein anything was right so long as all members of a peer group did it together.

The roots of Winter's *Suburban Captivity* could be found in *The Organization Man* and in the work of C. Wright Mills. Throughout his book, Winter examined the ethos of the suburban church, of the denomination, and of the ideology of the organization that drove them both. But while Whyte's idea of the organization played a leading role throughout Winter's work, Winter ultimately was not satisfied with Whyte's admonition to rebel within the system. *Suburban Captivity* conveys a much greater class consciousness and class critique than *Organization Man*. Winter joined Mills in seeing the present predicament of middle-class culture, including suburban religion, as the outcome of two hundred years of industrial development. Rebelling within the system was an insufficient response, indeed an impotent response, to a corrupt and corrupting way of life. The solution proposed in Mills's work—that of class consciousness—proved to be the first step in Winter's plan for the renewal of the churches. The churches and their members must, he believed, first become aware of their domestication within the private sphere, their irrelevance to the public's spheres of political and economic life, and then make a conscious effort to hold themselves to more comprehensive standards, reaching out across the lines society had drawn to contain them. The particular standards Winter advocated were religious ethical standards derived from the biblical prophets and the teachings of Jesus. They were standards which insisted that religious ethics and practices extended to all facets of human life and were not contained in some restricted spiritual sphere. The standards were explicitly religious, but the process for their implementation was not; it was a Millsian strategy of consciousness raising.

Finally, viewed together, Peter Berger and Dwight Macdonald appear as soulmates. They both shared a style, a mastery of the formal essay, and an inclination to attack even their closest allies over comparatively minor points. These similarities, however, signaled a deeper affinity between their works. Berger and Macdonald were united in the belief that the "middlebrows" in their respective fields did not know what they were talking about and were in fact dangerous. For Macdonald, it was the intellectual supporters of popular culture who he feared would utterly destroy Shakespeare in the name of bringing him to the masses in bowdlerized form. For Berger, the enemies were the clergy who were content to preach a version of the gospel tailor-made to the needs of the culture in order that religion might remain popular on the culture's terms.

Macdonald's solution to his problem was a hermetically sealed elite high culture. Berger's solution was an anti-institutional movement of Christian elites. For one, the subject was culture and for the other it was Christian theology, but in both cases the intellectual move was the same; the beloved object could only be preserved by an elite intellectually committed to the highest standards and ready and willing to suffer unpopularity for the sake of the cause.

The three religious jeremiads had much in common with their secular antecedents. Yet they also represented three distinctive responses to the phenomena of religion's popularity in the postwar era. At the risk of being too typological, we will propose that these responses be viewed as three faces of a common neo-orthodoxy and be designated biblical neo-orthodoxy, ethical neo-orthodoxy, and theological neo-orthodoxy. There were other religious jeremiads that took suburban religion as a dominant subject. They both preceded and followed the work of Herberg, Winter, and Berger, but their exclusion in this work is for a purpose. First and most obviously, *Protestant, Catholic, Jew*, *The Suburban Captivity of Churches*, and *The Noise of Solemn Assemblies* proved to be, over time, the best-selling, most read, and most influential of their genre. More importantly, however, they represent the major intellectual lines of attack on postwar religion. The religious cultural criticism that has proven to have a more enduring reputation found in the work of Reinhold Niebuhr, Paul Tillich, Abraham Joshua Heschel, John Cogley, and Gustav Weigel—the last two Catholics, an as-yet unrepresented group in the religious-cultural dialogue—was arguably more satisfying because it was a more complex body of criticism that combined the different major approaches of critique. Yet because even these eminent theologians did not go beyond the outer bounds of the three faces of neo-orthodoxy, it is most instructive to view the lines of response in their pure form.

Will Herberg's concept of biblical faith best typified biblical neo-orthodoxy. As the name suggests, neo-orthodoxy involved a return to the tradition of "right opinion," or alternatively, "correct doctrine." Furthermore, as the "neo" implied, this return to tradition was not a return to precritical ways of thinking about faith and about the Bible. Fundamentalism was the anti-intellectual path of response to the Enlightenment, liberal theology, and to the findings of historical criticism of the Bible. Neo-orthodoxy, by contrast, accepted the methods of liberal theology and the findings of biblical criticism without accepting their conclusions. So it was with all three of the religious critics that their programs reflected the determination to reassert aspects of religious tradition in a post-liberal, post-critical way. Herberg's solution of biblical faith was characteristic in this regard. The assertion that the biblical tradition was normative for Jews and Christians did not depend on a doctrine of the verbal inspiration of the Bible. It did not require that factual claims made within the Bible—such as that Jonah spent three nights in the belly of a big fish—be true. This biblical neo-orthodoxy did not even require most of the material within the Bible to be incorrupt or textually well preserved in order to be useful. Rather, the biblical materials were of use as true standards and guides to behavior because they came out of the real human experiences of dealing with God. As such they revealed the ambiguity, tragedy, uncertainty, and grace of human life in relation with God. It is useful to remember that Herberg's appropriation of these materials was not only influenced by Niebuhr, but also by Martin Buber's and Paul Tillich's existentialism. The Bible, therefore, spoke most truly because it spoke most humanly and honestly to the depths of human joy and sadness, and of the limits of freedom and finitude. Herberg and others for whom neo-orthodoxy was of the biblical variety believed that the Bible spoke the words modern culture most needed to hear. They believed this to be true because the Bible spoke in a narrative form, in sayings and aphorisms, in parables and poetry to a culture that wanted black and white answers and sought to escape its own complexity by making of religion a place to find and ratify simple solutions.

Biblical neo-orthodoxy could afford to be interfaith. Since the Bible spoke most humanly, it also spoke most universally. Because it refrained from entering into the language of denominations, heresies, and theological parties, it could not be said to be true for Lutherans and not for Jews. Biblical neo-orthodoxy also served as a nice exterior standard for humanity in relationship with God and in community. Biblical neo-orthodoxy tended, therefore, to be antitheological. Of course, this propensity applied to the selections from the Bible that it deemed relevant. The teachings of Jesus and the book of Job, for example, were primary material. By contrast, Paul and his Christology did not receive much priority in the attentions of Herberg and others among the intellectual advocates of a renewed appreciation for the wisdom of the Bible. These included literary figures such as Archibald MacLeish, author of a Broadway drama about Job, and younger theologians such as Robert McAfee Brown, author of the enormously popular neo-orthodox book of theology for high school–aged Protestants entitled, *The Bible Speaks to You*.

To see the call to biblical religion as a form of intellectual attack on the popular identification of religion with culture, it must be remembered that the purpose of the jeremiad is to condemn some practices and convince one's audience to change its ways. In the hand of intellectuals like Herberg, biblical neo-orthodoxy said to the adherents of popular religion: "First of all, your religion is shallow. Secondly, it isn't *really* the Jewish or Christian faith you think it is." To the extent that Jewish and Christian Americans were disturbed about having a shallow faith, or concerned that they belonged to a religion which in practice corresponded to its historical foundations, the criticism was effective. What biblical neo-orthodoxy took away with one hand, it returned with the other, by saying, in effect: "The historic faith represented in the Bible is both authentically Jewish and Christian, and moreover, it is rich, deep, profound, faithful; not shallow."

Of the three faces of neo-orthodoxy, biblical neo-orthodoxy was the most gentle, least elite, and most popular. Its overall purpose was to constructively make a 5,000-year-old faith tradition existentially acceptable and relevant to twentieth-century youths and adults, by demonstrating that contemporary struggles and answers were to be found in the ancient book. This had been Herberg's theme in *Judaism and Modern Man* and would also be his purpose in his third book, *Four Existential Theologians*. Biblical neo-orthodoxy was at root a return to the basic source of American religiosity—the Bible—coupled with the claim that what was most ancient, biblical faith, was at the same time most modern.

Of the three religious critics, Gibson Winter most completely represented the second face of neo-orthodoxy, ethical neo-orthodoxy. Throughout his text Winter used terms such as "the responsible church" and "the responsible society." Responsibility is essentially a moral category, as are integrity, accountability, obligation, and faithfulness—other favorite words of Winter's. Winter also frequently used the term mission, a phrase that would be used frequently in the sixties and seventies to mean church activity in general. As Winter used it, mission was meant to convey the active mood that was desired within the church. To this way of thinking, the standard by which to judge religion was what it did. Ethical neo-orthodoxy, therefore, was characterized by the belief that religion and religious people were to be appraised on the basis of what they did in contradistinction to what they believed and what organizations they joined.

It is important to note that ethical neo-orthodoxy was not a standard that was completely independent of biblical neo-orthodoxy. Matthew 25—"Even as you have done it for the least of these, you have done it unto me"—and the book of James—"Faith without works is death" —were key texts for ethical neo-orthodox thinkers. But ethical neo-orthodoxy distinguished itself from the biblical variety by searching the Bible for overall lessons that could be reduced to simple propositions which could be used as ethical yardsticks. Ethical neo-orthodoxy therefore had much in common with the social gospel movement of the Progressive era. The social gospel's standard—"the Fatherhood of God and the brotherhood of mankind"—was another such attempt to make clear what biblical religion expected of human beings in a social context.

Given Winter's concern for urban areas, the poor, and the marginalized, and given his conviction that the response of the church was sub-Christian, it is not surprising that he conceived of the task of religion in moral terms. The problems in the contemporary world and religious establishment about which Winter was most concerned called for the kind of solution ethical neo-orthodoxy could provide.

Viewed as a form of attack upon the popular religious synthesis of the day, ethical neo-orthodoxy was notable for the sweep of its charges. Contemporary religion, it argued, was individually and corporately selfish. It sanctioned the lifestyle of the middle class while conveniently defining the lower class outside of the church's fellowship. Ethical neo-orthodoxy therefore found the religious culture of the 1950s defective in its concern for the poor and lacking in its social consciousness. Yet it also provided a positive standard by which Christians and their churches could redeem themselves. The name Christian would be deserved by individual and church alike if it was earned through faithful obedience to the ethical standards the Bible revealed as interpreted by contemporary social prophets. Such a program was well suited to the activist streak in the American character, and, of all of the intellectual criticisms of popular religion from the side of neo-orthodoxy, it probably had the greatest effect. The religious civil rights and antiwar movements, religious movements for and against abortion, women's rights, economic justice, against nuclear weaponry—indeed, a whole host of the religious special interest groups that have proliferated since the 1960s—owe in no small measure to the kind of thinking Gibson Winter was doing in *The Suburban Captivity of the Churches*. Viewed from the perspective of over thirty years, ethical neo-orthodoxy succeeded to an appreciable degree in convincing some religious persons that their faith commitments necessitated social and political commitments.

In chapter 2 a three-part model of religion was offered. It was argued that under the general title of religion at least three kinds of religion can be distinguished: *popular religion*, the religion of the general society; *ecclesiastical religion*, organized religion, usually having a professional cultic leadership; and *elite religion*, religion as conceived by intellectual elites within a culture such as monks, theologians, philosophers, and seminary professors. The contention of the analysis at that point was that religion in the 1950s was characterized by a great deal of overlap between the spheres of popular and ecclesiastical religion. It was further argued that elite religion exercised little or no influence over either of these spheres. It has been the purpose of this book to argue that the suburban jeremiads represented an attempt of elite religionists to try to reassert influence over ecclesiastical religion by persuading those persons simultaneously involved in ecclesiastical and popular forms of religion that the demands of being involved in ecclesiastical religion— Christianity or Judaism—required a rejection of much of the contents of popular religion. To a greater or lesser degree, this attempt to win the hearts and minds of those involved in churches and synagogues to elite conceptions of the duties and allegiances of Christianity and Judaism was present in all three varieties of neo-orthodoxy. It is, however, in theological neo-orthodoxy, as represented here by Peter Berger, that the case of the religious elites was put forward with the most force.

Theological neo-orthodoxy owed its roots most clearly to the so-called father of neo-orthodoxy, Karl Barth. Berger and others who would make the theological case against popular religion followed Barth in making a distinction between religion and Christian faith. Barth began by accepting the criticisms of nineteenth-century critics, philosophers, and anthropologists, such as Weber, Nietzsche, and Durkheim, about religion. Religion was an opiate of the people, a crutch for the fainthearted, a rationalization for wealth and privilege. Christian faith, however, was not a religion, Barth argued, for as soon as human beings made of Christianity a religion, it was no longer a faith. Even before Berger, theological neo-orthodoxy constituted an attack on the identification of a particular religion with the general religion of the culture. The only way for a particular religion to be authentic was for it not to be a religion at all, but rather "faith." The great claim of theological neo-orthodoxy was even more exclusive than this, however, for it was Barth's conviction that Christianity alone, with its access to revelation, constituted a "faith," while all other religions were simply that—"religions." Unlike biblical neo-orthodoxy under Herberg, theological neo-orthodoxy had no prospect of being interfaith.

Theological neo-orthodoxy also owed a debt of gratitude to Dietrich Bonhoeffer, because it was Bonhoeffer who went even further than Barth and argued that Christianity itself constituted a religion. Therefore

Christianity was something in which Christians should have little or no interest. Thus, even before Berger applied theological neo-orthodoxy to the American religious establishment in the late fifties, theological neo-orthodoxy had an anti-institutional foundation.

In Berger's hands, theological neo-orthodoxy constituted an attack not only on popular religion, but also on ecclesiastical religion, for to the degree that Christians were concerned with the success of their religion *as a religion*, they were participating in something other than the Christian faith. In the place of the secular standard of religion's success—the number of people professing adherence—Berger proposed a singular religious standard: intellectual truth. Though convinced like Barth that access to some truth was only through revelation in life and death of Jesus Christ, Berger maintained that such truth would not fall outside rationality. Intellectual honesty and integrity, therefore, favorite concepts of even secular intellectual elites, were the standards theological neo-orthodoxy proposed to judge faith by; any individual practice or belief should stand or fall accordingly.

Theological neo-orthodoxy was the most elite of the three faces of neo-orthodoxy. It punctured the pretensions of churches and religious leaders. Indeed, it even made organized religion seem at best a compromise, at worst unnecessary. It did, however, have positive appeal for some. For ministers, priests, seminarians, and college students who read Berger (or who read Bonhoeffer's *The Cost of Discipleship* or the work of Søren Kierkegaard, authors who in the late fifties and early sixties were just becoming popular in their own right in the academy), the message of theological neo-orthodoxy came as a relief. The intellectual compromises that the church and religious organizations seemed to inevitably make were both intelligible and tragic, but were not the end-all and be-all of Christian faith. For many, theological neo-orthodoxy would become the basis of an intellectually satisfying, noncompromising faith within, or outside, the compromised church.

The three forms of neo-orthodoxy—biblical, ethical, theological neo-orthodoxy—formed three separate but related attacks on the part of religious elites upon the religious cultural synthesis of their day. That the return to religion of the postwar period was under serious attack from the mid-1950s on, there can be no doubt. Since it was attacked from so many angles, it was unlikely that the synthesis would last long. Under the pressure of events—Selma and Birmingham, political assassinations and the Vietnam War—the central conviction of American culture in the 1950s, that everything within the country was basically good and under the special favor of God and his three favorite religions, was put sorely to test. The religious jeremiads in some ways simply represented an early attempt to put that conviction to the test on the grounds of biblical, ethical, and theological considerations. The legacy of such attacks, however, was greater than the mere fact of the shattering of such a key religious and cultural assumption. For though the religious critics were united in condemning the religious-cultural synthesis of 1950s America, they painted quite divergent alternative versions of what religious faith and practice should be. Once the religious cultural consensus was shattered, these visions of religious integrity would form part of the raw material out of which religion in the 1960s would construct its own theologies, movements, and identities. Sooner than perhaps any of popular religion's advocates and critics ever expected, the past became prologue.

5

Among the Ruins of Certainty: Religion in the Sixties

■

When one thinks of religion in the 1960s, it is common to associate it with its cultural outcroppings, the media images and news stories about religion. Thus among the religious things remembered most vividly are the Berrigan brothers and William Sloane Coffin counseling and exhorting young men not to submit themselves to the draft. Those alive during the sixties remember an antiwar movement involving not only the religious left, but also Richard J. Neuhaus, Abraham Joshua Heschel, and Michael Novak. They remember Bishop James Pike's public wonderings about the spirit world, and the image of his car abandoned in an arid and desolate place in Israel. They also might remember the colorful covers of Malcolm Boyd's books of angst-ridden popular prayer and religious poetry; books with titles like *Good Old Plastic Jesus* and *Are You Running with Me, Jesus?* Other strong sixties' images of religion include the *Time* magazine cover story that asked "Is God Dead?" and news photos of black ministers with neckties and white clergymen wearing collars together leading marches for civil rights in the deep South. Few whites who saw television interviews with Malcolm X in the early 1960s will ever be able to get rid of the image of the intense man who calmly pointed out that whites were devils and the implacable enemy of blacks. Martin Luther King, Jr.'s funeral was the decade's televised religious event that stuck in the mind in a way that was only equaled by Lee Harvey Oswald's on-screen murder and Neil

Armstrong's walk on the moon. Other salient images of religion in the 1960s endure—nuns in short, bright skirts, long-haired youths calling themselves Jesus freaks, ecumenical worship services featuring Protestant ministers with Roman Catholic priests and guitar music.

The major religious news stories of the sixties also indicated that a more radical, less conciliatory mood characterized the decade. In 1962, a group of ten Protestant denominations embarked on a process of discussing whether the differences separating Episcopalians, Methodists, Congregationalists, and Presbyterians could be cast aside to form a single church. The Second Vatican Council (1962–65) brought revolutionary changes to the Roman Catholic Church—that institution which in American religion had changed least in the fifties. Later in the decade came the news that denominations like the Protestant Episcopal and United Presbyterian churches and a few wealthy congregations like New York's Riverside Church were seriously considering a positive response to Black Power advocates led by James Forman, who demanded that they pay reparations for the collective misdeeds of white America in four hundred years of oppression against blacks. Other mainstream churches opened their doors to black radicals in need of a place to meet.[1] Meanwhile, the Six Day War in Israel recast American Jewish identity overnight, creating an interest in a Jewish state that had been noticeably lacking in the Jews of the American diaspora. In California, a different kind of countercultural movement was underway, as Episcopal priests such as Alan Watts and Jewish poets like Allen Ginsberg shed their mainstream upbringings to become advocates of Eastern religions and "forms of consciousness."

Not everything changed. Billy Graham still crusaded. Conservative Protestant and Pentecostal churches continued to grow exponentially. And some individuals maintained their fervent belief that prayer had a positive effect on plant growth. Still, these were not the news events they had been in the 1950s. At least in the media, religion wore a decidedly liberal face in the sixties. Even so, digging below the surface of news coverage about what was religiously new in the 1960s, one discovers that far from all religious individuals shed their conservative religious backgrounds, opinions, and practices. J. Howard Pew, the wealthy scion of the Sun Oil Company fortune, founded the Presbyterian Lay Committee to stand up to liberalizing trends in his denomination. A group of conservative but nonetheless prominent clergy from mainline Protestant denominations also sponsored an ongoing attack on the legitimacy of the National Council of Churches, the ecumenical discussions about church union, and liberal social action programs in general. They believed themselves to be the guardians of the churches against a liberal, clergy-led heresy of major proportions, as evidenced by the title of one of their tracts, *Your Church— Their Target*.[2] On the Catholic front, while Vatican II made eating meat on Fridays permissible for Roman Catholics, it did not necessarily make them feel good about it. A pre–Vatican II piety seriously contended with the new theological and ecclesiastical understandings of Vatican II. In many respects, large portions of the two dominant faith groups exhibited a traditional popular piety with remarkable staying power.

Given the persistence of religious outlooks that understood religion as sanctioning traditional families, providing first and foremost a personal relationship between God and the individual, and creating a better society only by creating better individuals, the flowering forth of 1960s religious liberalism is all the more striking. This book has been concerned with locating the origins of this liberal religious explosion and placing the transformations of American culture of the postwar period in their religious context. In the second chapter, a typology of religion and culture was offered that delineated three types of religion—popular, elite, and ecclesiastical. Using the typology, the religious culture of the 1950s was described as one in which all three forms of religion were in ascendancy in the culture and in fairly close convergence with one another. The next portion of the book developed the thought of a particular group of thinkers working in the 1950s and early 1960s, who focused on the religious nature of American culture. The remaining interpretive task is to show how the thought of these critics bore fruit in the three different types of religion in the sixties and in turn affected the role of religion in the society. The overall premise of this history is that the missing link between the wildly popular, culture-supporting religion of the 1950s and the confrontational, politically fractious religious ethos of the 1960s and following years is in large measure the intellectual move made by the critics of suburban religion.

When the solutions proposed by the writers of the jeremiads are examined in light of what came next in the sixties, it appears that these proposals formed the major basis for the directions elite and ecclesiastical religion would take. Acting on those proposals in the sixties also had consequences for the role of various forms of religion in the life of ordinary persons, and for the relationship of religion to the larger society. The balance of this book is about the impact of the ideas enunciated in the suburban jeremiads in three portions of the culture germane to the religious and social transition between the 1950s and the 1960s. These cultural segments are: religious bodies and their clergy; the religious academy; and religion in the common experience.

Religious Bodies and Their Clergy

As American clergy began to take to heart the ethical demands of their faith as interpreted by persons like Gibson Winter, they spoke and acted out on all manner of issues. Denominational statements proliferated during the sixties. Early successes in using moral suasion to change social behaviors, as for example in the case of Vanderbilt Divinity School, where students and faculty shamed a southern university into fair treatment of black students, led some religious leaders to overestimate their own political clout and social significance. Meanwhile, intramural debates over the authority for such acts were waged. The Methodist ethicist Paul Ramsey challenged the assumption of religious leaders and denominational decision-making bodies that they represented millions of church members when they made pronouncements on political issues. In his 1967 book, *Who Speaks for the Church?*,[3] Ramsey made it clear that, for Protestants at least, the authority to make decisions about denominational polity did not carry with it the authority to do much more than speak to the church. But while church leaders and academics fought over who could legitimately speak for the churches, a more apt question would have been, "Who listens?"

Whether individually in the pulpit or collectively in the councils of churches, interfaith groups, or denominational governing bodies, religious leaders spoke out, based upon the idea that if they spoke loudly and with one voice, their followers would have no choice but to accept the religious leaders' moral position or place themselves outside the religious fellowship. It was as if America's religious leadership had taken their cues from Berger and Herberg, who had said, in effect, tell them what it is to be authentically Christian or Jewish, do not stint on the truth, and if they don't like it, they will have to leave. Yet there was another possibility that neither Herberg, nor Berger, nor most religious elites had even considered. Just because members of religious groups heard conflicting messages from their churches, places of work, and political parties did not mean that they had to either accept their religious leader's view or get out. In fact, they tended to remain members of their churches and synagogues despite pronouncements from religious elites with which they disagreed. At the same time, they often did not like what they heard. It was perhaps at this point that neo-orthodoxy and, indeed, the assumptions on which religious elites based their actions, were most badly out of tune with the reality of religious America at large.

Even if the belief that religious ideas mattered greatly proved to be a fallacy, it was an understandable conviction for religious elites to embrace. For religious intellectuals like Berger, ideological seekers like Herberg, and clergy who had dedicated their lives to living in response to theological truths, religious ideas did matter. It was quite intelligible that their own experience of the relationship between values and behavior should be mistaken for human religious experience in general. The nature of fallacies is that they are the result of mistaking particular experience for general experience. It was intellectually clean and emotionally satisfying to accept Paul Tillich's definition of religion as ultimate concern and then to say—as did the neo-orthodox elites—that those who did not share their ultimate concern with biblical faith and relevant moral action were worshipping some other god than the God of Abraham, Isaac, and Jacob. But this neat theological standard, while perhaps useful for defining who was in some kind of Augustinian City of God, did not help address the problem of those who did not subscribe to the standard but still remained within the membership of actual churches in this world. To be sure, some religious people did vote with their feet. More, however, did so in subtle ways, remaining church members and investing loyalty in their local churches, in its small groups, and in their individual priests, ministers, or rabbis, but becoming disaffected with the programs and public-policy stands of counciliar and denominational bodies. Meanwhile, liberal church activists in nearly every denomination kept hammering away at a progressive social agenda, seeing their scars as signs of progress in the cause.

The politicization of organized religion was also intelligible. The 1960s posed ethical problems to the churches more acutely than had the early postwar years. The civil rights movement could not be avoided. Segregation was, as Winter had pointed out, endemic within the domestic sphere the church had chosen to occupy. Black Power was even more of a challenge, and even more divisive insofar as its demand was not for mere fair play, but for going the second mile in the form of reparations. Vietnam also divided the religious community unlike previous wars—the issue was the morality of a particular war when the government only provided the opportunity to religiously object to all war. Again and again, political questions of the day demanded religious answers.

The tension between ways of looking at and living religion were experienced most directly in the lives of the clergy. They were, by dint of position, cast in the role of liminal men and women. They were caught between masses of individuals comfortably practicing an ecclesiastical religion influenced by popular piety and the denominational elites and theologians who counseled the perfection of obedience to biblical ideals even if faithfulness brought unhappiness. The religious elites could afford to counsel, and even seek, this perfection, for they were institutionally insulated from religion as practiced by most people. Clergy, on the other hand, while wanting in their hearts to think as did their seminary professors and speak out courageously against every injustice as did denominational leaders, were confronted daily by the truth about ministry. People wanted clergy to be counselors and social directors, while receiving assurance and status confirmation from their church, not a more strenuous ethic by which to live.

The jeremiad's function in the 1950s and early 1960s was, as it had always been, social correction. Even so, the people it most worked to correct were the clergy. Jeremiads reinforce social systems by recalling their hearers to the claims that they have accepted in the past, and in the 1960s it was the clergy who had made the greatest personal and professional commitment to the faith and felt the sting of unfaithfulness most acutely. Working out of a biblical neo-orthodox framework, they tended to convert faith into ethics. Clergy thus found that their faith called them to do something about their cultural locations, and so brought their concern to bear on the congregations in which they worked. The more successful ones still tended to pastoral duties. Others cast all else aside and converted their church situations in the 1960s into a crisis.

One cleric who felt the sting more fiercely than most was a young minister in Syracuse, New York. The Reverend Grover E. Criswell, pastor of the Union Street Christian Church, resigned his pastorate from the pulpit in 1968, announcing to his congregation that he was awaiting assignment to a hospital chaplaincy. Criswell used the Sunday morning sermon to tell his congregation that he was leaving because he no longer thought very much of the parish and its ministry. He found "the most creative ministries have gone around the parish." He castigated the parish church for being "more concerned about the symbols of success than about ministry in the name of the Lord." He went on to apply the suburban jeremiad's critique to every aspect of church life. The parish church equated "love with a pleasantly abstract euphoria, and hope with an optimistic outlook on life." It was "comfortable in its self-centeredness." It had become a "club for the like-minded" whose tenets "merely echo[ed] the mores and values of Americanism."[4] The charges that had been leveled in books read by clergy were now being directed from the pulpit against an actual congregation. Nor was this an isolated instance, for by the late 1960s, all across the United States, ministers and priests were resigning from their parochial duties to pursue other expressions of ministry or other lines of work. Though most clergy used more tact than Criswell, their reasons for religious dissatisfaction with the parish ministry were not all that different from his.

The sociologist Benton Johnson has proposed that the reason Criswell and many others were unable to stay in the parish given the intelligentsia's critique of bourgeois religion was that the neo-orthodox clergy had no positive cure of souls. "Puritan preachers criticized the laity as harshly as did the pastor in Schenectady," Johnson writes, "but the doctrines available to them could cause their flocks to mend their ways because these doctrines spoke directly to their fears and their hopes. Modern evangelicals can command the laity's loyalty by promising material and spiritual advantages both here and hereafter. But religious liberals do not have the resources for engaging the laity that their predecessors had."[5] Criswell and other religious liberals had only the appeal to guilt available to them. Having already sided with the poor against the middle class, and having abandoned supernatural rewards and sanctions, a generation of jeremiad-influenced clergy lacked the language to communicate a way of being faithful to those laity prepared to hear in the familiar languages of individual piety, rewards, and sanctions. The 1950s religious boom brought many bright young persons into the mainstream churches' ordained ministry, but because they were generally of good educational stock and trained in neo-orthodox theology and higher criticism of the Bible, even the pastorally inclined could not bring themselves to say that heaven would make up for all past injustices, personal or otherwise.

Meanwhile, like Criswell, many clergy were headed into nonparish ministries. The jeremiads helped legitimate specialized ministries. At the same time, the success of the 1950s and the unrelieved economic boom funded an expansion of denominational staff and special ministry positions. The insulation from direct-market pressures functioned for Protestant clergy in much the same way as religious orders had for centuries for Catholics—it gave some clergy a place where they could develop separately from the opinions and interests of the laity. What Jeffrey Hadden later called the "gathering storm," to refer to an attitudinal cleavage between clergy and laypeople, was mitigated somewhat by proximity to laity for parish-based clergy, but almost not at all for specialized clergy.[6] Some clergy went into community organizing or another form of urban ministry, often funded by church judicatories, but only rarely paid for by those directly served. Others went to work as campus ministers, again supported by a larger church organization. On the campus, however, a study by Phillip Hammond released in 1966 demonstrated that campus ministers were much more permeable to the campus ethos— becoming quite tolerant of student morality and the atheism of faculty— than they were to the church ethos they supposedly represented.[7] Some clergy thus escaped to the campus from the church where they could represent the kind of religion a college student could believe in, but not the kind he or she would find after returning home upon graduation. Even those clergy who held on to their pastoral positions in local churches by being pragmatic found themselves wondering if they were successful because they were not being faithful.

Many of the effects discussed here were not evidenced until the late 1960s among Roman Catholics. When they came, however, they arrived with a vengeance. Priests were caught in the bind of conscience and a changing church, a church that, though hugely changed, was not changing quickly enough to keep up with American society. The papal encyclical letter *Humanae Vitae* was made available to the public on 29 July 1968. In it, Pope Paul VI showed definitively that there were certain issues about which he was not interested in change. One of these was contraception. Another had been clerical celibacy, which he took off the agenda of Vatican II in 1965. Not accommodating to the world on these issues would have its price as years went by, though the issue of clerical celibacy passed almost unnoticed at the time. The sharing of the magisterium, or teaching authority, with all the bishops of the church was also a promise that now seemed to have its limits, for the U.S. Catholic Bishops had themselves issued a statement of pastoral concern for married persons who continued to utilize artificial contraceptive measures, urging all confessors to exercise patience and understanding toward those persons. After the media turned the bishops' statement into a story of American bishops standing up to the Pope, they then needed to reverse course and make clear their full obedience to the teaching authority of the Pope.[8] By 1968, the Vatican's stands on clerical celibacy and contraceptive use, along with the relaxation of some religious obligations, were having an effect. An immediate drop in weekly attendance set in. Where 74 percent of Catholics had attended church on a typical Sunday in 1958, 65 percent did in 1968. That weekly attendance rate would drop further by 1973 to 55 percent, and again to 52 percent in 1978, where it would remain stable through the end of the 1980s.[9] The drop in religious observation could be viewed merely as what Catholics might do once released from church sanctions for not attending the mass. They became more like Protestants, who were likewise under no strong theological obligation for weekly church attendance, or like Jews, for whom the religious justification of weekly synagogue attendance was extremely weak.

Another trend was much more ominous for Catholics than mass attendance statistics: the decline in priestly vocations. Total enrollments in religious and diocesan seminaries dropped from the 1958–60 level of 49,100 seminarians to 43,500 in 1968. The decline to 88 percent of 1960 levels appears even more dramatic when the effects of the baby boom are taken into consideration. At a time when there were more and more Catholic young men in the population of potential priests, fewer and fewer were making themselves available to the church. At a press conference to discuss the trend, Father T. William Coyle expressed his concern about the nationwide decline in vocations, but expressed his view that the celibacy controversy was not immediately responsible, because the drop started before celibacy became a major issue.[10] Whether or not celibacy was the crucial issue for the young persons considering the priesthood or religious life, it was certainly true that sexuality issues, together with internal and external politics, had come to the fore in the Roman Catholic Church. Indeed, by the middle years of the 1960s, no religious body could any longer make a credible pretense to freedom from politics.

The Religious Academy

In May of 1958 the symposium hosted by John Cogley on "religion in a free society" revealed that the jeremiads had captured in a popular way the underlying mood of religious elites' view of popular and ecclesiastical religion. At that event, the religious giants of the day—Reinhold Niebuhr, Abraham Joshua Heschel, Paul Tillich, Gustave Weigel, and John Courtney

Murray—all expressed sentiments in keeping with the main thrust of the jeremiads then emerging. Religion was too precious a thing to be embraced for its culture-supporting effects. God also stood in judgment of human culture and even all human religion. This critical insistence that those who embraced religion were playing with fire would only intensify in the coming decade as religious intellectuals attempted to reclaim religious ideals and language from the uses to which they had been put in the 1950s. A theological war was being waged against the return to religion, and the three great jeremiads discussed in the previous chapter represented only the beginning of the elite attack on American religion as it was practiced in the popular and ecclesiastical spheres.

The intellectuals' debate over religion's place in society that was initiated in the 1950s by the suburban jeremiads continued and took on more complex forms in the next decade. What had begun at a fairly popular level was translated to a much more theoretical and scholarly level in the years that followed. The creation of the American Academy of Religion in 1962 was symptomatic of a broad-gauged change taking place; religious thought and thinking about religion was increasingly becoming more like other academic disciplines and was escaping the influence of religious sects and their clergy. The popular sociological speculations of self-educated amateurs like Will Herberg would also be increasingly replaced with the more rarefied discussion of civil religion led by Robert Bellah, on the one hand, and by the "scientific study of religion" movement led by Rodney Stark and Charles Glock, on the other.

Meanwhile, popular jeremiads continued to be produced. Any number of Martin Marty's books could be cited, with *Second Chance for American Protestants* and *A Nation of Behavers* good early and late examples, respectively, of the genre. After Vatican II had begun to transfer power to the laity in the form of parish councils and to strip away some of the distinctive features that made Roman Catholicism more than just another Christian denomination, Catholics began to make the case against their church that the writers of the suburban jeremiads had made against the Protestant and Jewish faiths. Portions of Garry Wills's *Bare Ruined Choirs* read as a scathing lament that the Roman Catholic Church had given up its treasure too easily and had only preserved it as long as it had for the wrong reasons. Wills proved himself every bit as trenchant as Peter Berger in condemning hypocritical religious faith. In 1965 a Canadian journalist, Pierre Berton, wrote a book called *The Comfortable Pew* about the lukewarmness of religious commitment in his own country, which became not only the best-selling book by a Canadian to that date in

Canada, but also a runaway hit in the United States and the United Kingdom. The early jeremiads had made their mark, and the popular battle for the hearts and minds of religious people continued.[11]

As the religion-and-society debate developed in the academy and the jeremiad became an even more popular form of discourse in the religious community in the 1960s, the concerns raised by Herberg, Winter, and Berger began to be addressed in two distinct communities of discourse. The first was a group of academic theologians who sought to free God or, if that proved impossible, at least theology, from cultural captivity. The second community of discourse was a group of writers still attempting to address people of faith in general. Each of these groups continued to probe the relation between religion and society, but did so in ways that departed significantly from the fifties' critics.

Among the theological discoveries of the 1950s for American theologians were the writings left behind by the German theologian Dietrich Bonhoeffer. These writings reached their full impact in the 1960s. Peter Berger had been ahead of his time in incorporating Bonhoeffer's radical neo-orthodox views into *The Noise of Solemn Assemblies*, particularly Bonhoeffer's call for a "religionless Christianity." Bonhoeffer, a pastor, theologian, and leader of the Confessing Church, the church that openly resisted National Socialism in Hitler's Germany, had left behind a testament of sorts in his *Letters and Papers from Prison*.[12] Like Karl Barth, Bonhoeffer made a sharp distinction between religion as a culture-binding set of myths and rituals and Christianity as biblical faith, or the following of Christ, son of the one true God. He had also used the provocative words of death and absence to describe Western culture's relationship to God. Now, in the 1960s, a group of American theologians would explore and extend these insights further under the interchangeable names death-of-God theology and radical theology.

One logical outcome of the theological neo-orthodoxy represented by Peter Berger was the death-of-God theology. This was a form of religious criticism of contemporary religion conducted by religious intellectuals without the least thought of how it might impact the local church. At one level, it was a kind of intellectual's revenge on the church-culture synthesis. It was theology for its own sake, rather than for the church's sake, but also perhaps for the sake of the religious intellectuals themselves. Radical theology tended to divide into two camps, those who saw secularity as an accomplished fact and problem, such as Gabriel Vahanian and Berger himself, and those who embraced the secular world as a positive good, such as William Hamilton, Thomas J. J. Altizer, and Harvey Cox. On the whole, the former camp continued Berger's line of critique, while the latter group of writers accepted his account of the contemporary atheistic world and said in effect, "Yes, isn't it wonderful?" Paul Van Buren and Richard Rubenstein were two other thinkers associated with the movement whose work developed along less partisan lines.

Gabriel Vahanian was the first 1960s theologian to proclaim the death of God. In his 1961 book, *The Death of God*, Vahanian argued that the death of God was an accomplished cultural fact because modern culture had no place for God. The culture was immanentist, while the biblical view necessary for God to exist was transcendentalist. Modern persons could not, therefore, be fully acculturated and still affirm the reality of a wholly other being. Vahanian further believed that all the religiosity of the fifties revival simply proved his point. It was a religiosity, a "desperate caricature" of Christian faith, and in no way countered the modern human being's loss of a sense of transcendence.[13] The issue, therefore, was not the actual existence of God, but whether anyone was capable of worshipping the real God rather than themselves under the name of God.

More radical in his claims about the death of God was William Hamilton, a theologian at Colgate Rochester Divinity School. In an essay entitled, "Thursday's Child: The Theologian Today and Tomorrow," Hamilton suggested that the modern theologian did not actually believe in God, or that a God really existed. God, "the problem solver" and "need fulfiller," had disappeared from human experience. Hamilton tried for a while to maintain an expectancy for a God with other, less useful qualities, but eventually gave up that hope as well. His theological musings then shifted to the centrality of Jesus as showing Christians how to live in the world. Jesus was important not because he was divine, but because he was worldly, fully immersed in living, and waiting for appropriation by moderns. Jesus, in Hamilton's world, was "the place to be."[14]

Thomas J. J. Altizer issued the most sensational version of death-of-God theology. Altizer, an assistant professor at Emory University, blended all the sources of death-of-God thinking he could find in philosophy and literature—Nietzsche, Hegel, William Blake, Kierkegaard, and Bonhoeffer—and presented a case for "Christian atheism." If Hegel was right in claiming that the real must become concrete, then, Altizer reasoned, for Christians to claim that God had become human in Jesus Christ meant that God had ceased to be God by really, concretely becoming human. The source of Christian life was therefore to be found only in the radically immanent life of Jesus. Being a Christian required having no supernatural, transcendent God, for the true Christian knew that God had, of God's own volition, ceased to exist.[15]

For Paul Van Buren, God was not alive or dead. Statements about God were meaningless because they could not be verified. Verification of statements about anything in the modern, empirical, scientific, and secular world required that persons be able to specify what would count as evidence for or against the truth of each of those statements. Reference to a being operating outside the laws of nature and the realm of verifiable experience made speaking about God either impossible or misleading. To say that God existed was every bit as meaningless as to say that God did not exist. Van Buren, therefore, urged a moratorium on "God talk," arguing that most statements about God could be converted into statements about human beings and thus rendered meaningful in a secular sense. He pointed to the life of Jesus as unique, since he had shown how to be free by freeing others. To those who asked what was so special about Jesus if attendant theological claims were put aside, Van Buren was forced to admit there was nothing to prefer Jesus over Gandhi, the Buddha, or any other exemplary life, except that Jesus was part of his tradition and Jesus' life spoke to him. This kind of challenge subsequently led Van Buren to concentrate his work on interfaith issues.[16]

Richard L. Rubenstein contributed to the death-of-God theology from a distinctly different perspective. Writing first and foremost as a Jew in *After Auschwitz*, Rubenstein asked how it was possible for Jews to accept the traditional idea of God as a loving, caring being who created and sustained the world in the face of the evil of the Holocaust. The failure of God to intervene in the fate of millions of God's chosen people in the course of World War II made reliance upon that God both ludicrous and tragic. The lesson for all people, but for Jews particularly, was that they must rely upon themselves and not upon some deity. The God who changed history for the ancient Hebrews was effectively dead.[17]

Roman Catholic theologians did not produce any literature for the death-of-God movement. Yet they too increasingly employed death and absence language to discuss the relation of God to culture in the sixties. When *Time* magazine did a cover story on the death-of-God theology, prominent Catholics were among those who commented. The Jesuit theologian John Courtney Murray pointed to the cultural reality of the "atheism of distraction." People were often, Murray said, "too damn busy" to concern themselves about God. Edward Schillebeeckx, a Dominican theologian, linked the demise of God to the links the church had made between

God and a culture whose time had passed: "God has disappeared because of the image of him that the church used for many, many ages." The doctrines that were supposed to explain and convey God to believers had also lost their power. Michael Novak, then a member of the Stanford philosophy department, wrote: "I do not understand God, nor the way in which he works. If, occasionally, I raise my heart in prayer, it is to no God I can see, or hear, or feel. It is to a God in as cold and obscure a polar night as any non-believer has known."[18]

Evaluating the impact of radical theology is difficult. The movement became a *cause célèbre* for a season and then disappeared so far as academic theologians were concerned. However, the impact on the larger public who never understood the arguments offered under the label "Death of God" was probably more profound. After *Time* asked, "Is God Dead?" on its cover of the 8 April 1966 issue, readers reacted with passion. Some were angry that this question was posed the same week Christians and Jews celebrated Easter and Passover. Others, like R. A. Ellsworth, a retired Army colonel from Laguna Hills, California, were more sweeping in their judgments. "Sir," Ellsworth wrote, "*Time*'s story is biased, pro-atheist and pro-Communist, shocking and entirely un-American." A Lutheran minister from Tustin, California, Clyde Showalter, wrote *Time* to advise, "Spend some time reading the Word of God rather than the word of men, and you will be writing not about 'the Death of God' but about the 'God of death.' I Corinthians 15:55–56."[19] The most succinct responses to Time's cover question came from Norine McGuire of Chicago and Richard L. Storatz of the University of Notre Dame, who wrote in to reply, "Yes" and "No," respectively. The most elliptical responses, predictably, came from those who had a professional stake in the matter, including Joseph Lewis, President of the Freethinkers of America—"Not only is God dead, he never was"—and a ministerial student named Wilmer Reichmann, Jr., who wrote in to say, "God is dead to those who wish him so; he lives for those who hope in him."[20]

While the readers of *Time* continued to wage theological battle for weeks on its letters-to-the-editor page, the general public was simply unsettled. People in the pews knew that God was alive and did not care about making sense to philosophers, but they were disturbed that theologians were saying these things at seminaries their monies helped to support. Theologians, previously accepted as the brilliant—though perhaps too esoteric—defenders of the faith, suddenly became suspect individuals. The result was a further isolation of religious thought from religious life.

Not all products of neo-orthodoxy were so rarefied as the death-of-God theology. At the very time when white academic theologians were debating exactly in what sense God was dead, another product of neo-orthodoxy was taking shape in African American and Latin American hands. Like earlier calls for a return to biblical religion, these theologies began with the Bible. But instead of reading the prophets back to the dominant culture (as had Herberg and Winter), the theologies of liberation read the Exodus story as the normative account of how God acted in human history. It concluded that God was on the side of the oppressed, that God sought the liberation of all people, and that the oppressed and not the oppressors were the people with whom the church was to cast its lot. Black and Latin American theology thus posed a new challenge to Euro-American religion and culture in terms of the biblical theology adopted in the previous generation. Key early texts for these movements, however, did not appear until late in the 1960s, when James Cone's *Black Theology and Black Power* (1969) was published, followed by the publication of Gustavo Guitierrez's *A Theology of Liberation* in 1971.

One book coming out of the religious academy did reach an immediate and vast audience in the 1960s. Its author was a young theologian from Harvard named Harvey Cox, and the book was *The Secular City*.[21] As a critique of contemporary religion and American life, the book initially appeared to be in the lineage of the suburban jeremiads of the previous decade. In other respects, *The Secular City* was the clearest indication available of how religious concern for contemporary society had moved on from the narrow focus on suburbs and suburban religion. Cox's whole treatise was meant to address the religion and culture problem just as the jeremiads had. Yet his intention was to bless many of the outcomes other writers found disturbing as the authentic outcome of biblical religion.

Harvey Cox's book was an even greater publishing event than the jeremiads that preceded it. Like Peter Berger, Cox wrote what would be his most widely read book on a commission from a student Christian group, in this case the National Student Christian Federation. Writing quickly, and directing himself to a lay audience, Cox wrote with both lucidity and passion, even if without precision. Though Cox wrote *The Secular City* as a tract for an upcoming student-movement conference, his text very quickly eclipsed its original purpose and within a year sold more than half a million copies. It would go on to sell more than a million copies over the next twenty-five years. More importantly, it would regularly find its way into the hands of the public and onto reading lists of college courses on religion, values, and American society for another fifteen years.

One of Cox's real accomplishments through his book was to help reintroduce Americans to the symbolic. Sigmund Freud's use of symbol had largely been domesticated to discussions of sexuality. Carl Jung had made, to this point, very little impact on American thinking. Rudolph Otto and Mircea Eliade were, by this time, read by graduate students and applied mostly to the religions of other times and cultures. But here, almost alone, Cox discussed symbols and society as they concerned modern American society. Cox also managed to connect these gleanings from cultural anthropology and phenomenological approaches to the study of religion with the concerns of neo-orthodoxy for a "biblical faith." In short, Cox had set about upon a synthetic task of major proportions. *The Secular City* would bring together the concerns of the secular critics about mass society with the religious critic's concerns for biblical faith, ethical practice, and a religionless Christianity *and* analyze the whole situation through lenses borrowed from Emile Durkheim and Bronislaw Malinowski. The synthetic character of Cox's approach explained part of the book's appeal. Americans love the thesis that ties up all loose ends. Yet Cox's content and his overall evaluation of the contemporary scene provide another clue to the book's popularity. For unlike the secular and religious jeremiads of the 1950s, Harvey Cox's *Secular City* was a profoundly optimistic account of the way the world was heading.

Secularization, Cox believed, occurred "only when the cosmopolitan confrontations of city living exposed the relativity of the myths men once thought were unquestionable" (1). People in all ages believed that the gods lived as they did. If the Greeks saw the cosmos as "an immensely expanded polis" and the people of the Middle Ages saw it as a feudal manor on an infinite scale, Cox believed it was no trick that his contemporaries should experience the universe as "the city of man." This city was "a field of human exploration and endeavor from which the gods had fled." The world had become a human task and a human responsibility and had been liberated from the closed-system worldviews that had always interpreted it in the past. There was no "out there" out there, no gods or fates that could account for what went on in the modern world. Secularization, Cox wrote, happened when human beings turned their attentions "away from worlds beyond and toward this world and this time." He pointed out that secularization's Latin root, *saeculum*, meant "this present age," and recalled Dietrich Bonhoeffer's 1944 observation that secularization represented "man's coming of age." Cox went on to dismiss the idea that secularization was anticlerical or antireligious in nature: "The forces of secularization have no serious interest in persecuting religion. Secularization simply bypasses and undercuts religion and goes on to other things. It has relativized religious world views and thus rendered them innocuous. Religion has been privatized." What then of religion in the modern world? Modern religion was filled with believers convinced that they could be wrong and devotees persuaded "that there are more important things than dying for the faith." "The gods of traditional religion," Cox concluded, "live on as private fetishes or the patrons of congenial groups, but they play no significant role in the public life of the secular metropolis" (1–2).

If all the preceding statements concerning the state of religion in the modern world could be seen as troubling things for a young theologian to be telling a body of Christian students, what followed was even more startling. Secularization was not only inevitable, Cox contended, it was good, for it allowed human beings to see once and for all their proper place in the scheme of things. Secularization enabled them to see that in most human affairs the future was in their hands alone, and they could not displace responsibility off on some tribal god nor on some metaphysical system of spirits or life forces. The fate of the world, not to mention the structure of community, work, play, sexuality, and the church, was in human hands. Cox's central thesis, therefore, was one that combined a consistent antimetaphysicalism with a strong ethic of human responsibility. Ultimately, Cox would ground his position—like the neo-orthodox thinkers he followed—on a reading of the Bible as a normative description of what God intended for human beings. For Cox, secularization was, in the borrowed language of the German theologian Friedrich Gotgarten, "the legitimate consequence of the impact of biblical faith on history" (15). Cox laid the development of natural science, of democratic political institutions, and of cultural pluralism at the door of the Bible. Cox believed that biblical faith had contributed to secularization in three distinct ways: by disenchanting nature, desacralizing politics, and deconsecrating values. These processes he linked, respectively, to the biblical events of Creation, Exodus, and the Covenant at Mount Sinai.

Because the Bible affirmed that God created everything, the natural world was no longer an enchanted forest, where suns and moons exerted their wills upon human beings. Once the world became predictable, natural science became possible. Democracy was likewise made possible by the Bible, for as Cox pointed out, in a society where rulers ruled by divine right and where political authority was directly legitimized by religion, significant political and social change was almost "impossible" (22). The Exodus represented not only the pivotal event in the life of subject Hebrew people, but the potential deliverance of all people from claims of sacrapolitical authority.

To natural science and democracy, Cox added the goods of cultural relativism and pluralism. Historical relativism, Cox wrote, was the "end product of secularization. It is the non-religious expression of what Jews have expressed in their consistent opposition to idols, and Christians in their sporadic attacks on icons" (29). The consequences of biblically in-spired iconoclasm were far reaching. If individuals could understand their values to be historically conditioned, then each was in the uncom-fortable position of knowing that "the rules which guide his ethical life will seem just as outmoded to his descendants as some of his ancestor's practices now appear to him" (27). The loss of ethical certainty would clearly be disturbing to a wide range of Cox's readers, so he sought to reassure them that such a loss did not necessarily have to result in solip-sism, but rather could promote a much more constructive outcome. With the awareness that every individual's perspective was limited, a recogni-tion would grow that no one had the right to inflict his or her views on anyone else (27–28). Biblical faith had thus set the terms of faithful secularity. Now, Cox believed, it was the task of the community of the faithful to realize that biblical vision.

While the entire first portion of *The Secular City* amounted to a theo-logical celebration of the possibilities of the liberal, secular society, Cox turned in the second part of his book to radical proposals for the role of the church in the secular city. The church's proper role was to be God's avant-garde. Cox's essential critique of the church was that it was too tied to a particular answer to the theological question of the *form* of the church when the only important question was the *work* of the church. If the church was to be God's avant-garde then it must be prepared to do and become what it must in order to fulfill its function. One of the places where Cox's prescription for the churches went well beyond the subur-ban jeremiads was when he wrote of the need for the churches to heal the "powerlessness of certain groups in the cities." Here his writing took on a radical, biting edge. Groups of racial minorities and the poor in the con-temporary city were powerless in controlling their destinies, but worse, the churches helped keep them that way. The church's first response to the problems of the inner city in Cox's view had been simply to run away. Struck by pangs of conscience out in the suburbs, the church's next response had been to mount and finance urban ministries of various sorts. Cox faulted these ministries—some of Gibson Winter's very solutions to suburban captivity—as largely ill-conceived, flimsy, self-deluding, and even patronizing (120).

Cox singled out the weekend work camp in which suburban youth traveled downtown in order to help paint and fix up the ghetto as a particularly abusive practice. The work camps, he wrote, "have the advantage of bringing young people in an area they might never have seen otherwise, but the psychology of the situation is so unfavorable that, on balance, work camps probably do more harm than good." The weekend work camp did real harm in at least three ways, Cox believed. First, the suburban paint brigades often substituted for the pressure that should have been placed on landlords to maintain their rental property in the neighborhoods where the vast majority of residents did not own their own homes. The psychology of the work camp was likewise wrong, for it fostered an "attitude of dependency on the part of those who ought to be stimulated to take some action." Finally, the work camp was defective because it perpetuated an "attitude of condescension in those who should be confronted by their guilt in the structural inequities of metropolis" (121). Cox noted accurately that few suburban youngsters came home from these experiences and asked their parents about discriminatory zoning patterns, bank redlining, or the benefits that they themselves derived from unequal tax and service burdens of inner-city and suburban people in the metropolis. Instead, the leaders of these work camps usually wanted participants to have "a good experience" and "to return to their homes with less rancor and prejudice against inner-city people, especially Negroes." Programmatically, these camps were designed to foster personal relationships across lines of race and class. Yet, Cox pointed out, this strategy flew in the face of the contemporary civil rights movement, which had demonstrated that blacks were not as interested in "winning friends" as in "winning freedom, not interpersonal warmth but institutional justice" (122). In more general terms, Cox characterized the poor of the inner city as "people trapped in the prison house of urban injustice." Suburbanites then were seen as those on the "outside." The church needed to recognize that "inner-city people represent the oppressed to whom Jesus said he had come to bring not warm words but liberty" (124). This liberation motif is one that grew in use in the coming years.

Cox went on to suggest that the real work of the church was to more truly secularize sexuality, work, higher education and even talk about God. As it had mystified the understanding of all these aspects of the culture, so it was called to demystify them for the sake of the culture. A later reader is amazed at Cox's proposals for their inherent optimism, hope, and sense that the era of the sixties was on the brink of realizing the dreams of all human history. It is hard to find quite such a culture embracing religious books before or after *The Secular City*. In 1965 Cox stood at a divide between the self-doubt and second thoughts of the critics of the fifties, and the cynical mood that would dominate intellectual life and letters after the disappointments of 1968: wars, assassinations, and the election of Richard Nixon. Cox embraced secularity precisely because it rejected what was wrong with the old religion. Secularization became the occasion for escape from the suburban captivity and bourgeois middle-class town culture. Yet in baptizing the secular opportunity of the new era, Cox, like the other critics of the American church and synagogue, made institutional expressions of religion superfluous. Like Peter Berger, Harvey Cox offered no compelling reason to stick with the church as opposed to keeping the faith on one's own. Gibson Winter and Cox were alike in sharing a vision of what the church might be if it lived up to its high calling. Yet given the real nature of most churches, Winter and Cox's ethical yardsticks disqualified so many local faith communities that institutional religion became theoretically important but practically impossible.

Of course, writing books of criticism is largely a young scholar's and an old curmudgeon's game. Perhaps the truest critique of Cox's entire line of thinking was offered by James Gustafson. In his review of *The Secular City*, Guftason complained that Cox had little use for the pastoral functions of the church in his zeal for a theology of permanent social revolution. "Does not the pastoral function of the church increase, together with its moral functions, in the dislocations of secularization?" he wrote. "The persistent crises of death, broken families, loss of a sense of self, with their morally and spiritually sickening effects also come into the mission of the church and require a reconciling, healing personal ministry. Cox allows for this, but gives it little dignity."[22] Gustafson went on to explain that the source of his complaint was that Cox was able to affirm the moral ambiguity of the secular institutions and still proclaim their usefulness for bringing in the Kingdom, but was unable to accept a less-than-perfect church. This ecclesiastical demand Gustafson saw as unbiblical and sectarian. Cox had thus been too rough on the limitations of human faith communities and too unmindful of their real virtues. Yet the stunning sales of *The Secular City* suggest that once again the jeremiads were striking a nerve in at least some sectors of American religious experience.

Religion in the Common Experience

Intellectuals, motion picture producers, church members, city dwellers and suburbanites, the young and the old, newspaper editors, and television viewers all liked religion in the fifties. The suburban jeremiads went directly to the heart of this popularity and asked, "Is it a good thing that religion is so popular?" The response to this question by clergy and religious intellectuals in the sixties has already been assessed, but what of religion in the experience of individuals in the broader culture? How did religion change in the 1960s? Was it less culturally popular? Less or more important in the lives of individuals? More or less visible in the media? And if changes occurred, what if any role did the jeremiads play in those changes? A short answer to these questions is that religion in the 1960s was much less culturally popular than in the 1950s, though individuals' patterns of religious belief and participation in religious activity changed surprisingly little. Explaining these changes and relating them to the ideas of the suburban jeremiads takes longer to answer.

Some religious change was inevitable as the fifties gave way to the sixties. One of the ways in which the religion most people experienced began to change in the sixties was a side effect of its extraordinary popularity during the previous decade. No matter what the causes of the fifties' religious boom were—a convergence of childbearing patterns, a church- and synagogue-building wave that invited laypersons into the exciting process of institutional creation, or the comfortable correspondence between ecclesiastical and popular modes of religiosity—when those factors declined, the numbers of people in the churches inevitably dropped somewhat. A spirit of decline began to affect the churches. Reports of national membership losses beginning in 1966 only lent credibility to some people's belief that a declension from a 1950s golden age of religion had begun.

The jeremiads provided a theodicy of numerical decline for persons prepared to think in their terms. Nevertheless, an assertion that perhaps a church with fewer members was a better church than a church with more but less committed members was thin soup to those who had experienced a church or synagogue bursting to the seams in the 1950s. Furthermore, churches and synagogues in the fifties functioned better for young married adults with small children than they did for families experiencing the natural but disruptive events of adolescent rebellion and children leaving home for work or college in the sixties. For many, nothing would ever again equal the feeling of being young and living in a community of new families in new homes, with new schools and churches in suburban communities where death, disease, divorce, and dissension were virtually unknown.

Meanwhile, in urban churches and synagogues, the two decades of postwar suburbanization had depleted these congregations of the young, leaving behind older members. In the fifties, the bulk of the remnant urban congregation members had been in their late middle age or early retirement years. Consequently, they were often still married, had high disposable incomes, and were able to sustain downtown congregations during the 1950s without noticeable strain—despite the fact that they were not adding younger members to their number. When older, urban congregations of Christians and Jews continued to age and their resident members moved increasingly into periods of widowhood, infirmity, and declining financial resources in the 1960s, numerous congregations fell into hard times. Endowments allowed some "large steeple" churches to support exciting preaching ministries, but the relocation of the younger adults to the suburbs virtually assured that urban religious decline among white religious bodies would be dramatic. The prophets crying in suburbia in the fifties seemed more prophetic in their predictions of urban religious decline as the years wore on.

African-American religion in the cities was relatively untouched by the jeremiads. Fleeing the cities and their problems was not a moral issue for black Christians, since they were largely excluded from the suburbs. Residential segregation meant that moving to the suburbs and leaving the poor behind was not an option. Later, when residential opportunities for blacks opened up, they did so for the most part in the cities themselves in formerly all-white neighborhoods. But the crisis in the cities of the 1960s—the collapse of tax bases, departure of the white middle classes, decline of city jobs, riots, the intensification of institutional racism, and the diminution of city resources to fight crime, fires, and decay—did change the ethos in which the black urban churches had their being. On the positive side, the rising proportions of black to white voters in cities meant that the power to elect black governmental officials was widely employed, and big-city mayors and members of the Congressional Black Caucus largely came out of church backgrounds and related well to their religious constituencies. On the negative side, the decay of schools and economic opportunities in the cities meant that political freedoms were often rendered hollow by the inability of African Americans to afford the fruits of freedom. After white flight, the black church in many urban places continued to play its historic role of assisting the black community in bearing adversity and maintaining hope, while taking on responsibility as well for the larger institutions of government and education.[23]

And what of popular piety? The circulation of *Guideposts*, Norman Vincent Peale's inspirational monthly magazine, did not decline. But its readership tended to remain the same, aging with the magazine. Younger individuals had fewer examples of religious literature directed toward them, with a few important exceptions: Harvey Cox's *Secular City*, Alan Watts's popularizations of Zen Buddhism, and Malcolm Boyd's meditations. Gone from the religious literature of the young was the simple assurance of Peale's positive thinking. Instead, a Boyd prayer or meditation frankly bared the confusion the writer shared with the reader. In his most famous book, *Are You Running with Me, Jesus?*, Boyd offered prayers about going into a gay bar, counseling a young woman who was pregnant out of wedlock, and other problems of the day, but his greatest themes were loneliness and alienation:

You said there is perfect freedom in your service, Lord.

Well, I don't feel perfectly free. I don't feel free at all. I'm a captive to myself.

I do what I want. I have it all my own way. There is no freedom at all for me in this, Jesus. Today I feel like a slave bound in chains and branded by a hot iron because I'm a captive to my own will and don't give an honest damn about you or your will.

You're over there where I'm keeping you, outside my real life. How can I go on being such a lousy hypocrite? Come over here, where I don't want you to come. Let me quit playing this blasphemous game of religion with you. Jesus, help me to let you be yourself in my life—so that I can be myself.[24]

Malcolm Boyd was not the only figure troubled by religion at the time. Religious anxiety became a major feature of life in the sixties. During the previous decade, religion's popularity generated a sense of religious assurance. Each person within the religious world could think that when religion received a high approval rating in the 1950s, it was his or her own view that was being endorsed. The intellectuals who were elite religionists believed that their academic theologies were finding favor. The ecclesiastically identified, including much of the clergy, believed it was church religion Americans liked best. Finally, religion's popularity to Norman Vincent Peale's followers meant that more would find happiness through positive thinking. In the sixties, the latent conflict between contending views of religion came out into the open. The effort on the part of any one group to translate this apparent cultural popularity into power of various sorts exposed the real cleavages that existed between types. The secular theologies, the liturgical changes wrought by Vatican II, and moral decisions about fighting in Vietnam versus fleeing to Canada were all occasions of intense debate for religious parties in the sixties. The exposure of divisions between groups over what religion was, and why it was valuable, had the effect of making religion seem to be under attack in the sixties in a way it had not been in the fifties.

Since religion's definition and its value were simultaneously in the eye of the beholder, public opinion polls gauged how religion was viewed in the minds of the American people. By 1962, 31 percent of Americans believed that religion's influence was on a downswing. Just five years earlier in 1957, only 14 percent believed that religious influence was on the wane. The exact wording of Gallup's question was: "At the present time, do you think religion as a whole is increasing its influence on American life or losing its influence?" The figures for the percentage of people replying "losing influence" grew steadily during the sixties, reaching 70 percent by 1969.[25] But religion's loss of popularity was more apparent than real, for in terms of individual behaviors and beliefs, Americans changed little about how they personally related to religion.

When the question was asked in Gallup polls about how important religion was in the life of the individual respondent, very little decline in religious influence could be detected. In 1952, when Gallup asked, "How important would you say religion is in your own life—very important, fairly important or not very important?," 75 percent answered very important, and 20 percent fairly important. When Gallup next asked the question in 1965, 93 percent of respondents still deemed religion important in their lives, with 70 percent terming it very important. This latter result came from the same survey group in which those who believed religion's influence was on the decline outnumbered those who thought it was on the rise by a margin of three to two. Religion was thus holding its own rather well in the lives of individuals, even though these same people thought it was not doing very well in the lives of their neighbors.[26]

The continued high level of religiosity among Americans during the 1960s, when compared to the growth in the perception that religion was losing influence, leads to the question of what was understood as influence. Clearly, if religious influence meant that politicians paid lip service to religion, then the 1960s were less influenced by religion than the

1950s. The contrast could not be seen more clearly than in differences between the pious pronouncements of Dwight D. Eisenhower and the secular political rhetoric of Presidents John F. Kennedy and Lyndon Johnson. If religious influence meant that, in matters of public concern, religious leaders spoke with one voice and that voice was taken seriously as a moral and political authority, then religion's influence was also on the decline. Increasingly during the 1960s, national religious bodies found themselves at odds with their members over the pace and extent of civil rights progress, the morality of the war in Vietnam, and the need for either freedom or law and order in ghettos and on campuses.

One clue to what was going on in the growth of pessimism about religion's influence may be found in a 1962 opinion survey, in which young adults were far more inclined than older persons to believe religion was losing influence. Fifty-three percent of those between eighteen and twenty-four years of age said they believed religion was on the decline.[27] Those who had still been in adolescence in the 1950s had, as young adults in the 1960s, much less appreciation for religion than did their parents or other elders. Late in the decade, as religion's influence barometer continued to fall, the Gallup organization began to probe why people believed church influence was on the decline. They found four commonly voiced reasons. One was that younger persons found religion irrelevant to their issues and interests. Another was the belief that material pursuits had distracted people from higher things. Still another was the conviction that growing crime, violence, and immorality were expressions of the reduced influence of religion. (Persons truly influenced by religion, went the theory, did not commit crimes.) Finally, a commonly expressed opinion was that the church was not playing its appropriate role in society. Curiously, half of the last group believed that the churches were meddling where they did not belong, and the other half said that the church had failed to keep up with current social and political issues.[28]

What all the explanations for the perception of decline had in common was that they pointed to social factors outside the religious bodies themselves. The rapid social changes of the 1960s brought on by crime, affluence, and foreign wars, and exhibited in youth culture, civil rights, and the legal system, created an ethos where the appearance of stability was washed away. If a person believed that religion was the thing that bound societies and peoples together, it was difficult to assert religion's influence in the face of so much coming apart. If instead a person emphasized an ethical conception of religion—believing religion either preserved existing morality, or righted wrongs—then it was hard to maintain a belief in religion's influence in a time of so many changes for the worse, or at least painful changes from the past. As the Vietnam War heated up, the hawkish World War II veteran saw the young man's resistance to fighting the war as an affront to God and country, while the pacifist youth saw the war as an outrage brought about by moral bankruptcy. Neither side believed that religion's influence was very evident in the events of the day. In sum, the times gave religious faith and institutions a wide set of issues with which to respond to and did so on such a rapid schedule that they could not respond well to each and every challenge.

At the same time religion was undergoing a public perception crisis, other institutions—universities, government, big business, the military— were also suffering declines in their influence, and for similar reasons. Religion was different only in how far and fast it fell in perceived cultural significance, and perhaps also in how seriously this sense of malaise was internalized in the life of the institutions of organized religion.

Even with religion losing influence, radical discontinuity with past religious belief and expression did not characterize the religious lives of most people in the 1960s. The typical religious life during these years consisted of a further extension of trends underway for several decades. Most individuals were pragmatic in their faith, counting good deeds and a life well lived as more worthy in the eyes of God than fine words of theology, correct belief, or worship attendance. Americans were also becoming more tolerant of those of other denominations and religions. A Roman Catholic president was no longer unthinkable; neither was a mixed-faith marriage, or a divorced minister. The characteristic anti-intellectualism of Americans combined with their growing tolerance to form an easy going antidogmatism, one that undermined denominational barriers and made people much more willing than their parents to join a church of a different denomination than the one in which they had been raised.

As it was with individuals, so it was with churches and synagogues. Life in a typical 1960s congregation was barely touched by the suburban jeremiad literature. Whatever effects these criticisms had, they were indirect. This is not to say that these effects might not be intensely felt, as for example in the numerous cases where the clergy of a particular congregation might challenge the members to do something about Vietnam, napalm, restrictive zoning, or their "country club" ways.

Yet if the typical individual's life and the average religious institution were not changed directly and dramatically by the ideas presented in the jeremiads, that did not mean that no lives and institutions were changed. Two places where religious change was most noticeable was in mainstream religion's role in the political debate between liberals and radicals and in the shared experiences of the 1960s college generation.

Liberals, Radicals, and Religion

The neo-orthodoxy of the religious critics promoted a political liberalism that found its moment in the larger culture of the 1960s, but was soon superseded by radical thought and by liberalism's inability to deliver all that it had promised.[29] In the popular thought of the 1950s, religion was the soul of civil society. Be it Protestant, Catholic, or Jewish, religion provided the values by which America could be a great nation. It was against the easy assumption that religion was society's handmaiden that the jeremiads were uniformly arrayed. Because they came out of neo-orthodox assumptions, they did tend, however, to favor a secular political liberalism and stop short of endorsing radical political solutions.

Neither Herberg, nor Berger, nor even Winter were utopians. Their belief in the sinfulness of human beings and human institutions led each of them to dismiss the possibility of perfecting human institutions. But like the rest of the neo-orthodox, they keenly felt the obligation to try and achieve justice—knowing it would always be partial. Likewise, they each believed in reform, seeking to create more perfect institutions, while knowing these too would fall short. Harvey Cox was more optimistic, more willing to use the language of revolution, though he also tended to presuppose the improvability of existing social arrangements as his celebrations of technocratic society and the Kennedy style in politics showed.

The background against which the suburban jeremiads had been cast was one of unbridled optimism about the American Way of Life. One way of marking the fifties off from the sixties, and thus delimiting the work of the fifties' critics, is to note the changes that were taking place in the American landscape by the early sixties. For one, the nation's mood was changing, and by the end of the Kennedy administration it was already becoming clear that the United States was a country with serious race problems and large pockets of remaining poverty. In the fifties, John Kenneth Galbraith's *Affluent Society* had invited Americans to use their society's immense wealth to provide for unparalleled social and educational benefits for all. Now, in the early sixties, Michael Harrington's *Other America* revealed the nation's failure to do anything of the sort for vast numbers of its citizens.[30] The optimism of the fifties concerning the eventual triumph of the American Dream was now mixed with a sense of real doubt about its prospects for fulfillment. Yet the criticism of the fifties had provided the means by which the more sober picture of American life could be seen in the sixties. This criticism had also been written in a spirit that did not engender cynicism about American shortcomings, but rather encouraged Americans to employ their natural activism to solve social problems. The bequest of the suburban jeremiads—religious and secular—to the general culture of the sixties was thus threefold. They enabled people to see culture and religion with less rosy vision, and they also spurred their readers to do something about the problems they portrayed. Finally, however, they also initiated an ongoing process of critical reflection on religion and culture that later became quite destabilizing in other hands.

As it turned out, liberals were not the only heirs of the fifties' social and religious critics. The New Left and religious radicals also traced their roots to the same few figures. And therein lay the source of the 1960s political culture crisis. The critique of liberal technocracy offered by writers such as C. Wright Mills, Dwight Macdonald, and Paul Goodman would be picked up most forcefully by the young. One June day in 1962, while John F. Kennedy was telling Yale University graduates that ideology was dead and remaining social problems could be solved by technology, a group of fifty-nine persons gathered at a Michigan labor resort and debated and revised a political treatise drafted by Tom Hayden, a college newspaper editor and a leader in Students for a Democratic Society (SDS).[31] The "Port Huron Statement," as the document was known, became the founding charter of the New Left, a broad coalition of young Americans who called for change in the way things were being run in American society, especially by liberals such as Kennedy. Its introduction began with the ominous words, "We are people of this generation, bred in at least modest comfort, housed now in universities, looking uncomfortably to the world we inherit."[32] The young of the 1960s thus proved themselves capable of issuing a jeremiad of their own. Two portions of the statement were especially noteworthy. The first of these was the section on "values," in which the students depicted modern America as trapped in a spiritual crisis where "doubt has replaced hopefulness—and men act out of a defeatism that is labelled realistic," and where "to be idealistic is to be considered apocalyptic, deluded."[33] Against this background, the students articulated their belief that human beings were "infinitely precious

and possessed of unfulfilled capacities for reason, freedom and love."
The goal of human life, therefore, was articulated in the statement in
terms very similar to those used by the older critics. Human independence, personal authenticity, transcendence over feelings of powerlessness, and a willingness to learn became the watchwords of the new
order.[34]

The second remarkable feature of the "Port Huron Statement" was its
call for "participatory democracy." For, though it was ill-defined in the
document and in subsequent use, the term's endurance as a slogan
would prove that even the New Left was capable of making a lasting
contribution to American political thought. Participatory democracy was
a direct challenge to liberal elites' view that only the most knowledgeable
should rule, arguing that all citizens were stakeholders in policy decisions
and thus to be included in political decisions. The potency of this slogan
was such that it outlived the movement that coined it, becoming a new
political value widely shared by the American public. But before participatory democracy entered the American mainstream, it first became the
rallying cry of a generation of college and university students.[35]

The long-term religious effect of having two political alternatives—
liberal and radical—to the American Way of Life was to divide communities of faith further into more polarized camps of conservatives, moderates
(liberals), and radicals. The suburban jeremiads had counseled people of
faith to avoid an identification of religion with contemporary American
culture, but they provided almost no guidance as to how countercultural
religion should be. Meanwhile, the values of an entire generation were
being challenged, stretched, and reshaped by the events and currents of
the nation's campuses.

Going to College in the 1960s

In some ways, the suburban jeremiads had used figures of speech that
would sound hollow with time. The suburb itself as a metaphor for all that
was wrong with postwar society—its affluence, its materialism, its separation of old and young, rich and poor, white and black—was one of
these soon-dated terms. Everybody criticized the suburbs, but increasingly, everyone came from them, too. Many of those who came from the
suburbs were the young who filled the nation's colleges and universities,
and later its barricades.

In the early fifties, there was much concern voiced by religious observers for the college generation and its relationship to the church. When the college generation boom actually occurred between the late fifties and the early seventies, however, the churches would find that it was the first generation in American history they would substantially "lose." As Theodore Roszak perceptively noted, from sources as varied as Allen Ginsberg's "Howl" and *Mad* magazine's cynical satire of American politics, movies, schools, and religion, by the mid-sixties the young had been exposed to years of jabs at the middle-class culture of their parents.[36] To see one's own parents as foolish and laughable was no great trick, but to see their entire generation as contemptible was peculiar to the sixties. The churchly religion of their fathers' and mothers' generation was just one of the victims of youthful distrust of the received culture.

If the young did not share the faith of their parents, then the religious worldview of the sixties' college generation can be described as simultaneously contrarian and idealistic. By 1965, more than half of all Americans were under twenty-five years of age, and a huge majority of these were still in school and not yet in the adult world. The social criticism of the 1950s had prepared the way for this new majority to see itself in contradistinction to that adult sphere of life. Since, as the jeremiads taught the young (either directly when they read the books in college, or indirectly as they heard the jeremiads' slogans), the great problem in American religion was adult and institutional hypocrisy, then the young would seek religious integrity through coordinated belief and action.

The idea that faith was as faith does—that the test of religious faith was the social good it produced—was compelling to a surprisingly large number of the young in the 1960s. It also moved many into action. The idealistic young provided the bodies for the civil rights movement, opposition to the war in Vietnam, the Peace Corps and Vista, various campus movements, and the ecology movement of the late 1960s. These movements also became "the church" for many younger adults, a foreseeable result of the critique of suburban religiosity. The ethical neo-orthodoxy that Gibson Winter represented appealed to the activist nature in many Americans. Yet even as it enlisted persons to the good causes of the day, it helped to found a faith that did not need the church, even if it did need other corporate expressions, movements, and causes.

The pursuit of autonomy and authenticity extended to the spiritual life of this college generation as well as to its political activity. Practicing religious authenticity led some of the young into political activity. This was largely a foreseen and—from the perspective of the 1950s critics—

desirable consequence of taking the suburban critique seriously. Other students turned eastward to Buddhism, Taoism, or Transcendental Meditation, or adopted more conservative and strenuous expressions of Christianity or Judaism. Still other young Americans avoided religious hypocrisy by rejecting religion altogether. The number of young Americans expressing no religious preference and no belief in "God or a Supreme Being" became the fastest growing segment of the population, albeit an extraordinarily small one by European standards.

All the religious options exercised by younger adults in the 1960s can be seen as extensions of acceptance of the suburban jeremiads. Taking religion seriously enough to do something about it in relation to race relations or the war was an obvious internalization of the criticism of the fifties' apathetic piety. But so too was leaving aside normal churches and synagogues in the quest for other, more beloved communities. Even removing oneself from the practice of institutional worship entirely was a foreseeable consequence of Peter Berger's call for intellectual integrity.

Conclusion:
The Suburban Jeremiad
in Purpose and Consequence

The debate over the place of religion in American society would take a variety of forms in the years after 1965, as serious scholars of religion joined clergy and social critics, radicals and college students, in examining the role of religion in the nation. Even so, the debate in its initial, most popular phase was passing.

The suburban jeremiads, without exception, had been structured to accomplish the twin purposes of conviction and correction. They first sought, at length, to convince their readers that the author's worldview was correct and that the culture or religion—or some combination of the two—was headed for disaster if things kept on in the direction they had been going. The corrective portion of the jeremiad then showed that there was a way out of this decline if only the people would return to their God (or alternatively, depending on the writer, seek autonomy, practice individualism, develop class consciousness, or reject middlebrow culture). For every problem, therefore, there was a means of salvation. Still, when one turns from structure to function, from the question of what these texts were designed to do toward the question of what they actually accomplished, one discovers that these texts proved more important in the long run for their compelling ability to capture in a word or phrase an acute sense of what was wrong with religion and society in America.

Louis Hartz, in his classic analysis of American politics, *The Liberal Tradition in America*, argued that America was a country born free, a liberal, Lockean nation that having had no aristocracy, had likewise no need for ideologies to defend or overthrow feudalism.[37] Because of this fact America was a nation whose political and social discourse was singularly devoid of ideas. In the place of ideas, slogans functioned as labels for things good and bad, as surrogates for more complete analysis, as banners under which to rally, and as encapsulations of problems and solutions. The genius of the suburban jeremiads was that they made use of this fact of American culture and provided popular slogans to represent their ideas, even as they lamented the lonely role of the contemporary intellectual. To a remarkable degree the titles of these books conveyed their contents. The idea of an organization man was an idea that could be readily understood and manipulated by the average person, apart from the reading of William Whyte's book. Likewise, when Will Herberg said that "we worship the American Way of Life," he coined a slogan that would function independently of his book without betraying his analysis. The "noise of solemn assemblies" was often applied in the years following Berger's use of the term to disparage the activities of the institutional church. Gibson Winter's phrase, "the suburban captivity of the churches," was also a self-explanatory slogan of considerable power for religious journalists and activists to bandy about.

The religious jeremiads proved to be powerful texts in part because their writers were intellectuals who had not disdained to fight on popular ground and provide the slogans popular discourse required. But they also were successful because they captured what many individuals were already thinking themselves. Herberg's *Protestant, Catholic, Jew* became an assigned text in many college religion courses well into the 1970s. There it fed students' sense of dissatisfaction with the hollowness of their culture. Berger's *Noise of Solemn Assemblies* became an underground classic. It started off as a privately commissioned and printed work, and became so celebrated and remains so popular that Doubleday still keeps it in print. Gibson Winter's *Suburban Captivity of the Churches* was a preacher's book; it did not reach the circulation that the other two books had in lay culture, but there are few ministers of a certain age who do not have it on their shelves.

The sales of these books indicated that their authors were not just prophets crying in the wilderness, but also prophets speaking for a people. People bought and read these books to confirm what they did not want to be, or be a part of. The religious jeremiads also articulated, as we have argued, the major responses to the 1950s religious-cultural synthesis. When the sixties came to the religious communities, the avenues of countercultural expression had already been anticipated. Did these jeremiad writers cause the sixties? No. Yet they did help people think about the religious problems of postwar society and thus hastened the sixties' discontent in coming. Their work set the foundation for key developments in the sixties and provided slogans that helped to concisely articulate religious and social problems and suggest solutions to those problems.

Martin Marty has written of Will Herberg's *Protestant, Catholic, Jew* that the world Herberg described did not last long. This world, he writes, "emerged only during the Second World War and changed considerably after the Eisenhower revival."[38] The same might be said about the worlds described by virtually all the social critics of the 1950s and early 1960s. Moreover, some of the problems these critics sought to address did not endure. Consensus and conformity, for example, did not last. And yet, to depict the jeremiad writers as working only on short-lived issues is terribly wrong. For their real legacy is that they rekindled perennial questions about the identity of American culture, the integrity of religion as practiced in the nation's churches and synagogues, and the moral responsibility of those with resources toward those without them. The jeremiads succeeded most, therefore, in moving these religious and cultural issues to a central place of concern in American society. Though solutions proved elusive, the suburban jeremiads' formulation of American culture's unfinished business still abides.

Notes

■

Preface

1. Sydney E. Ahlstrom, "The Radical Turn in Theology and Ethics: Why It Occurred in the 1960s," *Annals of the American Academy of Political and Social Science,* January 1970, 1–13.

1. Life in a Suburban Culture

1. Benita Eisler, *Private Lives: Men and Women of the Fifties* (New York: Franklin Watts, 1986), 29.
2. William H. Whyte, Jr., *The Organization Man* (Garden City, N.Y.: Doubleday Anchor Books, 1956), 353.
3. Robert Wuthnow, *The Restructuring of American Religion: Society and Faith since World War II* (Princeton, N.J.: Princeton University Press, 1988), 26.
4. *Christian Century,* 7 June 1950, 718.
5. William McKinney and Wade Clark Roof, "Liberal Protestantism: A Sociodemographic Perspective," in *Liberal Protestantism: Realities and Possibilities,* ed. Robert S. Michaelsen and Wade Clark Roof (New York: Pilgrim Press, 1986), 41.
6. *Christian Century,* 22 March 1950, 362.
7. Ibid.
8. Morris Freedman, "New Jewish Community in Formation: A Conserva-

tive Center Catering to Present-Day Needs," *Commentary*, January 1955, 36–37; for another view of suburbia from a Jewish perspective see Harry Gersh, "The New Suburbanites of the 50s," *Commentary*, March 1954, 209–221.

9. Freedman, "New Jewish Community," 47.

10. Marshall Sklare, "Church and the Laity among Jews," *Annals of the American Academy of Political and Social Science*, November 1960, 60.

11. E. Brooks Holifield, *A History of Pastoral Care in America: From Salvation to Self-Realization* (Nashville: Abingdon, 1983), 260.

12. Ibid., 261.

13. Ernest Havemann, "Unlocking the Mind in Psychoanalysis," *Life*, 28 January 1957, 82, 119.

14. Ibid., 271.

15. Seward Hiltner, "Religion and Psychoanalysis," *Journal of Pastoral Care* 4 (1950): 35.

16. Martin Buber, *I and Thou* (Edinburgh: R. & R. Clark, 1937).

17. Holifield, *History of Pastoral Care*, 271.

18. *Christian Century*, 11 January 1950, 41.

19. William L. O'Neill, *American High: The Years of Confidence, 1945–1960* (New York: Free Press, 1986), 229.

20. Charles Clayton Morrison, "America's Atomic Atrocity," *Christian Century*, 29 August 1945.

21. Harold E. Fey, "Fifteen Years in Hell Is Enough," *Christian Century*, 3 August 1960.

22. Wilbur Smith, "The Atomic Bomb and the Word of God" (Chicago: Moody Press, 1945). For more on Smith and an explanation of how Peter could write of atomic principles without knowing about them, see George Marsden's excellent study of Fuller Seminary, *Reforming Fundamentalism: Fuller Seminary and the New Evangelicalism* (Grand Rapids, Mich.: William B. Eerdmans, 1987), 23.

23. Quoted in Thomas Hine, *Populuxe* (New York: Alfred A. Knopf, 1986), 136–137.

24. O'Neill, *American High*, 77.

25. *Time*, 14 July 1952, 60.

26. For an example of this, see William B. Kennedy, "Neo-Orthodoxy Goes to Sunday School: The Christian Faith and Life Curriculum," *Journal of Presbyterian History* 58 (Winter 1980), 326–370.

27. National Council of Churches, *Christian Faith in Action: Commemorative Volume* (New York: National Council of Churches, 1951), 150–151.

28. *Christian Century*, 22 March 1950, 357.

29. Edwin S. Gaustad, *A Documentary History of Religion in America*, vol. 2 (Grand Rapids, Mich.: William B. Eerdmans, 1982), 489.

30. Some of the more prominent examples of the genre were James Hastings Nichols's *Democracy and the Churches*, Samuel Stumpf's *A Democratic Manifesto*, Winthrop Hudson's *The Great Tradition of the American Churches* and "Theological Convictions and Democratic Government," John MacKay's "Letter to Presbyterians," and Bromley Oxnam's *I Protest*. Catholic intellectuals were arguing along similar lines in *Democracy and Catholicism in America*, by

Currin Shields, and in *The Churches and the Public*, edited by John Cogley for the then-new Center for the Study of Democratic Institutions.

31.   Reinhold Niebuhr, *The Irony of American History* (New York: Scribner, 1952), 2.

32.   The incident in question involved a youth from Chicago, Emmett Till, who was lynched in Mississippi in 1955.

33.   Ralph Ellison, *Invisible Man* (New York: Random House, 1947); Richard Wright, *Black Boy* (Cleveland: World, 1945). For more on Robinson, see Carl T. Rowan and Jackie Robinson, *Wait till Next Year* (New York: Random House, 1960).

34.   United States Supreme Court, 347 U.S. 483 (1954).

35.   For an unparalleled account of the relation between the legal, personal, and political aspects of the civil rights movement at mid-century, see Richard Kluger, *Simple Justice: The History of Brown v. Board of Education and Black America's Struggle for Equality* (New York: Alfred A. Knopf, 1976).

36.   August Meier and Elliot M. Rudwick, *From Plantation to Ghetto: An Interpretive History of American Negroes* (New York: Hill and Wang, 1966), 221–225.

37.   *Christian Century*, 29 March 1950, 412.

38.   Lerone Bennett, Jr., "When the Man and the Hour Are Met," in *Martin Luther King, Jr.: A Profile*, ed. C. Eric Lincoln (New York: Hill and Wang, 1970), 13.

39.   Ibid., 137–138.

40.   Martin Luther King, Jr., "Non-Violence and Racial Justice," *Christian Century*, 6 February 1957.

41.   Ibid.

42.   *Christian Century*, 21 March 1956, 360.

43.   *Christian Century*, 1 February 1956, 147.

2. The Return to Religion

1.   Robert T. Handy, "The American Religious Depression, 1925–1935," *Church History* 29 (March 1960), 3–16.

2.   H. L. Mencken, "Protestantism in the Republic," *Prejudices*, 5th ser. (New York: Alfred A. Knopf, 1926), 104–105, 115.

3.   The so-called religious depression, it is important to note, was largely a Protestant phenomenon. Catholics and Jews at the time were having problems of their own, particularly the problems associated with second-generation immigrants not continuing the religious practices of their parents, and the financial difficulties of trying to build an ecclesiastical infrastructure at a time of general economic depression. Still, they were not directly caught up in the theological and urban-versus-rural conflicts that had done so much to bring

Protestantism to its low state. Yet insofar as attacks against Babbittry and Gantryism were applied to religion in general, all religions suffered from lowered public esteem. Such was the nature of Protestantism's still culturally dominant position in American life that an assault on Protestantism was commonly taken as a strike against all religion.

4. *Newsweek*, 1 September 1952, 59.

5. *Time*, 2 April 1951, 81.

6. Nathan Glazer, "The Jewish Revival in America: I," *Commentary*, December 1955, 493–495.

7. Ibid.

8. For pictures of some of the most notable examples of 1950s church architecture, see *Time*, 19 September 1955, 76–81.

9. *Good Housekeeping*, November 1954, 32f.

10. *Holiday*, December 1952, 146–147.

11. Clarence W. Hall, "The Churches Rise Again," *McCall's*, June 1955, 34–37.

12. Ibid., 112.

13. Ibid.

14. See "The New Churches," *Time*, 26 December 1960, 28–33, for a retrospective view of the architects involved in ecclesiastical design in the 1950s and the styles they employed.

15. Booton Herndon, "How to Build Your Own Church," *Saturday Evening Post*, 19 May 1956, 54–55.

16. Ibid.

17. Freedman, "New Jewish Community," 41.

18. Advertisement quoted in Jackson W. Carroll, Douglas W. Johnson, and Martin E. Marty, *Religion in America: 1950 to the Present* (New York: Harper and Row, 1979), 19.

19. *Newsweek*, 20 October 1952, 106.

20. "99 to 1," *Time*, 20 October 1954, 64; "Proof of God," *Time*, 10 January 1955, 60; "I Believe in God," *Newsweek*, 20 October 1952, 106; "Glory, Glory, Glory," *Newsweek*, 22 February 1960, 63.

21. "The Proof of God," *Time*, 10 January 1955, 60.

22. Howard Whitman, "What Soldiers Believe," *Collier's*, 2 June 1951, 18, 68–71.

23. Howard Whitman, "What Scientists Believe," *Collier's*, 11 August 1951, 26–27.

24. Ibid.

25. Ibid.

26. James Bender and Lee Graham, *Your Way to Popularity and Personal Power* (New York: Coward-McCann, 1950).

27. James Bender and Lee Graham, "Prayer That Gets Results," *Coronet*, May 1952, 98–100.

28. Eddie Cantor, "Greater than the H-Bomb," *Reader's Digest*, September 1953, 7–8ff; Madame Chiang Kai-shek, "The Power of Prayer," *Reader's Digest*, August 1955, 52–58; Fulton Oursler, "What Prayer Can Do," *Reader's Digest*, January 1951, 6–10.

29.   Adelaide Kerr, ed., "How to Pray and What to Pray For; Religious Leaders Answer Questions," *McCall's*, September 1956, 79.

30.   Ibid.

31.   Douglas MacArthur, "A Father's Prayer," quoted in Jim Bishop, "Day of Final Appeal," *Good Housekeeping*, November 1954, 32.

32.   *Newsweek*, 14 January 1952, 75–76.

33.   *Newsweek*, 2 April 1952, 118.

34.   Charlie W. Shedd, *Pray Your Weight Away* (New York: Lippincott, 1957). For an intellectual's contemporary review of this now out-of-print classic, see Gerald Weales, "A Family That Prays Together Weighs Together," *New Republic*, 25 March 1957, 19.

35.   "Power of the Brief Burst," *Time*, 13 April 1959, 95.

36.   "Yes, You Can Dial Prayer," *Good Housekeeping*, September 1958, 125.

37.   *Newsweek*, 4 July 1955, 23.

38.   *Newsweek*, 3 September 1956, 56.

39.   "Prefab Church Seats 180," *Popular Mechanics*, December 1956, 86ff; "New Look for Churches: Modern Design Takes Over," *Popular Science*, December 1954, 112–113.

40.   Nancy Wilson Ross, "Religion's Root Meaning," *Mademoiselle*, December 1956, 56ff.

41.   Henry Morton Robinson, *The Cardinal* (New York: Simon and Schuster, 1950).

42.   Alice Payne Hackett, *Sixty Years of Best Sellers, 1895–1955* (New York: R. R. Bowker, 1956), 84.

43.   James C. G. Conniff, "When Men Find God," *Coronet*, April 1956, 48.

44.   Eric F. Goldman, *The Crucial Decade—And After: America, 1945–1960* (New York: Vintage Books, 1960), 217.

45.   "Religion in Popular Culture," *Commonweal*, 7 October 1955, 5–6

46.   "To Pray or Not to Pray" *Time*, 8 August 1960, 63.

47.   *Senate Miscellaneous Reports II*, 83d Cong., 2d sess., Report 1287.

48.   *Congressional Record*, 83d Cong., 2d sess., 1954, 100 pt. 2: 1700.

49.   Gerard Kaye and Ferenc M. Szasz, "Adding 'Under God' to the Pledge of Allegiance," *Encounter* 34 (Winter 1973): 52–56.

50.   *Congressional Record*, 84th Cong., 2d sess., 1956, 102, pt. 10: 13917.

51.   *America*, 7 March 1953, 612.

52.   *U.S. News and World Report*, 30 January 1953, 13.

53.   ". . . Is Our Religious Revival Real?" *McCall's*, June 1955, 25.

54.   *Life*, 26 December 1955, 12.

55.   Edward Morgan, ed., *This I Believe: The Living Philosophies of One Hundred Thoughtful Men and Women in All Walks of Life: As Written for and with a Foreword by Edward R. Murrow* (New York: Simon and Schuster, 1952).

56.   343 U.S. 306 (1952), 313.

57.   See Carroll et al., *Religion in America*, 28–34.

58.   Henry C. Link, *The Return to Religion* (New York: Macmillan, 1936).

59.   Matt. 16:25; see also Matt. 10:39; Luke 9:24, 18:33; Mark 8:35; John 12:25.

60.   Norman Vincent Peale, *The Power of Positive Thinking* (New York: Prentice Hall, 1952).

61.   Fulton J. Sheen, *Treasure in Clay: The Autobiography of Fulton J. Sheen* (Garden City, N.Y.: Doubleday, 1980), 359.

62.   Ibid., 69.

63.   Ibid.

64.   William Griffin, ed., *The Electronic Christian: 105 Sermons from Fulton J. Sheen* (New York: Macmillan, 1979), 200.

65.   Ibid., 202.

66.   Ibid., 203.

67.   Ibid., 205–206.

68.   See Reinhold Niebuhr, *The Children of Light and the Children of Darkness* (New York: Scribner's, 1944), xi–41; and Richard Wightman Fox, *Reinhold Niebuhr: A Biography* (San Francisco: Harper and Row, 1985; 2d ed. 1987), 215–234.

69.   Sydney E. Ahlstrom, "Theology and the Present-Day Revival," *Annals of the American Academy of Political and Social Science*, November 1960, 23.

70.   David Riesman, "Freud, Religion and Science," *American Scholar*, July 1951, 271.

71.   Ibid., 272.

72.   Ibid., 273.

73.   Liston Pope, "Dilemmas of the Seminaries," *Christian Century*, 26 April 1950, 20–21.

74.   Howard Lowry, *The Mind's Adventure* (Philadelphia: Westminster, 1950).

75.   Nathan M. Pusey, "A Religion for Now," *Harper's*, December 1953, 21.

76.   Ibid.

77.   *Life*, 26 December 1955, 107.

78.   "God at Harvard (Contd.)," *Time*, 22 June 1959, 56.

79.   Goldman, *Crucial Decade*, 305.

80.   John Cogley, "All This and Heaven Too?" *Commonweal*, 2 April 1955, 29.

81.   Ibid.

82.   ". . . Is Our Religious Revival Real?" *McCall's*, June 1955, 25.

83.   Nathan Glazer, "The Jewish Revival in America: II," *Commentary*, January 1956, 18.

84.   Gustave Weigel, "The Present Embarrassment of the Church," in *Religion in America*, ed. John Cogley (New York: Meridian Books, 1958), 224.

85.   Paul Tillich, "Freedom and the Ultimate Concern," in Cogley, *Religion in America*.

86.   Abraham Joshua Heschel, "The Religious Message," in Cogley, *Religion in America*.

87.   Reinhold Niebuhr, "Varieties of Religious Revival," *New Republic*, 6 June 1955, 15.

88.   Ibid., 14.

89.   Catherine L. Albanese, *America: Religion and Religions* (Belmont, Calif.: Wadsworth Publishing Company, 1981), 6.

90.   The problems lie chiefly in finding a pure case of either kind of religion and in using the distinction to explain the muddled religions one encounters in real-life situations.

91.   Hine, *Populuxe*, 35.

92.   Ibid., 36.

93.   *Saturday Evening Post*, 29 March 1952, 34.

94.   See Patricia J. Tracy, *Jonathan Edwards, Pastor: Religion and Society in Eighteenth-Century Northampton* (New York: Hill and Wang, 1979), 91–122, for an analysis of the effect of the premature death of a teenager on the numbers of conversions among the youth's cohort; see also Mary Ryan, *Cradle of the Middle Class: The Family in Oneida County, New York, 1790–1865* (New York: Cambridge University Press, 1981).

95.   Wuthnow, *Restructuring of American Religion*, 37.

3. Critics of the American Dream

1.   David Riesman, Reuel Denney, and Nathan Glazer, *The Lonely Crowd: A Study of the Changing American Character* (New Haven: Yale University Press, 1950; 2d ed., 1960).

2.   Erich Fromm, *Man for Himself* (New York: Rinehart and Company, 1947); C. Wright Mills, "The Competitive Personality," *Partisan Review* 13 (1946): 433ff.

3.   Allan Bloom, *The Closing of the American Mind: How Higher Education Has Failed Democracy and Impoverished the Souls of Today's Students* (New York: Simon and Schuster, 1987), 144.

4.   William H. Whyte, quoted in Ann Waldron, "Advocate of the Livable City," *Princeton Alumni Weekly*, 30 September 1987, 21.

5.   William H. Whyte, Jr., *The Organization Man* (Garden City, N.Y.: Doubleday Anchor Books, 1956).

6.   C. Wright Mills, *White Collar: The American Middle Classes* (New York: Oxford University Press, 1951).

7.   C. Wright Mills, *The Power Elite* (New York: Oxford University Press, 1956).

8.   C. Wright Mills, "A Pagan Sermon to the Christian Clergy," *Nation*, 8 March 1958, 199–202.

9.   Bernard Rosenberg and David Manning White, eds., *Mass Culture: The Popular Arts in America* (Glencoe, Ill.: The Free Press, 1957).

10.   Richard H. Pells, *The Liberal Mind in a Conservative Age: American Intellectuals in the 1940s and 1950s* (New York: Harper and Row, 1984), 174.

11.   Ibid.

12.   Ibid., 175.

13.   Quoted in ibid., 178.

14.   Dwight Macdonald, "A Theory of Mass Culture," *Diogenes* 3 (Summer 1953): 1–17; reprinted in Rosenberg and White, *Mass Culture*, 59–73.

15.   Macdonald, "Theory of Mass Culture," in Rosenberg and White, *Mass Culture*, 59.

16.   The question has arisen as to why these social critics were so popular, and in what sense they can be called "prophets" if they were successful in getting a hearing for their message. Recent observers have argued that Americans have a peculiarly strong need to hear how bad they are and therefore have been eager consumers of critics from David Riesman to Allan Bloom. While I would agree that this is the case and will return to the issue of Americans' fondness for the jeremiad, it seems to me that given a somewhat greater historical perspective the interesting question to ask is why these particular Jeremiahs, the sociologically inclined critics, were so popular. To pose this question is to ask why the great moral tracts of the times were not coming from the pulpits of New England, nor from the muckraking journalists, nor from the left-of-center novelists, as they once had. It is to ask what made the social critics the new preachers of morality. The answer, I would suggest, lies in the mid-twentieth-century transfer of cultural authority to science and particularly social science, as discussed in chapter 1. Finally, it is fair to call them prophets given their popularity, for the designation prophet can be applied to one who addresses a society at its points of stress and who articulates a vision in tension with its consensus.

4. Critics of the American Way of Religion

1.   Harry J. Ausmus, *Will Herberg: From Right to Right* (Chapel Hill: University of North Carolina Press, 1987), 55.
2.   Quoted in ibid., 65.
3.   Ibid., 71.
4.   Ibid., 78.
5.   Ibid., 80.
6.   Ibid., 86.
7.   Ibid., 91.
8.   Ibid., 92.
9.   Will Herberg, *Protestant, Catholic, Jew* (Garden City, N.Y.: Anchor Books, 1955, 2d ed., 1960).
10.   Barbara Ward, "Report to Europe on America," *New York Times Magazine*, 20 June 1954; Oscar Handlin, *The American People in the Twentieth Century* (Cambridge, Mass.: Harvard University Press, 1954), 222; quoted in Herberg, *Protestant, Catholic, Jew*, 1.
11.   For negative appraisals of the revival by intellectuals, see particularly Goldman, *Crucial Decade*, and Seymour Martin Lipset, "Religion in America: What Religious Revival?," *Columbia University Forum*, Winter 1959.
12.   Oscar Handlin, *The Uprooted: The Epic Story of the Great Migrations That Made the American People* (Boston: Little, Brown, 1951), 3.

13.   Marcus L. Hansen, *The Problem of the Third Generation Immigrant* (Rock Island, Ill.: Augustana Historical Society, 1938), 7.

14.   Ruby Jo Reeves Kennedy, "Single or Triple Melting Pot? Intermarriage Trends in New Haven, 1870–1940," *American Journal of Sociology* 49, no. 4, January 1944.

15.   Richard Wightman Fox, "Always in Love with Absolutes," review of *Will Herberg: From Right to Right*," by Harry J. Ausmus, *New York Times Book Review*, 30 August 1987, 15.

16.   See for example, J. B. Code's review in *Catholic World*, which reads in part, "While there is a great deal in this book to recommend it to those especially interested in the religious situation in this country, it falls short of being an adequate appreciation of American Catholicism. . . . This book shows originality and industry. . . . But it should be read in conjunction with John J. Kane's *Catholic-Protestant Conflicts in America*" (*Catholic World* 182 [December 1955]: 234). By contrast, what the sociologists liked about the book was its history. Lee Braude wrote, "In brief compass this book presents the American histories of the three major religious groups in this country" (*American Journal of Sociology* 61 [May 1956]: 646), J. Milton Yinger deemed it "certain to be a stimulus to the development of the sociology of American religious life" (*American Sociological Review* 21 [April 1956]: 237).

17.   Gibson Winter, "The Church in Suburban Captivity," *Christian Century*, 28 September 1955, 1112.

18.   Ibid., 1113.

19.   Ibid.

20.   Ibid., 1114.

21.   *Time*, 10 October 1955, 73.

22.   Gibson Winter, *The Suburban Captivity of the Churches: An Analysis of Protestant Responsibility in the Expanding Metropolis* (Garden City, N.Y.: Doubleday, 1961), 9.

23.   Peter L. Berger, *The Noise of Solemn Assemblies: Christian Commitment and the Religious Establishment in America* (Garden City, N.Y.: Doubleday, 1961).

24.   Robert and Helen Lynd, *Middletown in Transition* (New York: Harcourt Brace, 1937), 402.

25.   Martin Marty, *The New Shape of American Religion* (New York: Harper, 1959).

26.   Emile Durkheim, *The Elementary Forms of the Religious Life* (Glencoe, Ill.: Free Press, 1947); Bronislaw Malinowski, *The Foundations of Faith and Morals* (London: Oxford University Press, 1936); J. Milton Yinger, *Religion, Society and the Individual* (New York: Macmillan, 1957).

27.   W. Lloyd Warner, *The Living and the Dead* (New Haven, Conn.: Yale University Press, 1959).

28.   T. W. Adorno et al., *The Authoritarian Personality* (New York: Harper, 1950); Gordon Allport, *The Nature of Prejudice* (Cambridge, Mass.: Addison-Wesley, 1954).

5. Among the Ruins of Certainty: Religion in the Sixties

1. John R. Fry, *Fire and Blackstone* (Philadelphia: Lippincott, 1969).
2. Kenneth W. Ingwalson, ed., *Your Church—Their Target* (Arlington, Va.: Better Books, 1966).
3. Paul Ramsey, *Who Speaks for the Church?* (Nashville: Abingdon, 1967).
4. James H. Leggett, "Hope for the Churches?," *Schenectady Union Star*, 1968, as quoted in Benton Johnson, "Reinhold Niebuhr and the Cure of Souls," 1984, unpublished ms., University of Oregon, 1.
5. Johnson, "Niebuhr and the Cure of Souls," 4.
6. Jeffrey K. Hadden, *The Gathering Storm in the Churches* (Garden City, N.Y.: Anchor Books, 1970).
7. Phillip Hammond, *The Campus Clergyman* (New York: Basic Books, 1966).
8. Felician A. Foy, O.F.M., ed., *1969 Catholic Almanac* (Garden City, N.Y.: Doubleday, 1969), 177–182.
9. George Gallup, Jr., "Religion in America—50 Years: 1935–1985," *The Gallup Report*, no. 236 (May 1985): 9, 42.
10. By 1985 the number of Catholic seminarians would drop to below 11,000 students. By contrast, Protestant seminary enrollments during 1960–70 rose 51.4 percent. Foy, *1969 Catholic Almanac*, 176; Felician A. Foy, ed., and Rose V. Avato, assoc. ed., *1986 Catholic Almanac* (Huntington, Ind.: Our Sunday Visitor, 1986), 518, 525. Calculation of 1960–70 Protestant seminary enrollment growth is based on figures reported for schools in John C. Fletcher, *The Futures of Protestant Seminaries* (Washington, D.C.: The Alban Institute, 1983), 31.
11. Martin Marty, *Second Chance for American Protestants* (New York: Harper and Row, 1963); idem, *A Nation of Behavers* (Chicago: University of Chicago Press, 1976); Garry Wills, *Bare Ruined Choirs* (Garden City, N. Y.: Doubleday, 1971); Pierre Berton, *The Comfortable Pew* (Philadelphia: Lippincott, 1965).
12. Dietrich Bonhoeffer, *Letters and Papers from Prison* (New York: Macmillan, 1962).
13. Gabriel Vahanian, *The Death of God: The Culture of Our Post-Christian Era* (New York: George Braziller, 1961), 69–75, 228–231.
14. William Hamilton, "Thursday's Child: The Theologian Today and Tomorrow," *Theology Today* 20 (January 1964): 487–495.
15. Thomas J. J. Altizer, *The Gospel of Christian Atheism* (Philadelphia: Westminster Press, 1966).
16. Paul M. Van Buren, *The Secular Meaning of the Gospel* (New York: Macmillan, 1963).
17. Richard Rubenstein, *After Auschwitz: Radical Theology and Contemporary Judaism* (Indianapolis: Bobbs-Merrill, 1966).
18. "Toward a Hidden God," *Time*, 8 April 1966, 82–89.
19. *Time*, 29 April 1966, 19.

20. *Time*, 15 April 1966, 13.

21. Harvey Cox, *The Secular City* (New York: Macmillan, 1965; rev. ed., 1966).

22. James M. Gustafson, "A Look at the Secular City," in *The Secular City Debate*, ed. Daniel Callahan (New York: Macmillan, 1966), 13.

23. C. Eric Lincoln and Lawrence Mamiya, *The Black Church in the African American Experience* (Durham, N.C.: Duke University Press, 1990), 2–7, 196–235.

24. Malcolm Boyd, *Are You Running with Me, Jesus?* (New York: Holt, Rinehart and Winston, 1965), 13, used with permission of the author.

25. The percentage of individuals responding to Gallup that in their opinion, religion was "losing influence," grew from 31 percent in 1962 to 45 percent in 1965, 57 percent in 1967, 67 percent in 1968, and to 70 percent in 1969. Gallup, "Religion in America—50 Years: 1935–1985," 8, 16.

26. Ibid., 22.

27. Ibid., 8.

28. Ibid., 22.

29. Allen J. Matusow, *The Unraveling of America: A History of Liberalism in the 1960s* (New York: Harper and Row, 1984), xiii–xiv.

30. John Kenneth Galbraith, *The Affluent Society* (Boston: Houghton Mifflin, 1958); Michael Harrington, *The Other America* (New York: Macmillan, 1962).

31. John F. Kennedy, "Yale University Commencement Speech," *New York Times*, 12 June 1962, 20.

32. "Port Huron Statement," reprinted in James Miller, *"Democracy Is in the Streets": From Port Huron to the Siege of Chicago* (New York: Touchstone, 1987), 329.

33. Ibid., 331.

34. Ibid., 332.

35. See ibid., 142ff., for a discussion of the multiple meanings of participatory democracy and the uses to which these meanings could be put.

36. Ibid., 24.

37. Louis Hartz, *The Liberal Tradition in America* (New York: Harcourt Brace Jovanovich, 1955).

38. Martin E. Marty, *Pilgrims in Their Own Land* (New York: Penguin Books, 1984; 2d ed., 1985), 424.

Index

■

About the Author

JAMES HUDNUT-BEUMLER is Dean of the Faculty and Associate Professor of Religion and Culture at Columbia Theological Seminary in Decatur, Georgia. Previously, he worked for the Lilly Endowment in Indianapolis.